Palgrave Studies in Prisons and Penology

Edited by: **Ben Crewe**, University of Cambridge, **Yvonne Jewkes**, University of Leicester and **Thomas Ugelvik**, University of Oslo.

This is a unique and innovative series, the first of its kind dedicated entirely to prison scholarship. At a historical point in which the prison population has reached an all-time high, the series seeks to analyse the form, nature and consequences of incarceration and related forms of punishment. *Palgrave Studies in Prisons and Penology* provides an important forum for burgeoning prison research across the world.

Series editors:

BEN CREWE is Deputy Director of the Prisons Research Centre at the Institute of Criminology, University of Cambridge, UK and co-author of *The Prisoner*.

YVONNE JEWKES is Professor of Criminology, University of Leicester, UK. She has authored numerous books and articles on the subject and is editor of the *Handbook on Prisons*.

THOMAS UGELVIK is Postdoctoral Fellow in the Department of Criminology at the University of Oslo, Norway and editor of *Penal Exceptionalism? Nordic Prison Policy and Practise*.

Advisory Board:
Anna Eriksson, Monash University, Australia
Andrew M. Jefferson, Rehabilitation and Research Centre for Torture Victims, Denmark
Shadd Maruna, Queen's University Belfast, Northern Ireland
Jonathon Simon, Berkeley Law, University of California, USA
Michael Welch, Rutgers University, New Jersey, USA

Titles include:

Vincenzo Ruggiero, Mick Ryan
PUNISHMENT IN EUROPE
A Critical Anatomy of Penal Systems

Phil Scraton and Linda Moore
THE INCARCERATION OF WOMEN
Punishing Bodies, Breaking Spirits

Peter Scharff Smith
WHEN THE INNOCENT ARE PUNISHED
The Children of Imprisoned Parents

Thomas Ugelvik
POWER AND RESISTANCE IN PRISON
Doing Time, Doing Freedom

Marguerite Schinkel
BEING IMPRISONED
Punishment, Adaptation and Desistance

Mark Halsey and Simone Deegan
YOUNG OFFENDERS
Crime, Prison and Struggles for Desistance

Palgrave Studies in Prisons and Penology
Series Standing Order ISBN 978–1–137–27090–0 (hardback)
(*outside North America only*)

You can receive future titles in this series as they are published by placing a standing order. Please contact your bookseller or, in case of difficulty, write to us at the address below with your name and address, the title of the series and the ISBNs quoted above.

Customer Services Department, Macmillan Distribution Ltd, Houndmills, Basingstoke, Hampshire RG21 6XS, England

Young Offenders
Crime, Prison and Struggles for Desistance

Mark Halsey
*Professor of Criminology, Centre for Crime Policy and Research,
Flinders University, Australia*

Simone Deegan
Project Officer, Flinders University, Australia

© Mark Halsey and Simone Deegan 2015
MyCopy version of the original edition 2015

All rights reserved. No reproduction, copy or transmission of this publication may be made without written permission.

No portion of this publication may be reproduced, copied or transmitted save with written permission or in accordance with the provisions of the Copyright, Designs and Patents Act 1988, or under the terms of any licence permitting limited copying issued by the Copyright Licensing Agency, Saffron House, 6–10 Kirby Street, London EC1N 8TS.

Any person who does any unauthorized act in relation to this publication may be liable to criminal prosecution and civil claims for damages.

The authors have asserted their rights to be identified as the authors of this work in accordance with the Copyright, Designs and Patents Act 1988.

First published 2015 by
PALGRAVE MACMILLAN

Palgrave Macmillan in the UK is an imprint of Macmillan Publishers Limited, registered in England, company number 785998, of Houndmills, Basingstoke, Hampshire RG21 6XS.

Palgrave Macmillan in the US is a division of St Martin's Press LLC, 175 Fifth Avenue, New York, NY 10010.

Palgrave Macmillan is the global academic imprint of the above companies and has companies and representatives throughout the world.

Palgrave® and Macmillan® are registered trademarks in the United States, the United Kingdom, Europe and other countries.

DOI 10.1057/9781137411228

This book is printed on paper suitable for recycling and made from fully managed and sustained forest sources. Logging, pulping and manufacturing processes are expected to conform to the environmental regulations of the country of origin.

A catalogue record for this book is available from the British Library.

Library of Congress Cataloging-in-Publication Data
Halsey, Mark, author.
   Young offenders : crime, prison, and struggles for desistance / Mark Halsey, Professor of Criminal Justice, Flinders University, Australia; Simone Deegan, Project Officer, Flinders University, Australia.
     pages cm — (Palgrave studies in prisons and penology)
  Includes bibliographical references.
  1. Juvenile delinquents—Legal status, laws, etc. 2. Juvenile justice, Administration of. I. Deegan, Simone, author. II. Title.
K5575.H35 2015
364.36—dc23   2014028135

Springer.com/mycopy

For Jason (1988–2009)

and

For Stewart (1963–2009)

Dear MyCopy Customer,

This printed, personal Springer eBook is a unique service that is available at a low cost, only on link.springer.com because your library purchased at least one Springer eBook subject collection. This book is an exact, monochrome copy of the eBook on SpringerLink.

MyCopy books are strictly for individual use only, and not available for resale. You can cite this book by referencing the bibliographic data and/or the DOI (Digital Object Identifier) found in the front matter.

MyCopy is the ideal format for anyone who wants a physical copy for page-by-page study.

My Book, MyCopy.
Enjoy reading.

Contents

Acknowledgments	viii
Introduction	1
1 Setting the Scene	11
2 Approach to the Field – Data	26
3 On Track	35
4 Recurring Breakdown	62
5 Major Derailment	104
6 Catastrophic Turn	127
7 Points of Unrest	177
8 Points of Light	210
Concluding Remarks	227
Custodial-Grams	233
Notes	245
References	247
Index	258

Acknowledgments

Mark Halsey

This book would not have been possible without initial funding from Flinders University and successive grants awarded by the Australian Research Council (DP0556471 'Understanding recidivism and repeat incarceration among young male offenders: A biographical and longitudinal approach', and DP094562 'Generativity in young male (ex)prisoners: Caring for self, other, and future within prison and beyond'). For such funding I'm extremely thankful.

The book would also not have happened without the cooperation of the South Australian Department for Correctional Services and the Department for Communities and Social Inclusion (formerly Department for Families and Communities). Particular thanks is due to Nerida Saunders, Karen Barry, Wendy Dale, Howard Pfeffer, James Armitage, Sam Armitage, Phil Miller, Peter Severin, David Brown, Anne-Marie Martin, Jackie Bray and Kevin Harkin. I'm indebted to Joe Decicco, Fran Hawkins and Trevor Richardson who have assisted with updating the whereabouts of participants over many years. To all who assisted with access to juvenile training centre residents and prisoners within the grounds of various facilities I offer my sincere thanks. The content of this book, however, is not necessarily reflective of the views held by current or former employees of any government department.

Colleagues near and far have offered insight and support either directly in conversation or through their writings. I'm particularly indebted to Shadd Maruna, Stephen Farrall, Fergus McNeill, Alison Liebling, Ben Crewe and Jonathan Simon. Closer to home, Andrew Goldsmith has been a genuinely great colleague and friend and has helped shape my thinking in countless ways. David Bamford and Kathy Mack offered consistent encouragement. Sharon Pickering provided sage advice over the years. Ken Polk, Chris Cunneen and Eileen Baldry all inspired and supported the work in ways probably unknown to them.

Kim Clarke did a fantastic job as research assistant. Vandra Harris conducted some of the interviews. Andrew Groves designed the custodialgrams.

To Ben and Adam, you've both been along for the entire journey and then some. I can't thank you enough for your friendship.

To Alby, Chris, Greg, Marc and Hamish, thanks for being such great mates and for taking an interest in the research.

To Simone, thank you for developing such a respectful rapport with certain of the participants in the latter stages of the project.

To Kate, I know this work has taken a toll in so many ways – ten years is a long time to stick at anything. I literally couldn't have done it without you. 'Thank you' doesn't really say it. But I offer my heartfelt appreciation to you.

To my wider family. Thank you.

Finally, to each and every interviewee, I offer my deepest gratitude. It is a remarkable thing to open one's life up to another – let alone a researcher or 'stranger'. I take the weight of what you have all said over many years extremely seriously. Simone and I have tried to write this book in a way which pulls no punches but also in a manner which, we hope, does justice to you and/or who you might wish to 'become'. In the end, this book only exists because each of you agreed to speak on record about your lives. This, therefore, is your book as much as it is ours.

Simone Deegan

I would like to dedicate my work on the 'Generativity in young male (ex)prisoners: Caring for self, other, and future within prison and beyond' project to the young men and their families who invited me into their homes and into their lives, no questions asked. Also to the young people around the world who find themselves living on the margins of their communities.

I am so very thankful for all of the help and support I received while writing this book. First and foremost: to Mark, for your unflagging support and bottomless stores of patience across the project. I benefited enormously from the opportunity to tackle serious analysis and interpretation of data and for that I am indebted to you.

I appreciate very much the assistance of Kim Clarke. Thank you for all your hard work and fine sense of humour.

To Brian O'Reilly, thank you for your tireless representation of every client I sent your way. Keep fighting the good fight.

To Terry Deegan, thank you for (literally) taking the journey with me. You're the best, Dad.

To Phillip Brook, thank you for giving me a sanctuary to clear the 'clutter' when it got too much. Who knew hitting a ball could teach you so much about life?

Last but not least, to the home team: Mark Alessandrini and Elton, for your unwavering love and support (gym sessions and group hugs!) Thank you for 'keeping it real'.

Introduction
Young Offenders: Crime, Prison and Struggles for Desistance

It's a strange thing watching someone 'known' to us for over a decade get a hefty term of imprisonment. Chris was in his mid-twenties and had just received 14 years for a series of violent crimes committed shortly after his last release. It took the State over four years to resolve his matters – an exceedingly long time on remand by anyone's estimation. The sentence brought Chris a degree of closure but also new opportunities to sink deeper into the mire of prison life. He'll be well into his thirties before having any chance of making parole. It's strange also, when, as researchers, we were able to see the train wreck coming but powerless to avert the impending damage. Perhaps, in the tradition of positivist detachment from the field, one has no quarter to try and influence the trajectories of those we study. Still, there can be no denying the substantive emotional investment tied to prison and post-release research (see Liebling 1999; Bosworth et al. 2005; but also Campbell 2002). The 'field' – be it policing, courts, prisons, the street more generally – is populated by countless affective moments. Courtrooms, in particular, are a haven for extreme emotional turbulence (Freiberg 2001). There, even the prosecution team agreed Chris had one of the most troubled and deprived early life-courses they had encountered. Still, he had to pay for what he'd done. He had to pay even though it was broadly acknowledged that his was a life bereft of the building blocks necessary for carving out any semblance of a conventional existence.

This circumstance brings sharply to the fore one of the curious things about the neo-classical system of justice. Typically, the impact of particular social milieus and key turning points in defendants' lives are forensically mined, but only to the extent that these do not interfere with the capacity to render each culpable for 'her/his' actions. It's as if the background reports, the psychological assessments, the social need inventories, and the like, can only push so far into the terrain of *societal and systemic failure*. As Deleuze and Guattari (1996: 159) write, 'You will be a subject, nailed down as one'. Chris, you will be an *offender*. And to help reinforce this, a lengthy prison sentence awaits. After all, you yourself told the court of feeling irretrievably institutionalized. So again, a custodial facility will become your place of residence – a place where you've spent more than 95 per cent of your days from age 13.

The colloquial definition of insanity is doing the same thing repeatedly in the hope that a different result will arise. With over 20 release events under his belt by the age of 21, a kind of systemic insanity came to characterize the dynamic at play for Chris (and for others whose stories feature in this book). Even victims of crime – perhaps, especially victims – know that retribution doesn't really fix anything. It doesn't deter others from doing similar acts. It rarely deters the incarcerate her/himself from reoffending. Something, it would appear, is broken. For too long, the bureaucratic emphasis has been on *fixing the offender* (more cognitive behavioural therapy, anger management, 'thinking straight' programs), *playing with the spatiality of crime* (manipulating objects, hardening, removing and surveilling targets) and *creating social awareness of risky situations* (educating potential victims). Perhaps it's time to look in another direction. Perhaps the juvenile and criminal justice systems as well as the social worlds in which they sit need to be overhauled.

If so, this would, at minimum, mean acknowledging that many of the ways in which we police and punish offenders inadvertently helps create (rather than rehabilitate) 'dangerous' or socially marginalized individuals. It would mean directing attention more broadly to communities of interest – communities in need of urgent economic investment – rather than gearing operations and policies around 'persons of interest'. It would mean thinking about social obligation as well as individual responsibility. It would mean, in short, acknowledging the fundamentally criminogenic nature of so much social and criminal justice policy. It would, in turn, entail decoupling such policy from the expediency of short-termism (election cycles, personality driven politics, 'shock-jock' commentary) and knee-jerk punitive responses (law and order campaigns). Or, perhaps, more simply, offenders could 'do the right thing'. They could obey the formal conditions imposed on them by the courts and correctional agencies as well as those imposed informally by society. They could *desist* from further offending – literally just 'shrug off the past' and conform. Society would then be a better place because the unruly would have been made to comply.

Except compliance is not the same thing as (re)integration – that is, becoming a fully functioning and participating citizen. Compliance doesn't really have anything to do with real change – with putting people on a substantively different path. And it doesn't do much to dislodge society's preoccupation with the idea that offenders can only ever become, at best, *ex*-offenders. The rock icon David Bowie once said, 'I am only the person the greatest number of people believe me to be' (ABC1 Television 2014). In this sense, people exiting custodial facilities – *especially* such people – need the community on their side in order to build and claim a master status that breaks free from the offender/ex-offender dyad.

This book, reduced to its simplest dimension, is about 14 young men and their struggles to find such status. Certainly, this has been an immensely difficult if not impossible task for the majority of them. Most remain entrenched in the cycle of crime and incarceration – not because they 'want' to be in that situation, but because it is what they know best. Prison, it is true to say, 'works' well for some people. It gives them an identity – albeit one with limited value in the wider law-abiding community. As one Georgia State prisoner put it, 'I'm somebody in prison and nobody at home' (ABC2 Television 2014). A few of the young men, though, *have* built new lives – lives which make the years spent in and out of juvenile and adult custodial facilities seem like a blur – almost like it never happened. Almost. As will become apparent, scratching the psychic surfaces of these young men results in a complex mix of matter-of-factness ('We had a big argument [and so] I strangled her') and emotional reflexivity ('I've caused so much pain. It needs to stop'). We hope something of this complexity is captured in the book.

At the same time, we are cognizant that a book cannot completely encompass the range of issues canvassed in multiple conversations over many years. Some events must inevitably take a back seat to others – this is part and parcel of a grounded approach to analysing interview data (Glaser 1992). We have, though, been appropriately attentive to scenarios that don't fit neatly into the more prevalent themes and sub-themes emerging from analysis of transcripts. This is a critically important part of qualitative work – to remain attuned to moments which at first glance seem insignificant to determining the main game, but which, on closer inspection are in fact central to such. Knowing the bus loops, chancing a lift to the social security office, bumping into an old 'associate', catching a break from a police officer, living in one street not another – all these 'small things' can make the world of difference between a desistance process which stays on track or runs more or less seriously off the rails.

Of course, class, gender and socio-economic factors all structure life in undeniably important ways. These too are integrated into our analysis.

Study location

The young men at the centre of this book were interviewed repeatedly within and beyond custody in South Australia from, in most instances, late 2003/early 2004 to the end of 2013. South Australia has a population of around 1.7 million with the majority (80 per cent) residing in the capital city, Adelaide. In geographic terms, South Australia is equivalent in size to about one quarter of the United States of America ('US'). It shares a border with Western Australia, Northern Territory, Queensland, New South Wales and Victoria. Colonized in 1836 by Europeans, South Australia was, for some 40,000 years, originally home to numerous Aboriginal nations. Their precise population at the time of 'settlement' is unknown but is generally recognized to be around 20,000 people. They lived near the coast and in the deserts (the 'interior') and used their songlines to meet and connect with other nations/tribal groups from what are now known as Australia's states and territories (see Chatwin 1988). Presently – through a combination of disease (such as smallpox) and appropriation of lands – less than 2 per cent of the South Australian population are Indigenous (that is, identify as Aboriginal or Torres Strait Islander). However, such persons, as a group, make up 50 per cent and 25 per cent of, respectively, juvenile and adult custodial numbers. The overall incarceration rate in South Australia is roughly 170 per 100,000 relevant population. This puts it more or less on par with states such as Maine, Minnesota and Rhode Island in the US and with the incarceration rate of the United Kingdom ('UK') generally.

Like most cities, Adelaide evinces some stark disparities between its wealthier and economically marginalized communities. By the most conservative estimate, about 12 per cent of Adelaide's population live below the poverty line (Australian Council of Social Service 2012). This rises to 20 per cent when a slightly different threshold of disposable income is invoked. Unsurprisingly, all of the young men in our study grew up in suburbs or towns with high rates of youth unemployment (approaching 20 per cent in some areas), high rates of public housing of varying but typically dilapidated condition, high rates of crime, and low accessibility to good schools, adequate public transport, good leisure activities, cultural pursuits, and the like. Large-scale blue-collar industries – revolving particularly around automobile manufacture – have come and gone or are soon to go. General Motors has recently announced it will cease making cars at its Elizabeth (northern Adelaide) plant from 2017. Mitsubishi closed its doors several years ago in Adelaide's south. Ford will shut down its manufacturing plant in the neighbouring state of Victoria by the end of 2016. Toyota has announced it will do the same. The car industry provides about one half of 1 per cent of all jobs in South Australia and, until recently, just over 6 per cent of the state's manufacturing jobs (van Onselen 2014). Such industry closures only add to the social and economic strain in areas (such as Adelaide's northern, western and southern suburbs) where intergenerational long-term unemployment is not uncommon. A recent national report rated Adelaide's northern suburbs as the third worst area nationally in terms of youth unemployment. In the two-year period 2012–14, the youth unemployment rate rose in Adelaide's western and northern suburbs by, respectively, 45 per cent and 34 per cent. In some regional centres (for example, Whyalla in South Australia's mid-North) the rate increased by a staggering 67 per cent (a good portion of participants interviewed have lived or currently live in such places). By 2016, the youth unemployment rate in these areas is forecast to approach close to 27 per cent (Brotherhood of St Laurence 2014). Significantly, the suburbs in these locations are also disproportionately home to families experiencing significant rates of intergenerational incarceration. Halsey and Groves (unpublished) found almost half of 240 prisoners who had experienced two or more generations of incarceration grew up in just three areas (Port Adelaide, Elizabeth and Noarlunga). Participants in our work describe certain streets in these places as akin to 'the Bronx'. All were only too aware they came from the 'wrong side of the tracks' and that it was a long journey – irrespective of getting involved in crime – to the other side.

The youngest participants were aged 15 when first interviewed and the oldest was 29 years when last interviewed. Over time, some of these young men have featured prominently in print, TV and web-based media on account of their (alleged) offending. Others have been fortunate enough to avoid such public attention and condemnation. In this book, we draw on interview data and field notes to explicate the circumstances associated with desistance from crime and/or intensification of serious repeat offending in each young man's life. In particular, we examine the changing relationships surrounding – and attitudes toward – crime, incarceration, family, work, education and intervention programs as each young man progresses in age from his mid- to late teens through to his mid- to late twenties. We also draw on repeat interviews (conducted since 2009) with each young man's nominated significant others ('NSOs') (girlfriends, parents, aunts, grandparents, close friends and the like) as a means for understanding progress or decline in the struggle to desist (see Halsey and Deegan 2012, 2014). This data is additionally enriched by one-off interviews with all prison managers and offender development/rehabilitation managers in South Australia as well as select prison officers at various facilities where the young men served and/or continue to serve time (for further participant details, see Chapter 2, 'Approach to the Field – Data').

In search of generativity

Although the book is about the struggle for desistance (and resumption of offending), it is in equal measure a study of *generativity* (McAdams and de St Aubin 1998). Erikson (1982: 67) conceives generativity as a particular stage of human development that entails 'a widening commitment to take care of the persons, the products, and the ideas one has learned to care for'. Typically occurring around middle adulthood, the struggle to become generative is waged against the 'easier' option of becoming self-absorbed. In the latter scenario, personal stagnation prevails over personal growth. Recent work (see studies cited in Halsey and Harris 2011 but especially Maruna et al. 2004a) has drawn a strong link between generativity and desistance from crime, particularly where (ex)offenders 'make sense of a damaged past by using it to protect the future interests of others' (McNeill 2004: 432). McNeill and Maruna (2008: 232) note the narratives of former offenders are often 'care-oriented, other-centered and focused on promoting the next generation' (see also Barry 2006; Healy and O'Donnell 2008; Walker 2010). It makes sense, then, to propose that prisoners who have meaningful opportunities to 'give back' will be more likely to show interest in, and resilience during, the struggle to desist. This is by no means a hard and fast rule but it is one we believe makes intuitive sense and is backed by emerging evidence.

In our work, we conceive generativity as the desire and/or capacity to care for self, other and future in meaningful, non-violent and enduring fashion within prison and/or beyond. The combination of (ex)prisoner and significant other interviews permits, we hope, rare insights into the nature of change (or stagnation) in the early to mid-life course of a group of young males – all of whom share prolific offending profiles in their teenage years across a wide range of offences (armed robbery, endangering life, home invasion, aggravated assault, motor vehicle theft, to name several). Interviews with prison officials/officers lend the book an appropriately calibrated realism about what 'doing time' does or should entail, and, more pointedly, about the day-to-day challenges associated with trying to transform (or, as the case may be, 'shut down') oneself within and beyond prison. To get to grips with generativity – to understand desistance from, and persistence of, offending – we hone in on three modes of care: care of self, care of other and care of future. These concepts come to the fore in later chapters but we offer brief comment here.

Care as generative moment

The concept of care is a pivotal yet under-researched dimension of the penal landscape. Erikson considers it the defining 'virtue' in the struggle between becoming generative and becoming self-absorbed. In the correctional context, care extends well beyond the state's duty to look after those in custody (that is, to ensure safe and humane conditions for prisoners and staff alike). More specifically, care has a deeply *introspective dimension* encompassing care of mind, body and reputation chiefly within but also beyond custody. Care also has a *bridging dimension*. It is a device through which prisoners attempt to maintain links with significant others in the quest to do 'good time'. Care also has a substantively *projective dimension* insofar as it helps connect the present to the possibility of a future distinct to the past. Like the concept of hope, care of future enables (some) young prisoners to imagine living in conventional and non-violent ways. The experience of care – being cared for, and being given the opportunity to care for others – can in turn ignite and sustain hope (the latter being a positive yet potentially destructive force during incarceration and release) (see Halsey 2007b). The three modes of care are conceived and analysed throughout the book as indices of generative and stagnative dispositions. These dispositions, in turn, we view as impacting the likelihood of desistance – and whether, at a more basic level, someone forms the inclination to turn away from crime.

Foundational work on generativity references events such as becoming a parent, volunteering or entering a particular profession (such as social work, nursing, teaching) as archetypal generative acts. These are to an extent apparent in our study cohort. But we also found evidence of less 'visible' generative moments such as prisoners helping fellow prisoners with literacy and numeracy, with distress following receipt of 'bad news', and with the provision of 'moral' support for those on the cusp of acting out or going, literally, 'stir crazy'. Equally, we explicate the generative acts of young men's NSOs (such as child-raising, supplying money, writing letters and making legal inquiries) and how these impact the dispositions of each (ex)prisoner. The question of whether and how prisoners can meaningfully 'return' the gift of generativity (especially when locked up, but also following release) is central to the book. This book is therefore the first to specifically examine how generativity emerges, is sustained or thwarted in the context of young (ex)incarcerated males who have expressed the desire (if not always the capacity) to cease offending. Accordingly, two key questions guide the remainder of the work: 1) Who or what is it possible for young offenders to care about within and beyond custody? and 2) What are the events and processes which nurture and/or interrupt (temporarily or permanently) generativity and desistance from crime in the lives of these young men?

Overview of chapters

The book unfolds in the following way. Chapter 1 outlines the concept of desistance and demonstrates why it is important from social *and* economic standpoints. We earmark the need for a 'close' qualitative longitudinal study of how (ex)incarcerated young men interpret and respond to the range of social and institutional pressures/controls during what is arguably a little understood key transitional period in their lives. This period, we argue, involves the sometimes brief but frequently more extensive blurring of the well-known (and much lauded) distinction between 'adolescence limited' and 'life-course persistent' offending (Moffitt 1993). The chapter (as well as the book more broadly) affirms the precariousness and possibilities of this phase.

The second chapter provides an overview of the research design and evolution of the study since 2003. It describes the methodologies engaged for collecting and analysing data as well as the ethical dilemmas posed by doing longitudinal qualitative work with a cohort of (ex)prisoners and their loved ones. The fine line between 'researcher' and 'advocate' is given attention, as are issues of 'objectivity' versus 'emotional' investment in the data collection and analysis stages.

Chapter 3 ('On Track') describes the life-course of three young men (Billy, Charlie and David) who have – despite each having served significant custodial time and who were, at various points, 'written off' by magistrates, judges, youth workers and like as 'incorrigible' – managed to desist from crime for the last several years. We examine in detail the factors that have uniquely converged and underpinned the success of each young man – chiefly their capacity to transition from generative commitment to generative action. The perspectives of nominated significant others are drawn on in order to highlight how this success is a collective event involving hardship and uncertainty but also hope and a real sense of progress.

In the fourth chapter ('Recurring Breakdown') we focus on the young men (Joel, Paul, Reggie and Ben) whose motivation to desist from crime is resolute but whose capacity to do so has been repeatedly undermined by a combination of personal and situational circumstances. Typically, these breakdowns have resulted in many periods in the community interspersed by multiple custodial sentences of a fairly short duration (generally several months to a year). We describe the range of generative commitments extolled by each young man as well as their prospective and retrospective accounts of the breakdown in each of their attempts to desist from crime. Again, the views of NSOs help to unpack the nature of setbacks.

Chapter 5 ('Major Derailment') provides an in-depth account of the circumstances associated with major interruptions to attempts to desist from crime. Our focus here is with two young men (Lee and Matt) whose commitments to desist came to an abrupt halt due to further serious offending. In such cases, their crimes were of the same or similar kind to what they had previously engaged in and served time for. Through interview excerpts, we explicate the social and psychological dimensions of the moment where, from each young man's viewpoint, there appeared to be no possibility of pulling back from the (reoffending) brink.

The sixth chapter ('Catastrophic Turn') tells the stories of the three young men (Sam, James and Chris) whose journeys take them into the realm of public notoriety. It relays their life stories up to and including their current terms of imprisonment and explicates the catastrophic results for loved ones, for the community and, not least, for each young man. In contrast to participants in previous chapters, the most recent offending by these young men is of a demonstrably more serious type than their previous criminal behaviour and has led to long custodial sentences. We situate these stories against the backdrop of juvenile and adult custodial facilities as well as post-release services that, collectively, profess a clear commitment to 'rehabilitation'. Crucially, we explore attempts by NSOs who, in highly volatile circumstances, try to 'talk sense' to their loved one – to get each to 'do the right thing'. Through the vicissitudes of three lives, we ask and analyse how things could go so terribly wrong.

In Chapter 7 we comment critically on the factors that make it so difficult for many young offenders to 'leave the life' and, with specific reference to the work of Moffitt (1993), examine the relative merits of 'adolescence-limited' and 'life-course persistent' offender categories for our participants. We also explicate the key themes emerging from the stories told in previous chapters. These include: *parentification* (the damage done to children who must bring themselves and/or their siblings up from a very young age); *personal need versus systemic offerings* (the disconnect between what is required to desist from crime as to what is available to support such); *beckoning help* (the issue of young men's reluctance to reach out to a trusted other (or service) before or when things turn bad); and *managing the scorned self* (humiliation as both a catalyst for offending and as reproduced by prison and post-prison environments).

The final chapter offers some tentative suggestions for improving young offenders' rehabilitation and reintegration prospects. Our suggestions are based on the idea that desistance is not an 'internally' driven or 'self-willed' venture but a much more complex collective endeavour. We posit ways in which (ex)prisoners' generative commitments might be more frequently turned into generative actions within and beyond custody in order that desistance from serious repeat offending occurs by 'design' rather than, as would seem to be the case, by accident. To our knowledge, young men in and out of custodial facilities have rarely been asked to narrate the kinds of constraints and 'enabling niches' (Taylor 1997) impacting the nature and intensity of generative desires and actions within and following repeat periods of incarceration. The book aims to do just that.

1
Setting the Scene

In their influential work *Shared Beginnings, Divergent Lives*, Laub and Sampson (2006: 145) pose the question: 'Why do some offenders stop offending?' Their response was as follows:

> It appears that offenders desist as a result of a combination of individual actions (choice) in conjunction with situational contexts and structural influences linked to important institutions that help sustain desistance. This fundamental theme underscores the need to examine both individual motivation and the social context in which individuals are embedded.

It has taken considerable time for criminologists to arrive at this type of explanation – one whose 'validity' might now seem obvious. But if the combination of personal and social factors underpinning desistance (engagement of pro-social networks, overcoming drug and/or alcohol problems, gaining meaningful employment, enjoying a stable family life, being mentally and physical well, successfully dealing with issues of stigma, guilt and shame) are indeed reasonably clear, the actual convergence of any or all these elements in would-be desisters' lives is less common than it should be. Desistance, in short, is a complex business. Some people 'fall' into it – just as some 'fall' into crime. Others consciously make the effort to desist – sometimes lapsing in minor ways, sometimes in major fashion, sometimes with catastrophic results. Still others harbour no pretense toward stopping their offending. Each of these scenarios will be evident in the lives discussed later in the book. And each life discussed will bring to light just how difficult it is to strike the right combination of personal, situational and structural factors integral to getting desistance going and for sustaining it. For now, though, we raise the question of *why desistance matters*. In other words, why is it important to care about or study desistance from crime? In order to respond to this question, the scope of the problem of desistance – at least in terms of street/violent offenders – needs to be understood. In addition, and perhaps more pertinently, the economic benefits of desistance also need explication. Coming to terms with these aspects will help frame the significance of desistance from crime (and the value of generative action) in clearer, more pragmatic terms.

Who are (potential) desisters?

A good place to start looking for potential desisters is within the 'deepest' end of the criminal justice system – specifically, in the cohort of *sentenced* persons released annually from prison.[1] The focus on sentenced persons is important because not everyone who goes to prison has cause to desist from crime. Some are remanded, bailed, released off court, and/or eventually found innocent of all charges. It is therefore inappropriate, at least methodologically, to include these people in the population of potential desisters. Desistance requires, at minimum, having a history of offending to desist from (see below this chapter, 'Conceptualizing desistance'). In Australia, around 25,000 sentenced prisoners are released from prison annually. In the US the equivalent figure is about 700,000 (which *excludes* the several million persons released each year from US jails). In the UK around 80,000 persons per year are released from a determinate sentence (Sabol and West 2010; Ministry of Justice 2013). Of course, a good many persons released from prison do not, in fact, desist from further offending. In Australia 'about one in four prisoners will be reconvicted within three months of being released' (Payne 2007: xi) and around 40 per cent will return to prison under sentence within two years (SCRGSP 2013: C22). Such reincarceration rates hold for countries as diverse in their prisoner numbers as the US (Langan and Levin 2002; Pew Center on the States 2011: 10-11), UK (Prison Reform Trust 2013), New Zealand (Nadescu 2008) and Canada (Bonta et al. 2003) – although the latter evinces a lower rate of reincarceration of around 30 per cent within two years of release.

In more pointed fashion – and in terms of those who are likely to have more 'heavy lifting' to do when it comes to desistance – one could examine the population of persons who have been sentenced to a period of imprisonment on multiple occasions. Australian Bureau of Statistics snapshot data for 30 June 2012 shows that 55 per cent of prisoners had served at least one term of 'prior adult imprisonment under sentence'

(ABS 2013a: 21). In a study of 3352 sentenced prisoners released in Victoria in 2002–03, Holland and colleagues reported that one fifth had served *four or more* prior periods of imprisonment (Holland et al. 2007: 14). They also found the number (and length) of past incarceration episodes significantly influenced the rate at which people returned to custody. Specifically, '[f]ewer than one in five of those released from their first term of imprisonment returned to prison within two years, compared with close to two-thirds of those who had been imprisoned six or more times' (Holland et al. 2007: 15–16). In New Zealand, a study of nearly 5000 prisoners released from April 2002 to March 2003 showed that 7 per cent 'had served more than ten previous terms' of imprisonment (Nadescu 2008: 13). A four-year follow-up of the cohort revealed that 30 per cent of first-time incarcerates were reimprisoned within 48 months. This again sits in stark contrast to those who had served more than ten previous periods of incarceration – 78 per cent of whom were reincarcerated during a four-year follow-up window (Nadescu 2008: 13). The message here is clear: *imprisonment begets imprisonment*. More accurately, serving multiple short to medium-term sentences seems substantively linked to higher prospects of reincarceration (Holland et al. 2007: 15).

Of course, the problem of incarceration and its likely impacts on desistance begins, for many, well before adulthood (the stories in this book graphically illustrate such). To that end, a significant proportion of prisoners will have been incarcerated as juveniles. In a recent survey of 214 prisoners drawn from nine adult custodial facilities in South Australia, 75 per cent reported being incarcerated in their juvenile years, with most reporting first being locked up between ages 10 and 14 years (Halsey and Groves unpublished). A much larger study by the New South Wales Bureau of Crime Statistics and Research reported that of the 10 to 18-year-olds first appearing before the Children's Court in 1995 (n=5,476), 13 per cent (n=714) received at least one prison sentence in the eight-year follow-up period (Chen et al. 2005). Those whose first appearance occurred between 10 and 14 years of age were twice as likely to have received an adult custodial sentence (Chen et al. 2005: 4). In the US, data from New York State and South Carolina indicates that between 70 and 80 per cent of those serving time in a juvenile facility will likely be incarcerated for new offences in adulthood (see Mendel 2011: 10–11). In New Zealand, about half of all prisoners are likely to have first been incarcerated in their juvenile years (Nadescu 2008: 18). On any day there are around 850 juveniles in detention around Australia with around 80 per cent likely to be 'subject to supervision (community or custodial) by a corrective services agency within seven years [of release]'. Remarkably, 'almost half will be imprisoned as an adult' (Payne 2007: xii). More starkly, there is evidence to suggest Indigenous young men 'progress' from juvenile to adult custodial facilities at rates approaching 100 per cent (Lynch et al. 2003).

Penal statistics tend always to become more alarming when viewed through the lens of Indigeneity (see Cunneen et al. 2013). In Australia, Indigenous males are far more likely than non-Indigenous males to be reincarcerated (particularly in the first six months following release) (Holland et al. 2007). This is to say nothing of the shocking (and worsening) incarceration rates for Indigenous people in Australia generally. Recent figures put the overall Indigenous adult incarceration rate at 18 times that of non-Indigenous persons (SCRGSP 2013: 8.6).[2] Indigenous juveniles, on the other hand, are presently incarcerated at 24 times the rate of non-Indigenous juveniles (437 as against 18 per 100,000 persons aged 10 to 17 years) (SCRGSP 2013: 15A.188). In the US, 'Blacks' are incarcerated at roughly ten times the rate of 'Whites' and at three times the rate of 'Hispanics' (West and Sabol 2010: 28). Gender also matters when speaking of the population of potential desisters. On the whole, females are generally less likely than males to return to prison. But it is also known that females face incredibly heavy burdens (socially and economically) when trying to rejoin the general community (Rumgay 2004). In addition, the impact on children stemming from their mother's incarceration (whether for extended or shorter episodic periods) is likely to be more pronounced than the extended or repeat incarceration of their father (Hagen and Foster 2012). This is especially so where mothers may have formed the last – if precarious – line of defence against (total) family disintegration (Halsey and Deegan 2014).

Community correctional data gives some further clues as to the size of the population of potential desisters (and, by default, potential repeat offenders). In the 2012 December quarter, the daily average number of people under community correctional supervision in Australia was 54,312 – including, around 32,000 probationers, 12,500 parolees, and 8,200 persons on a community service order (ABS 2013b: 8). A good many of these will never receive a further community sanction (some estimates, for instance, put the general community correctional recidivism rate at a low 15 to 25 per cent). But many will end up in prison and have again to start the journey of desistance. Data from New South Wales shows that 75 per cent of the 17,000 prison receptions spanning July 2009 to December 2010 had previously served a community corrections order (with 66 per cent having served a prior custodial sentence) (Corrective Services New South Wales 2013). The US has around 4 million people on probation or parole on any day – a number roughly equivalent to the general population of Melbourne, Australia. In the UK, well over 200,000 people are on probation at any time (Ministry of Justice 2013: 12).

In sum, the combined statistics concerning a) people coming back to prison within two years of release, and b) people on probation or parole indicates there is a sizeable cohort of persons who have tried, will try again, or are trying, on any single day, to desist from crime (more on the definition of desistance later). This is to say nothing of the likely thousands of people convicted annually who do not serve a prison sentence (or who avoid probation or community service) but who nonetheless reoffend (those convicted and fined for driving offences are apposite here).

But this, of course, is still only a small fraction of the larger world of desistance – or what might be called 'the community of desisters'.[3] This community also extends to the family members and/or circle of friends in would-be or 'socially certified' desisters' lives. On that count alone, one could imagine that the horizon of desistance (ex-offenders and their support persons) in Australia, stretches out to at least a few hundred thousand persons. Internationally, that community would likely number in the millions. Prevalence data from the US Bureau of Justice Statistics shows that as at the end of 2001 there were 1,319,000 people in state and federal prisons. Beyond this, though, there were 4,299,000 persons who, since 1974, had *ever* been incarcerated – about 1.2 million of whom were still under some form of community correctional supervision (leaving around 3 million 'free' former incarcerates) (Bonczar 2003). Taking the early 1970s as the base, and working on a 4 to 1 ratio (i.e., four 'ever incarcerated' persons living in the community for every incarcerated person) would mean, *very* roughly, that the desisting or would-be desister population sits around 320,000 persons in the UK, 120,000 in Australia, 60,000 in Canada and about 40,000 such persons in New Zealand. Each of these individuals is positioned somewhere on the persistence–desistance continuum.

Economics of desistance

Beyond the fact that (potential) desisters and their support persons constitute an important fraction of the general population, there are other good reasons to be intensely interested in desistance. The best reason – the humanitarian reason – is to help minimize the cycles of pain, hardship and trauma which so often accompany repeat offending and reincarceration. Desistance from crime enhances the social and cultural fabric and improves the personal and familial circumstances of people's lives. Accordingly, the political value of desistance – a potentially powerful (if underutilized) rallying point for leaders and policy-makers – is that it has the capacity to increase levels of community safety. But there is another reason to be concerned with desistance and it is one that avoids tedious debate around whether offenders 'deserve' a second (or even third, fourth, etc.) chance to 'make good' (Maruna 2001). Desistance should be championed because it makes economic sense.

Since 2002, the average daily prison population in Australia has increased by nearly one third (31 per cent) from 22,492 to 29,381 (ABS 2013a: 9). This is almost four times the rate of growth occurring in the general population over the same period.[4] *Managing prisoners is a very expensive business.* In 2011–12, the national real net operating expenditure[5] on prisons totalled just over $2.4 billion[6] (SCRGSP 2013, Table 8A.8).[7] This figure excludes, it should be noted, the $103 million spent annually on moving prisoners around (that is, transport and escort services) (SCRGSP 2013, Table 8A.6).[8] In the same period, the real net operating expenditure for community corrections was $452 million (SCRGSP 2013: Table 8A.10) – a division that manages, on any day, nearly double the number of people in prisons, and which does so at one-fifth the cost. In a major Australian study, Allard et al. (2014) examined the economic costs of offending at ages 10 to 25 associated with a cohort of 41,377 individuals. Total costs (including policing, adjudicating, incarcerating, supervising offenders in the community, and supporting victims of crime) amounted to more than $1.1 billion across the group (Allard et al. 2014: 95). The really crucial determination, though, was that just under five per cent of the cohort 'accounted for 41.1 per cent of the total costs' (Allard et al. 2014: 94). This small subsection – labelled 'adolescent onset (chronic)' and 'early onset (chronic)' offenders – 'consumed' a vastly disproportionate quantum of resources to 'address' their offending. In fact, they 'cost...over 20 times more than individuals in the two low offending groups' with roughly $220,000 spent on each chronic offender (Allard et al. 2014: 94). The young men in this book fall squarely, as shall be seen, into these chronic categories. In fact, compared with the majority of offenders in the Allard et al. (2014) study, the costs associated with the offending of the young men in our study are likely to be much higher both on account of their crimes and on account of their considerable custodial periods. For example, the cost of incarcerating for 12 of the 14 young men in their juvenile years amounted to around $12 million.[9]

The Prison Reform Trust in the UK cites data from the National Audit Office showing 'Reoffending by all recent ex-prisoners in 2007–08 cost the economy between GBP9.5 and GBP13 billion' (Prison Reform Trust 2013: 1). A major recent report on recidivism in the US determined that 'If [...] the 10 states with the greatest potential cost savings reduced their recidivism rates by 10 per cent, they could save more than $470 million in a single year' (Pew Center on the States 2011: 26). The US correctional budget currently stands at more than US$50 billion per annum with 'one in every eight state employees work[ing] for a corrections agency' (Pew Center on the States 2011: 5). For every US$14 of public money spent, one dollar is spent on state and/or federal corrections (prisons, community supervision, and the like). The cost of running police, courts and prisons in the US in 2007 was just short of a staggering US$230 billion (Kyckelhahn 2011).

As with the US and UK, the bulk of the annual criminal justice budget in Australia goes to policing. In 2011–12, $9.4 billion (of a total justice sector budget of $14 billion) was spent on police services ($7.2 billion of which was devoted to salaries and payments) (SCRGSP 2013: 6.5 and C.9). Notionally, at least, the detection and apprehension of offenders makes up a sizeable proportion of police work – with repeat offenders accounting for a disproportionate amount of resources. In fact, around 20 per cent of offenders proceeded against by police in 2010–11 were subject to a proceeding on two or more separate occasions. In New South Wales, Queensland, South Australia, Tasmania and the Northern Territory, five per cent were subject to four separate proceedings in a 12-month period (SCRGSP 2013: C21). The costs associated with juvenile offenders are substantial as well. 'Total recurrent expenditure on detention-based supervision, community-based supervision and group conferencing was approximately $640.1 million across Australia in 2011–12'. This represented around 20 per cent of the total annual budget allocated for out-of-home care and child protection services – a budget which has increased by more than three quarters of a billion dollars over the past five years (SCRGSP 2013: 15.15–15.16). Keeping kids incarcerated cost nearly $400 million during the 2011–12 period (SCRGSP 2013: 15.67).

In light of the monumental costs associated with policing, judging, confining and supervising offenders, it seems obvious that increases in desistance from crime have the potential to free up large portions of public funds.[10] Allard et al. (2014: 83), noting the work of Cohen and Piquero (2009), observe 'The value of saving a 14-year-old high-risk youth from a life of crime was found to be between US$2.6 and US$5.3 million in 2007'. In the period spanning mid-2009 to the end of 2010, roughly two-thirds of all prisoner receptions in New South Wales were found, immediately prior to admission into custody, to be on 'Centrelink benefits' (equivalent to social security, health or housing benefits in the US and UK) (Correctional Services New South Wales 2013). Assuming an average benefit payment of $240 per week, that all admissions were unique individuals, and that all *avoided* incarceration for 18 months, such persons (n=12,922) would each have received just under $19,000 – a collective public tariff of around $242 million. However, if the same cohort all spent 18 months in prison, the cost would amount to around $113,000 per person or *$1.46 billion* (based on the 2010–11 cost per day per prisoner of $207). Even with various caveats (such as the fact that many will be released after only a few days), this very simple numbers game is a salutary exercise in thinking about the relationship between public expenditure and socially beneficial outcomes. Why, as a society, would we not invest more directly in the things that keep people out of prison rather than waiting until the horse has well and truly bolted? Something, as previously mentioned, is broken.

Beyond the numbers game

Arguably, to bring about positive changes in rates of desistance one has to move well beyond a broad statistical understanding of crime and rates of return to custody. In particular, we believe it is essential to appreciate what works well (and not so well) in *real people's* struggles to desist from crime. There are a host of factors small and large which police, court and correctional data do not (cannot) capture regarding why people reoffend or cease offending. Our chief aim in this book is to explicate some of these factors. There will of course be some commonality concerning people's situations. But mostly the scenarios we discuss are idiosyncratic. Indeed, one of our major contentions is that *each series of stumbling blocks or moments of consolidation in the desistance process plays out in unique ways for each person*. Everyone, in other words, desists (and reoffends) in ways peculiar to their own needs and circumstances. Subtle and not so subtle differences feed into circumstances that at first glance appear very similar in people's lives. Unless we know of and account for these subtle differences, we risk misunderstanding how each person could, or otherwise would, desist from crime. Evidence shows that desistance from crime is likely to be a *collective* struggle/process (Farrall 2004; McNeill 2006) and is likely to span years – sometimes decades (Laub and Sampson 2006; Weaver 2008). Some people (the precise number is unknown) sustain serious interruptions to the desistance process well beyond the (arbitrary) two-year benchmark typically used to measure recidivism or whether one has succeeded in 'going straight'. Ross and Guarnieri (1996), for example, extended the window of survival time to seven and half years and showed, in a Victorian cohort of 838 offenders, that while the bulk of recidivism and reincarceration episodes occurred within three years of release, 12 per cent returned to prison in years four to seven. As they remind us, '[T]his [number] cannot be ignored as trivial' (1996: 30). The question of how to recognize desistance – *when* to say it has occurred – is accordingly a difficult one to answer. But, as shall become clear in our work, the response lies in something more than simple time elapsed from prison or a community sanction. The distinction between 'primary' and 'secondary' desistance is central to this determination.

Conceptualizing desistance

In spite of recent and concerted interest in desistance, knowledge regarding the process of giving up crime 'is still relatively limited' (Kazemian 2007: 5; see also Bushway et al. 2003; Farrall and Bowling 1999; Farrington 2003; Laub and Sampson 2001; Le Blanc and Loeber 1998; Piquero et al. 2003; Uggen and Piliavin 1998). Commentators have noted a number of difficulties concerning the definition of desistance (Bottoms et al 2004; Kazemian 2007; King 2013; Maruna 2001; Laub and Sampson 2001). For some, it is an empirical variable denoting the categorical termination of, or cessation from, offending (Farrington 2007). Shover (1996: 121) similarly conceives desistance in terms of the 'voluntary termination of serious criminal participation'. However, the way in which 'the criminal career literature traditionally imagines desistance as an event' (Maruna, 2001: 22) has been subject to growing scrutiny. In particular, questions have been posed regarding how best to distinguish a temporary break from offending (intermittent desistance) from a more durable hiatus. Further, some have queried whether desistance has to include a decline in the frequency, type *and* severity of offending (Bushway et al. 2001; Farrington 2007) or whether a diminution in severity alone is enough to say that some offenders have, for all intents and purposes, 'desisted'. If the latter applies, then how much time should elapse prior to 'legitimately' being able to conclude desistance has in fact occurred (Bushway et al. 2001; Laub and Sampson 2001, 2006; Maruna 2001; Piquero et al. 2003)? Another question concerns whether desistance requires a minimum prior frequency of offending or, as some have asked, 'can desistance occur after [just] one act of crime?' (Laub and Sampson, 2001: 6). As Farrington (2007: 128) reminds us, it is 'obvious that a high-rate offender ha[s] stopped but [desistance is] harder to distinguish from gaps between offences for low-rate offenders'.

Desistance as *process*

One way of resolving these issues is to conceive of desistance not as an abrupt 'event or state' (McNeill and Maruna 2008: 225) so much as a provisional and sometimes confounding movement towards accessing social supports or 'hooks for change' (Giordano et al. 2002: 992). Observing a 'process of "to-ing' and 'fro-ing", of progress and setback, of hope and despair' (McNeill 2009: 27) recent scholars have argued the path towards desistance is 'zig-zagged' (Healy 2010) rather than 'linear'. We certainly believe this best describes the situations of the young men in our study. Here, a movement 'towards desistance' (Bottoms et al. 2004) can oscillate between offending and significant 'lulls' (Farrall 2002). As Haigh (2009: 315) puts it, a 'one-off decision to change is not the norm for most people attempting to change their lives'. Thinking about desistance as a process means, in effect, framing it in terms of its primary and secondary dimensions. Maruna (individually and with others) has 'pioneered' this distinction by, essentially, inverting Edwin Lemert's theory of criminal involvement as involving primary and secondary types of deviance (see Maruna et al. 2004; Maruna and Farrall 2004). In terms of desistance, these concepts are distinguishable by the 'length of time the individual has refrained from offending [i.e., primary desistance] and the subjective changes that they have experienced at the individual level [i.e., secondary desistance]' (King 2013: 148). Something happens in this process whereby the label 'offender' becomes superseded by the label 'non-offender' – or, put differently, the offender completes the long and complex journey of turning her/himself into a 'conventional citizen' (Maruna 2011). Many, of course, will not achieve this transformation. However, when secondary desistance emerges, individuals at the centre of that process tend 'to regard criminal activity as incompatible with their new identity' (King 2013: 149, drawing on Vaughan 2007). Capturing the nature of primary desistance (the cessation of an event) has, therefore, been a somewhat easier task than trying to explicate the dimensions of secondary desistance. The latter, as shall become clear in the stories told in this book, involves the timely convergence of personal, social as well as symbolic factors (Maruna 2001). But these tend to be in fairly short supply where the stigma of criminality and/or incarceration 'taints' the person trying to move toward the secondary phase.

'Antecedents' of desistance

Broadly speaking, three perspectives inform thinking about why people desist. These include: maturational reform, social bonding theory and narrative theory (for a detailed overview, see Maruna 2001). *Maturational reform* (or 'ontogenic') theories are based on the idea that offenders 'grow up' and desist from crime (Glueck and Glueck 1968; Gottfredson and Hirshi 1990; Moffitt 1993). In particular, the '[a]ge-crime curve' illustrates that most offending is a 'young person's game' (McNeill and Maruna 2008: 227) with most abandoning crime in their late teenage years (Moffitt 1993). It is hard to deny the merit of such a view. Studies of large-scale offender cohorts clearly illustrate the weight of maturational reform as an explanation for crime cessation. However, the perspective holds less weight for serious repeat offenders – especially for those whose age of onset is very young (less, say, than 14 years). It is manifestly obvious that many people do not stop offending in their early or even late 20s. The average age of prisoners the world over (early to mid-30s) is ample testimony to that fact.

Social bonding (or 'sociogenic') theories postulate that what matters most is whether 'good' things (such as stable employment or marriage) happen to 'bad' actors, thereby serving as a 'catalyst for sustaining long-term behavioral change' (Laub and Sampson 2006: 149). Here, importantly, and we think correctly, differential impacts of the same 'turning point' event are explained by the individual's level of motivation, 'openness to change' or interpretation of such events (Giordano et al. 2002: 1000). In so far as they permit offenders to 'knife off the past from the present' (Laub and Sampson 2006: 148–9), new social contexts promote opportunities for support and attachment whilst providing valuable structure and routine. Specifically, as the 'investment in social bonds grows, the incentive for avoiding crime increases because more is at stake' (Laub et al. 1998: 225). Again, we find this to be broadly so in our research. Certainly, the affirmative dimension of human (caring) relationships can inspire greater levels of civic participation and integration into 'conventional' roles (Barry 2006; Huebner et al. 2007;

McNeill and Maruna 2008). It is beyond doubt that many offenders are plagued by insecurity regarding their capacity to maintain a 'straight and legitimate lifestyle' (Haigh 2009: 307). Accordingly, simply having someone believe in their capacity to desist emerges as a key resource for many (ex)offenders (McNeill, 2004: 429; McNeill and Maruna 2008). Still, as the stories in Chapters 4, 5, and 6 will show, even having such support is no guarantee of success.

The third explanatory construct, *narrative theory* (or an 'identity change' perspective), emphasizes the capacity of individuals, through the development of a coherent life story, to 'resituate themselves and their identities, and subsequently to alter various forms of social activity' (King 2013: 150). Under these circumstances, changes in an individual's self-identity and worldview are seen also to prompt a reorientation of goals, desires and needs (Maruna and Roy 2007: 115). Consider, for example, the difference between 'a strong deviant identity and its associated behaviours [as against] the demands of [real or imagined] alternative, pro-social identities... [such as] partner, parent, churchgoer or employee' (Rumgay 2004: 407). As conventional roles assume greater relevance, individuals begin to reconceptualize their identities around new responsibilities and obligations while also identifying potential avenues that will assist 'longer-term moves away from crime' (King 2013: 155). These new 'pro-social' experiences become part of a 'reformed' person's burgeoning life story or script – one typically about redemption or giving back or 'becoming normal'. However, the motivation to desist is not necessarily synonymous with the belief that desistance will actually occur (Snyder et al. 1991: 570). To this end, Maruna (2001) found desisting offenders maintained an optimistic view about their futures and were driven chiefly by a 'redemptive script'. Active offenders, on the other hand, carried a negative view of their future and lived through the prism of a 'condemnation script'. We are undecided about the 'order' of events here – whether people build a redemption script ahead of having any hooks for change or whether the 'operationalization' of those hooks enables a redemptive (non-offender) narrative to slowly emerge (see Giordano et al. 2002; King 2013). Our sense is that these things happen in different order for different people. Certainly, in our small cohort, there is a mix of declarative statements regarding the desire to desist, the imagining of oneself to be a fundamentally 'good person', and, finally, of young men looking back at what they've achieved, and only then adorning their achievements with positive terminology. Here, in retrospect, a few speak of *now* being a 'normal person', living 'a regular life', and 'just getting on with things'. To our minds, these new identities – these emerging competent subjectivities – appear 'after the fact' as if taking each almost by surprise.

Desistance and generativity

We don't automatically discount any of the above perspectives as possible explanations for desistance. What we do discount is the possibility of a 'catch-all' theory. In a sense, this book 'tests' elements from all three perspectives and suggests that becoming generative is more or less central to the desistance process. Clearly, we recognize the body of work that connotes generative commitment and action as typically the domain of 'older' individuals. But we also find that young men who are able, through whatever means, to commence caring in meaningful (non-trivial) fashion for themselves, for others and for their future, are likely to be better placed to desist. For each of the young men in our study, this puts custodial environments (juvenile and adult) centre stage. Aged in their mid to late twenties, most have spent a total of eight to ten years behind bars. Sometimes, the 'pains of imprisonment' (Sykes 1958) are so pronounced as to seemingly *determine* their behaviour – a process more commonly called institutionalization. Chris, Sam and James – who feature in Chapter 6 – know something of this. Others have more or less been able to resist such. Accordingly, just as Liebling (2004) has asked whether prisons can be moral, we ask, in effect, whether incarceration can be generative – not of more harm, violence or humiliation, but generative, instead, of pro-social lives, of modelling respectful behavior, and of genuine opportunities for change. This is an immensely tall order for any custodial environment. Perhaps the most that could ever be expected is that those who work in such places believe that all prisoners are capable of change. The cultures of custodial facilities – how those on remand or under sentence are treated, how visitors (professionals or families/friends) are addressed, how a facility responds to 'trouble on the wing', how staff treat each other – goes fundamentally to how prisoners will 'do' incarceration and how they are likely to cope on release. In this way, Maruna and colleagues (2004a: 133) consider generativity to be a critically important part of reforming custodial *and* post-custodial environments:

> We contend that if the world of corrections were to become more of a *generative society* – that is, an environment in which generative commitments were modelled and nurtured, and opportunities for

generative activities were promoted and rewarded – it would simply be more effective at reducing repeat offending.

The size of our small cohort does not permit reliable statements to be made about whether this contention is categorically borne out. We do not seek generalizability of themes or 'findings' (for an eloquent defence of small but in-depth qualitative studies, see Maruna 2007; for an elaboration and justification of the [multiple] case study approach, see Stake 1995; Yin 2006). But we can say that the young men in our study were (and remain) acutely aware of when they were being treated badly within custody and, for that matter, while under community supervision (that is, when in the wider 'world of corrections'). We know this because there are so few examples of them telling us something positive about either of these domains. When something did arise, it was like finding a diamond in the roughest terrain.

The bigger picture

Prior, then, to outlining the method and nature of fieldwork undertaken, we think it important to remind the reader that the study of crime and desistance needs to be positioned within a much larger conceptual landscape. While we adopt, pragmatically, a critical realist stance (since we believe the harm caused through street/violent offending to be *real* and that it has *serious* repercussions for particular families and communities), we also recognize that the focus on people who commit such crime and their struggles to desist is but one very small part of the larger scene(s) of crime and violence which invest social and political systems (Matthews 2009; Frauley 2011). These 'systems' cannot be ignored. In fact, they are fundamental to the nature and extent of events typically labelled and policed as crime (see Greenberg 1993; Box 1983). This means that while 'crimes of the streets' take precedence hereafter over 'crimes of the suites', we acknowledge that understanding the onset of offending and desistance in the latter context remains a critically important but under-researched task (see South and Brisman 2013). To put it bluntly, if 'social harm' was taken as the basic measure, then desistance of white-collar and corporate offending would probably matter most – as would the link between 'corporate generativity' and the public good. The widely felt effects of the Enron scandal, various Ponzi schemes, the sub-prime mortgage debacle and other similar events amply attest to the social damage stemming from actors with the lion's share of political and economic power. Equally, the destruction to marine (and human) life caused by the malfunction of BP's Deepwater Horizon drilling rig, or by the meltdown of Japan's Fukushima nuclear plant, put the harms caused by 'run-of-the-mill' street offenders into sobering perspective. In short, we understand the ways in which power – seemingly implacable structural forces – frame particular events (mass unemployment, war, global warming, homelessness, poverty) as beyond the actions of any individual or group (as 'authorless'). Crime is an inherently political category used (that is, defined and policed) to benefit some groups over others. Understandably, therefore, the study of desistance from crime has been 'shorthand' for desistance from street/violent crime. This does not negate the importance of such work. But it does make it necessary to acknowledge the scholarly and personal-political choices associated with desistance-oriented research.

2
Approach to the Field – Data

This book was originally inspired by the work of Tony Parker – in particular, *Life After Life: Interviews with Twelve Murderers*. In that work, Parker somehow managed to step 'outside' the prose so that the stories could be told. He asked nothing of the reader – there was no explicit political, social or theoretical agenda being pushed. But the book had a curious way of imploring audiences to ask questions about the causes of crime, of deep personal trauma and about what might be done to prevent such. Equally, in a field often wedded to large cohort studies, Norman Mailer's *The Executioner's Song* was central to the current research. That work provided irrefutable evidence that delving into the trials and tribulations of a very small group of people could matter – that it could produce something worthwhile for readers (perhaps even for policy-makers and practitioners). It was and remains a master class in how to research the life of 'one' person and connect it so deftly to the lives of those who orbit around them.

More recently, the ground-breaking work of Shadd Maruna's *Making Good* has had a major impact on our thinking. The idea of asking people how they work their way out of crime – instead of into it – was simple but original. No other person has surpassed Maruna's contribution to the study of desistance. In addition, our study has also taken shape in relation to Kevin McDonald's *Struggles for Subjectivity* (we pay homage to this in the subtitle). McDonald draws extensively on various emergent 'identities' (graffiti writers, gang members, anorexics, 'ethnic' minorities) in an attempt to understand how young people create and hold on to a sense of self in the brave new world of globalization, of fundamental changes in the labour market, of significant fissures in the pathways to 'adulthood', and the like. In the final moments of that work he writes:

If we want to understand the emerging new world, if sociology [or, indeed, criminology] is to contribute to the struggle of imagining new ways of living, we must strive to understand such fragile struggles for freedom. We need to be up at dawn, listening to questions being asked in languages we do not yet understand (McDonald 1999: 218).

We take this challenge seriously. Specifically, we've tried to enact the principle of listening carefully to those whose voices remain obscured by the clang and clamour of public and political stereotyping or, more pointedly, by the conditions attending incarceration (where, we note, the very nature of existence revolves largely around being deprived of a voice). We have attempted to be sensitive to the nature of the struggles each participant believes her/himself to be engaged in – to relay them as far as is practicable from their perspective(s). At the same time, we are fully cognizant that as researchers (as authors), we are inextricably involved in (re)constructing events as much as we are involved in recording such (Presser 2009).

Two further and very recent works help to frame what follows. Adam Reich's *Hidden Truth* skilfully relays the challenges faced by young men in prison and beyond. His conceptual tools – chiefly, the 'game of law' and 'game of outlaw' – have influenced our thinking in important ways (for a review of his work, see Halsey 2013). Equally, Randol Contreras' brilliant *Stickup Kids* – an exposition of life and survival in the South Bronx – has left a lasting impression. His approach to the field and to storytelling is instructive. We don't presume to match such here, but we've done our best to convey the lives of participants in engaging fashion. The ethical and social imperative driving Contreras's work is also clear. As he reminds us, 'We must understand how despair can drive the marginal into greed, betrayal, cruelty, and self-destruction' (Contreras 2013: xix). For us, this quest to explicate the links between humiliation and violence is also paramount. We note, finally, the paucity of qualitative approaches to the longitudinal study of young people and crime (Laub and Sampson 2006: 61; Farrall 2004: 63; Farrington 2007: 130). We hope our work makes a small contribution in this regard.

Research design

The research design underpinning the data collection process for this book evolved over time. When the first interview was completed in September 2003, it was conducted as part of the small-scale research project *Negotiating Conditional Release: A Pilot Study of the Factors Affecting Recidivism Rates of Young Men in Secure Care*. That study aimed to determine reasons for the very high breach rates of young men on conditional release (the juvenile equivalent of parole). In all, 20 interviews (with 20 unique male participants, aged 15 to 18 years, lasting between 30 minutes and two hours) were completed over the period September 2003 to July 2004. Each young man had served at least one prior detention order of three months or more (making them eligible for conditional release) and had previously been breached and returned to juvenile detention while on conditional release on at least one occasion. Interviews explored three main themes: pathways into crime; experiences of being locked up; and transitions to release. The results of that project have been widely published (Halsey 2006a, 2007a, 2008b) and led to the recruitment and interviewing of a further ten unique participants (evincing the same base criteria for inclusion) through the latter half of 2004. These interviews (n = 30) subsequently paved the way for a major grant application to the Australian Research Council, and, in 2005, the lead author was awarded funds to undertake the four-year project *Understanding Recidivism and Repeat Incarceration among Young Male Offenders: A Biographical and Longitudinal Approach*. From 2005 to 2008, this project – again using the same base criteria for recruitment – expanded the cohort of 30 young men to 54 unique participants. Importantly though, the project was designed to 'follow' each young man into the adult custodial jurisdiction (if and when they progressed to such). In fact, 55 per cent (n = 28) of those interviewed in juvenile detention ended up in prison (this figure excludes the three interviewees who still held juvenile status, that is, who were aged 17 or below) during the project period. Follow-up (repeat) interviews were conducted with each young man subsequent to them being sentenced to a new period of incarceration. Interviews were *not* conducted with remandees or with those who were returned to custody for a minor 'breach' of parole conditions (such as failure to attend appointments). This was a methodological decision taken to keep the definition of recidivism as 'deep' and as 'tight' as possible.

From 2005 to 2008, 130 interviews were completed with 54 unique participants aged 17 to 24. Many (38 per cent, n = 21) participants were interviewed on three or more occasions consistent with their release, reincarceration and sentencing scenarios. Eleven participants were interviewed four or more times with one participant (Chris, see Chapter 6) interviewed on six separate occasions (reflecting, in other words, six episodes of release, reincarceration and sentencing for new offences in the study period). Including those conducted prior to 2005, 160 interviews were concluded from 2003 to 2008. Such data generated a rich six-year prospective and retrospective archive of custodial experiences, expectations prior to release (regarding housing, family, work and the like), and what actually occurred following release (scenarios of repeat offending and/or desistance of the 'primary' kind). Results of this work have also been widely published (Halsey 2007b; 2008a; 2008c; Halsey and Armitage 2009; Halsey and Harris 2011; Goldsmith and Halsey 2013).

In 2009, the lead author was again awarded funding from the Australian Research Council for the project *Generativity in Young Male (Ex)Prisoners: Caring for Self, Other, and Future within Prison and Beyond*. This project sought to explore the emerging link between desistance from (serious) crime and generative commitment and action among select young men interviewed in the aforementioned research (2003 to 2008). In early to mid-2009, 14 of the previous interviewees were invited to take part in the research (Indigenous = 1, Asian = 1, Caucasian = 12, with all but one born in Australia). At such time they were aged 17 to 24 years (1 = 17 years; 1 = 19 years; 1 = 20 years; 4 = 21 years; 2 = 22 years; 1 = 23 years; 4 = 24 years). They were chosen in accordance with their perceived position on the 'persistence-desistance continuum' with at least half having evinced good degrees of generative commitment in previous interviews (wanting to be a good parent, a good partner, a good provider and the like). Such commitment, as might be expected, was most prominent among older members of the cohort.

As at July 2009, ten of the young men were in prison, three were under community supervision, and one was 'free' from any order. Of those in prison, four were due for release in late 2009 (Reggie, Ben, Charlie, Joel), three in 2010 (James, Matt, Greg), and one in mid-2012 (Lee). One was about to start an eight-month period of probation (David) while another (Chris) was on remand. Of those in the community, one had just commenced a four-year parole period (Billy), one was on home detention bail (Sam) and another was on a community service order with court matters pending (Paul). Only one young man (Sean) was not under any supervision. There was a good mix of earliest release dates permitting, theoretically, opportunities to closely map the process of 'starting again' – for documenting the personal and social factors hindering or supporting moves toward desistance. The average age on first being admitted to custody was 13 years. All had served time in juvenile facilities and prison. Importantly, all had experienced at least ten prior release episodes from a custodial facility including supervised release (parole or like) and getting out end of order (as 'free' persons). Collectively, the 14 young men had committed a wide range of offences including, but not limited to, petty theft, hindering police, motor vehicle theft, home invasion (burglary break and enter), serious criminal trespass (theft from a business/public premises), armed robbery, endangering life, arson, serious assault, drug possession and supply, and more. Their familial backgrounds and circumstances of offending are described in later chapters.

From a research standpoint, this small group embodied demonstrably diverse positions from which to explore generative commitment and action over ensuing years (to the end of 2013). They also afforded – through interviews with family members and friends – the means to examine factors apt to derail such commitment. Significantly, nine of the original 20 young men interviewed in 2003–04 agreed to be a part of the study over the ten-year period of data collection (specifically, 12 of the initial 20 were approached with three declining to take further part). For the 14 young men, participation in the final part of the research meant committing to being interviewed twice yearly for four years no matter whether they were in custody or the community. On occasion, interviews occurred only once a year due to an inability to locate participants. In total, 86 interviews (including 31 community-based interviews) were completed with the 14 young men from late 2009 to late 2013. The majority (n = 9) were interviewed six to eight times during that period. Taking into account interviews conducted during previous projects, the distribution ended up as follows: one young man was interviewed on five occasions; three on seven occasions; two on nine occasions; two on ten occasions; three on 11 occasions; two on 12 occasions; and one on 14 occasions (n = 135 interviews with the 14 young males).

A further condition of involvement was that each was required to nominate up to three significant others capable, in the eyes of each young man, of narrating the challenges of incarceration and release from an 'external' viewpoint. As we have previously demonstrated, family and close friends of repeat incarcerates have a unique vantage point from which to view the struggles of such persons (Halsey and Deegan 2012, 2014). As might be expected, some young men found it easier than others to think of NSOs – persons who 'cared' for their welfare over a long period. Nonetheless, at least two significant others were interviewed for each young participant. Given the length of the project, some significant others came and went and were subsequently replaced, where possible, by new nominations. Fifteen males and 26 females were nominated resulting in 95 interviews (19 of which were conducted 'jointly' with, for example, the mother and (step)father of the young male participant). In the majority of instances, NSOs were interviewed once a year during the project period.

As a means for understanding the official objectives of incarceration, one-off interviews were undertaken with all managers of adult male custodial facilities (n = 7) in South Australia. With a view to ascertaining the scope for, and meanings of, 'rehabilitation', one-off interviews with offender development managers (n = 6) were also completed at the outset of the project. Given the pivotal role of prison in the young men's lives, interviews with 40 prison officers (10 female, 30 male), with varying levels of service (less than 2 years, 5 to 10 years, 10 to 20 years, and more than 20 years), based at five different facilities (one privately run, four publicly run, with a mix of security levels), form part of the project data. In total, 234 interviews were completed for the *Generativity in Young Male (Ex)Prisoners* project. When the interviews conducted with the 14 young men on previous projects are included (n = 50), the total number of interviews informing the book is 284. Excepting government employees, all participants were paid $30 to compensate them for their time and effort during interview.

Keeping in contact with interviewees occurred via three avenues. For those in prison or under community supervision, a key contact person from the Department for Correctional Services ('DCS') provided us with monthly updates of their whereabouts. Written consent for such information to be provided to us was given by each young man. With regard to NSOs, mobile phone (most commonly, texting) proved to be the key means of keeping in touch. Most often, when not in custody, this was the primary way of contacting the young men as well. As we quickly learned, the phone numbers changed frequently, and so we sought to obtain as many residential addresses and alternative contact numbers as possible across the interviewee cohort. Where phone numbers changed we sometimes travelled to relevant addresses to seek new contact numbers. Most participants, without any prompting, texted us their new contact details. We took this as a tangible measure of the trust established between them and ourselves. Our personal mobile phone numbers were given to all interviewees and we made it clear that they could contact us any time about any aspect of the project. Not infrequently, this meant having to work through a number of complex situations with various participants. These ranged across calls informing us that 'police were on the doorstep', to the more common theme, 'I'm falling apart' (Ben, Chapter 4). Occasionally, very occasionally, good news ensued. After many years of being denied the right to drive a vehicle, one young man (Charlie, see Chapter 3) called to say that he'd just obtained his licence ('Thought you'd want to know,' he said). Another sent a text extending an invitation to his wedding (Billy, Chapter 3). Beyond phone calls, many letters were written to the young men – especially when they were incarcerated. The correspondence was generally aimed at encouraging them to 'keep their heads down' and to do their time as well as possible. Christmas cards and the occasional birthday card were also sent. These seemed to offer some small respite for those doing it particularly tough. Of course, we reflected on whether such cards only made bad situations worse (reminding the young men of what they were missing). But most – at the next face-to-face meeting – commented on the gesture and thanked us for it (for 'showing an interest').

Longitudinal interview-based research – particularly when the same participants are interviewed many times over a lengthy period – has its own curious set of demands. We believe such research to be anything than a dispassionate endeavour (Liebling 1999). It is impossible to put emotions completely to one side over ten years when delving into the struggles – the lived experience of the pain, hopes, and fears – of highly marginalized people. It is difficult to resist 'taking sides' when it seems patently obvious that many of these people are being crushed by overwhelming institutional and systemic factors. Of course, it is essential to inject rigorous critical scholarship into such scenarios – to take, as it were, the longer and wider view of the social and penal landscape. This book attempts to do that. But the book is at one and the same time about generativity – specifically, the attempt by young (ex)incarcerated males to create the beginnings of a legacy they might one day look back on and be rightly proud of. It is appropriate therefore that we, as researchers, *also* put ourselves firmly within the generative frame – to try to show/model tangible degrees of care toward participants. As hinted at previously, one way we did this was to listen to their concerns and problems over the phone. Another involved talking face-to-face off-tape with them about 'stuff' before going on the record. At other times it meant helping out with a meal here or there, or connecting them to a mental health service, or acting as a 'go-between' when relations with partners or other family members were deeply frayed, and the like. These were some of the ways we sought to make the research process something other than a purely extractive exercise. *We wanted participants to be involved as equals in the project not as subjects of the project.* Without them, after all, there would not be a project.

Beyond this, one of the most important things we 'offered' participants was a commitment to write letters of support with regard to various scenarios which might play out in times ahead. As it happened, we were able to put our perspective on record in the contexts of participants' applications for parole, driver's licenses, and so forth. In several instances – and in what turned out to be quite high-profile cases – we were able to provide the court with detailed narratives of young men's lives in an effort to inform the sentencing process. Here, magistrates (in 'traditional' courts and in drug courts) and judges (in district courts) saw fit to cite our remarks in the official record. In these instances, separate consent forms were signed by the young men acknowledging that any letters tendered to the court would very likely mean their involvement in the research could become public knowledge (as researchers, we could therefore no longer reasonably be expected to protect their identity). Various amendments to the ethics applications were, therefore, sought and approved as the project unfolded.

During these 'generative' researcher-driven moments, we never ceased to be struck by how few persons were at hand to offer constructive support for the young men at key times in their lives (facing the prospect of 10 to 20 years in prison surely counted as such). All participants, in short, were genuinely taken aback by the fact that someone (researchers from a University, no less) took the time to listen to them, or, more simply, just to be present in court as a familiar face. It goes without saying that all letters were written on the basis that they would contain frank and fearless (if highly contextualized) information about each participant. If a letter concerned parole, we made it clear to each young man that their conduct within prison would be duly noted irrespective of whether that conduct was favourable or poor. One participant asked whether we could provide a reference for him as he was applying for a new rental property. We would oblige but he was reminded that we would likely be asked by the rental agent how we came to know him. That would mean saying something about the project and his past. On balance – and as much as it distressed us – he decided against putting our names forward. In sum, there were no 'free rides'. And participants knew and seemed to respect that.

In the ensuing chapters we bring to the fore the key turning points in each young man's life. We supplement their own narratives with those of significant others and, where appropriate, correctional personnel. Due to the sheer volume of interview material – all of which was *manually* read/coded – our presentation of participants' experiences is necessarily partial. In any case, an interview is a highly selective structuring/'editing' of experience to begin with. We have tried, though, to produce an appropriate balance between description (what happened) and analysis (why it happened). For each young man, an extended vignette is relayed which tries to capture the broad flow of events in their lives which have enhanced (put on track) or interrupted (derailed) their respective relationships to desistance. While we offer some limited critical reflection on each vignette *in situ*, the main analysis of such occurs in chapters 7 and 8. There we bring key emergent issues and themes together in an effort to earmark the theoretical and policy implications of the data.

Included in the book are a series of 'custodial-grams' depicting the history of admission and release for each participant. Specific permission to use this data was obtained from relevant government departments, and, of course, the young men themselves. In two instances, though, we were unable to track down participants to get their signed consent to use their data. As such, the stories of Greg and Sean feature less centrally in what follows and we do not reproduce a custodial-gram for these young men. In addition, we were unable to acquire official juvenile data for Paul (having instead to rely on his interviews and those conducted with his NSOs for approximate juvenile detention/remand dates). However, Paul did sign a form for release of his adult data and his custodial-gram (with a select juvenile component) is reproduced. To protect, as far as practicable, the identity of the young men, the custodial-grams do not display parole dates, or dates concerning breaches, major types of offending or significant life events. These are, though, hinted at in their life-stories. The singular purpose of the custodial-grams is to give an unambiguous sense of the relationship between total time spent in custody as against total time spent in the community and to illustrate changes in these durations over the years. We hope they add something of value to the work.

Over the next four chapters, we describe what happens in that liminal space and time where young men start to grapple with a sense of self that is simultaneously wedded to yet partly distinct from crime and repeat incarceration. The choices made (or omitted), the skills acquired (or forgone), the people befriended (or pushed away or who recede from view), the services engaged (or removed), the setbacks overcome (or that continue to impact), the scripts regarding self, other and future which emerge (or decline), all underpin the fragile project of what we call the assembling of the post-custodial or socially competent subject. As shall be seen, some fare far better than others in the struggle to put that subject together and to ensure it is kept alive.

3
On Track

This chapter relays the twists and turns taken by the three young men who, on the best evidence, are edging toward a secondary form of desistance – the stage, it will be recalled, which involves more than the slowing or cessation of offending to encompass, additionally, personal and social belief in a 'conventional', predominantly law-abiding self. Each of them, as shall be seen, consider themselves ex-offenders, or better still, in terms *other* than those which invoke reference to crime, prison, or the like. Minor forms of offending, though, persist in each case. But these are limited mainly to driving while disqualified (as juveniles, all had the prospect of applying for a licence cancelled by the courts), consuming the occasional alcoholic beverage (which contravenes parole conditions) or occasional consumption of illicit drugs. With these exceptions, Billy, Charlie and David are 'making good'. Their lives are fundamentally distinct from the days when they shared the same secure care unit as teenagers. Each, though, has taken a different path in the quest to get on track.

Billy

Billy is in his late twenties. He married Julie several years ago and they have three children. Two of the kids call him 'Dad' even though they know Billy is their stepdad. He proudly describes how they call him their 'good dad' – they don't see their 'bad dad' (he was repeatedly violent toward Julie and she managed, under very trying circumstances, to eventually leave him). Julie met Billy in the short period between one of his many release and reincarceration episodes. She waited six months for him and spoke with him three times a week on the prison phone and visited whenever she could. They now live in a quiet and well-located private rental property out of metropolitan Adelaide. Billy has just completed his parole period of four years. He has a job which enables him to work anywhere from three to six days a week. He found the job via Julie's small business network of customers. Like many young men, Billy has a passion for cars. He buys, repairs and sells cars from his backyard on a regular basis – dozens of vehicles might pass through his hands (legitimately, in most instances) – in a six-month period. The money he makes from improving cars supplements the seasonal nature of the income from his regular job. He is a reliable and hard worker and was recently given the opportunity by his employer to apply for promotion. Separate to this, and due to his extensive knowledge of cars, he was offered an apprenticeship through the Motor Trade Association of South Australia.

After more than a decade, Billy earned the right to apply for his driver's licence – a licence canceled at 'Her Majesty's Pleasure' in connection with his offending. The court awarded him that capacity not long ago – a real milestone in his journey toward getting on track (we were able to tender a letter of support for Billy and attended court). Billy's wife is self-employed and runs a small but increasingly successful business from their home. Billy and Julie are in semi-regular contact with their parents who help out with the kids where possible. Billy is also father to a child from a previous relationship and, after much negotiation (including court proceedings), spends most weekends with him. He is content with his lot but wants to save up to buy a property on a little bit of land – somewhere to give the kids a chance to grow up outdoors and somewhere further out of town.

Things, though, were not always like this. Indeed, Billy had all the hallmarks of being entrenched in long cycles of crime and violence. At 14, he was kicked out of school for hitting the principal. At roughly the same age he stole his first car and received his first detention order. He would tell in interview that at the core of his offending – the thing that sparked his overt anger toward others and the world generally – was finding out that his father was not, in fact, his biological father. 'When I turned 14...my uncle told me [that] my stepdad weren't my real Dad. And then my Mum told me. Then that's when I started getting into crime...I thought Mum didn't care. So I thought, "Oh well, if I do some crime, maybe she...might care".' The news about his 'father' literally shook his world and it took Billy many years to recover from it. He would subsequently spend his juvenile years in and out of detention serving longer orders on each occasion.

By his late teens to early twenties, he had escaped twice from custody (once as a juvenile and once as an adult), driven his vehicle into police cars to evade capture, committed aggravated robbery, breached his home detention, allegedly been bashed by prison officers, and served six separate detention orders of varying lengths. He also knows what it's like to have a police pistol pointed at him. Since first being admitted into custody at age 14, Billy spent nearly nine of the next 11 years in one or another facility. When being sentenced as an adult, the judge reminded Billy of his 'poor record' – he had racked up close to 100 charges in just a few years. He called Billy 'a menace to society'. Up until he was paroled, more than one third of his life had been spent behind bars. Just prior to his last release, in his mid-twenties, Billy reflected on and lamented the total custodial time he had served (just short of 3000 days) and the impact prison had on him: 'They reckon the system is supposed to... change [you]. It hasn't changed me. Like it's made me worse. But I'm trying to make that worser person go away.... I'm thinking of my family now to get out to.' He was committed to change – perhaps this was the defining impact of a five-year stint straight out of juvenile. Many prisoners – many people – talk about changing their life, but few actually do it.

In all his interviews, Billy was realistic about his chances of 'making it'. At the commencement of his four-year parole period he projected a *moderated outlook* – he was neither overly optimistic nor fatalistic regarding his situation: 'I see a different sense of future but there's that chance I could come back. I got four years hanging over me. So I can get done for maybe being in a pub or driv[ing] without a licence.... Just a little thing.' Billy knew that staying out of trouble – staying out of prison – would be no cakewalk. It required ongoing commitment. It wouldn't, in short, happen 'by accident'. A major push factor for Billy was his extreme reluctance to go back to prison. He spoke, as many much older ex-prisoners do, of feeling exhausted by the cycles of arrest, reincarceration and release that had marked his life for well over a decade:

I: [Y]ou've probably done better than anyone else that [we've] spoken to.... [W]hat do you put that down to [Billy]?
P: Just had enough of gaol.... Well, look at how many times I went in, fucking, every time I get out I had to set myself up and every time you go in you lose... your mates or someone rips you off, you lose your house, everything, your cars, you lose it all really. Every time I went in I've lost. Last time I went in for my adult charges I had two cars at that stage, books, everything. Gone. So... I walked out [of prison] with my clothes and my wallet. That's all I had. I lost everything else....

> I: What's kept you going?...
> P: First thing would have been [my son from a previous relationship].... [T]hat's why I handed myself in when I took off [from] home D.[1]... [And] I've... got the kids and [Julie] now.[2]

For Billy, the pains of imprisonment extended well beyond prison walls. It included loss of material items and personal relationships he had pieced together in the times he'd been 'free'. The trope of 'loss' is therefore key to Billy's 'awakening' from crime. By his mid-twenties he began to pay much more than lip service to the damage that crime and incarceration was doing not only to his own life but to those he cared about as well. In this context, his children became a key moral force in helping him to get (and stay) on track. Aged under ten years, Billy's children knew the consequences of their Dad taking a wrong step: 'Really, I shouldn't be on the road, but I reverse [the car] into [the driveway for Julie]. [The kids] always panic and go, "You're not supposed to drive, Dad. You'll go to gaol".... They know about the gaol situation. They know heaps about gaol.'

The longer he stayed out the higher the stakes became. In his later interviews, Billy seemed genuinely nervous about mucking up – he'd come a long way but knew that things were, in a sense, on a knife-edge. Julie spoke of the immense pressure involved in living with someone who had done a lot of prison time: 'It's all new to him still – I mean coming out... to a ready-made family... after pretty much living his whole life in prison .... And he's got no other support really and he never has [had] which is extremely sad.... [T]hat upsets me but [there's] not much we can do about it.' Billy's mother and stepfather did what they could to assist them. But they could only do so much and be there so often. They lived a considerable distance away, which hindered regular contact. Billy's father – himself an ex-prisoner – tried in his own way to help Billy and offered him many strategies for coping in prison (taking on a kind of 'wounded healer' role) (see Halsey and Deegan 2012). Perhaps most importantly, though, he counselled Billy to take care of the 'little things' while on parole so as not to give the authorities any reason to be suspicious of him or breach him.

> He is... slowly, slowly becoming normal. Because he's been institutionalized for so long, it's taken him a long time. He was getting anxious. He wants this. He wants that. Because he hasn't had ... much time out [of prison]. And I'm saying, 'Calm down, it will happen'. And he says, 'You know, I'm trying to get a job, but I need a licence'. So I helped him buy one of those motorized pushbikes... and I said,

'Put...lights on it...Put rear brakes on it...[otherwise] you'll be defected.' And he goes, 'How can I be defected?' I said, 'Because it hasn't got no rear brakes'. I said, 'No matter if it's a pushbike or not, they can still ping you.' And then his missus backed the car up, broke the manifold, and I'm going, 'Oh, God, you've got to be kidding me'. And so we dragged it down home, and I'm thinking, 'Shit'. So I had to drill it out, re-tap it, add spacers, add the manifold on for him so he...can use it, and I said, 'Use all your lights. Use your high vis[ibility] vest'. I said, 'You'll never have a problem with anyone.' And he's going, 'Yeah, I do, I do'. And I said, 'Well, I hope you fucking do'.

In addition to this moral and practical support, Billy was acutely aware of two very basic life-course equations. The first was 'more crime = prison = *harm to family*'. The second was 'more crime = prison = *harm to self*'. In short, there was an extremely powerful combination of push and pull factors in Billy's journey toward desistance. He articulated the pull factor (harm to family) in the following way:

> P: [I]f I do go back in gaol, I don't reckon [Julie] will stick around.... And if she did stick around, well, you might as well say she wouldn't be able to survive. Everything I've got will be sold. She'd probably have to sell the car to survive .... I reckon if I went back in, I reckon [Julie] would get kicked out of this house. She'd be probably end up going to the Salvos...just for some food, because she wouldn't be able to keep the rent, pay all the bills, keep the car going. She wouldn't be able to survive....
> I: And why do you care so much about that now...as opposed to like a year or two ago, [Billy]? What's changed?
> P: I don't know. We've got everything we want now. Like, it's only a rented house, but the house is suitable. We've got the cars we need. The girls have got their bikes, the pool, and all the toys now.... Everyone's got everything.

Coupled with this was Billy's unqualified belief that going back to prison would mean certain physical harm. He told of this 'push factor' in these terms:

> I saw one [of my mates], and he goes, 'Oh, come out tonight. We're going to get a few cars'....[And] sometimes I think when...I'm arguing with [Julie], the bills are coming in,...sometimes I think,

'Fuck, maybe I should go do something, get some more money coming in'.... But I just don't do it. It's like, how can I say it, [I'm] too worried about... going to gaol. And I've got one bloke who's... pretty big and wants to cave my head in pretty bad .... [H]e told one of my mates if I go back in, he's going to stab me in there... which he's known for.

Through ten years of interviewing this is the only time Billy acknowledged feeling scared or intimidated by prison or, for that matter, by another person. Paternoster and Bushway (2009: 1108) note that desistance involves 'working towards something positive and steering away from something feared'. It's difficult to know how much Billy's fear of being attacked kept him on track, but it certainly played some part. The key point is that this *push factor was coupled with the pull factor* of what Billy's reincarceration would do to his wife and his children. Of course, many could not care less about the damage incurred to one's family. But Billy took this responsibility seriously – perhaps because he knew what it meant to grow up in difficult circumstances. The specific factors pushing and pulling Billy cannot be engineered. They arose from his unique path. But the dynamic of push and pull elements would seem to be central to getting and staying on track.

Another key factor contributing to Billy's success involved the circumstances under which he developed a relationship with Julie. A friend had told Julie about Billy. Eventually she met him while dropping the friend off to a house opposite the place where Billy was residing. He in fact was on home detention. This was the final stage of his five-year custodial sentence which, if completed successfully, would turn into four years on parole. From across the street, Billy signalled to his friend and asked, 'Who's that?' They spoke only very briefly on that occasion. But the next time they met he had bought her children Easter eggs. Upon hearing her vehicle was 'stuffed up', he also lent Julie his car. The next time she heard from Billy was down the line of a prison phone. He had cut his home detention bracelet and tried to flee from police after his parole officer found out he'd not been attending his assigned place of employment. In fact, Billy, of his own making, had obtained work at a premises much closer to where he lived (meaning he could walk or ride a bike there instead of having to catch various types of public transport). He did not tell the authorities for fear they would not permit him to keep the job. Via the prison phone, Billy asked Julie to come visit him. Where many women might have balked at such a prospect, Julie used the prison to build her confidence around men – something that had been shattered due to a previously violent relationship.

> [Having Billy in prison at the beginning of our relationship] actually...worked very well for me, because...I've had a lot of issues with my ex. And so I've stayed away from men in general and I've been very uncomfortable around [them] and so for me to get to know another bloke, it was just about impossible because in the back of my head, I'm thinking, 'There's all these expectations and all this pressure and all that'. Whereas with him in lock-up,[3] there is not much you can do but talk and get to know each other. So it worked a lot better for me and that's what helped us.

Here, the prison became a safe space from which to build an intimate relationship. It helped create, ironically, a strong connection between Julie and Billy. The connection only grew stronger upon his release. Crucially, Billy had somewhere to reside and he had someone who was committed to a conventional life to reside with. Between the two of them they had about $400 per week to live on after paying rent and utilities. They made ends meet. Billy's parents paid for all the kids' Christmas presents to help ease the burden. But they faced other, more serious, pressures as well. Billy had major problems with his ex-girlfriend and her unwillingness to permit him to have access to the child he conceived with her. They eventually came to an agreement concerning 'hand-over' times and locations. But for a long period – and in successive interviews – Billy and Julie would tell how they feared for Troy's welfare. One day he was handed over with his hair teeming with lice. In desperation, Billy shaved his son's head as well as ensuring that he received the proper medical attention. They also noticed that Troy looked increasingly gaunt. He appeared to be wasting away. They wondered whether Billy's ex was feeding him properly. Julie took copious notes on the situation in preparation for a drawn-out family court battle. Billy's mother told in interview of being acutely distressed about the health and welfare of her grandson. To add to the weight of problems, Troy's mother was doing all she could to get Billy to slip up and go back to prison. This would, to her mind, prove to the courts that he was an unfit father.

Billy and Julie were provoked in all kinds of ways – emotionally and physically. This included Julie being struck with a baseball bat by a neighbour of Billy's ex. Billy came to her defence in a proportionate manner – he somehow kept his cool and let the judicial process take its course. This took monumental strength and personal restraint. For

Billy, the part played by his long parole period proved decisive: '[I]f I wasn't on parole and someone pissed me off, I reckon I would just punch them out.... I'd probably get bail anyway. But on parole I could get bail or I could go in for a breach because it's a new charge.... Because that parole's on me, that parole's there for a reason so I can't.' Eventually, Billy and Julie won the right to equal custody over Troy. Handovers occurred at a fast-food restaurant – that way, Billy said, everything was recorded on CCTV should anything go wrong. But just as this issue was resolving itself, Julie's ex started causing major problems. He was serving a sentence for armed robbery but had managed, according to Billy and Julie, to convince a friend to leave threatening messages on Julie's phone about her safety and that of her children. This went on for many months. Julie grew increasingly distraught regarding what her ex might do on release. She was told by the police that there was very little they could do. There was, after all, no conclusive 'proof' linking him to the abusive calls. She and Billy would just have to cope. And somehow they did.

As time passed, Billy slowly gained a new sense of self. Crucially, his emerging self was validated through several quarters. He had, first and foremost, the support of his partner:

> I always say that to her, ... 'Well, you know I've been in gaol. You know I've got a bad criminal record. Why did you go for me? Like, you stayed single for two years. Like, why?' She goes, 'It's different with you. I don't know. There's something there'. I said, 'All right'.

In addition, his parents and his brother also noted the major steps he had taken down the desistance path: 'Yeah, a lot of people have said I've changed.... I think the family are actually shocked that I'm still out.' His children reinforced his moral worth: '[My daughters] class me as [their] good Dad.' Beyond these persons, Billy also received validation from his employer – someone who understood the importance of second chances: '[O]nly certain people know about my parole there.... [My boss] ... he's just told me that everyone makes mistakes.' *Billy developed the capacity to care for others because some people cared for and about him.* As the months and years went by, the generative dimensions of his life came to the fore. Never one to overstate the situation, he seemed to inhabit the roles of father and provider without fuss or fanfare.

> I: ... And what do you enjoy doing with the kids most? What do you do with them?

> P: ... I don't know, ... bathe the baby and stuff, feed it, change the nappies.... Some days you go have a barbie, sometimes [go to] the park, or a friend's.... [T]hey've got their swings, trampoline, motorbikes, they've got their pushbikes, everything.... Just bought them new beds.... My motorbike, ... I might have to sell that, like usually I do, to look after them .... [And] actually, ... something's going to happen [that's] real big too – I'll be adopting the two girls.

Julie truly admired his commitment to her and to building a life around family.

> ... [H]e likes to earn money.... He loves to provide for us.... There's not many people – many men – that do that at all. Like the first thing he makes sure [of] is that everything we need is paid for before he even touches it. Like there's weeks where he will work the whole week and he won't even have $20 at the end of it himself sort of thing. He will make sure all bills are paid....

It is hard to believe this is the same person who – just several years earlier – was living in the segregation unit, in the most secure division, of any prison in South Australia. At that time, a prison officer had reprimanded him for not folding his blankets in the correct fashion. Billy told him to 'get fucked'. When the officer tried to put cuffs on him, Billy spat in his face. More officers joined the fray and he was promptly 'bashed' and 'thrown' into solitary (dressed in nothing but a canvas smock). He was there for a month. In fact, though, Billy is not the same person. With Julie by his side, he has slowly managed to accumulate a series of achievements (marriage, fatherhood, employment, completion of parole, right to apply for a driver's licence) which have given him tangible assets to hang a new sense of self on.

Postscript

After five years of being on track (and literally at the point of concluding the final edits), Julie called to say Billy had been admitted to custody. She said reduced hours at his place of employment combined with having to work nights caused him to look for a supplementary income. Occasional dealing in crystal methamphetamine (better known as 'ice') provided some monetary respite. But Billy himself started consuming the drug, and it transformed his behaviour. Visiting him recently in prison was a sobering experience. The reality of what he could lose – of what he had managed to build over time – hit Billy hard. It was almost as if he had become scared of his own progress. Julie intimated that the pressures of trying to stay on track are immense – that even the most stable life is underpinned by doubt and varying degrees of fatalism. We considered reassigning Billy's story to another chapter. But he has not been tried or convicted of any offence. His employer has since informed him he is willing to support Billy with further work if and when he is released from custody. Julie, although understandably apprehensive, wants and needs Billy in her and their children's lives. There are, in short, things to hold on to which could reignite and strengthen the desistance process. On that basis, we've chosen to leave Billy's story intact and to let it stand as testimony to the extreme fragility of the struggle to make good.

Charlie

Like Billy, Charlie is also in his late twenties. He met Michele – his current girlfriend – around four years ago and has been with her since his release in late 2009. They reside well beyond city limits and for some time lived with Michele's parents. Recently, they moved into their own place – a property owned by Michele's parents for which they pay them rent. He and Michele have recently had a child together. They have three children – the two older being from Michele's previous relationship. Her ex-partner has nothing whatever to do with her or the children. In Charlie's words, one day Michele 'found out something that he did really bad'. That meant the end of his relationship with his kids and with Michele. In the years since leaving prison Charlie has managed to all but overcome his heroin addiction. He has constantly sought work and has done all kinds of maintenance jobs, including cleaning toilets and like. After many years of being disqualified from driving – indeed after never having had a driver's licence – he recently earned the right to sit for his learner's and probationary permit. In addition to getting his own life on track, he has spent considerable time trying to steer his siblings away from crime as well. Some significant progress has occurred in that regard – no mean feat for a family that has notched up decades of custodial time between them. Through his commitment to fatherhood and his strong work ethic, Charlie has won the respect of Michele's family. The hard-won respect of Michele's father has been of particular significance to him. Charlie and Michele plan to get married but are waiting until one of them secures a steady job.

It's been a long road for Charlie to get to this point. He was first admitted to custody at 12 years of age and would cycle in and out of juvenile training centres until age 18 (amassing around 20 admission and release episodes during such time). This included four detention orders and numerous other 'short stays' for breaching his bail and/or failing to show up to court. He grew up in a notoriously crime-ridden part of Adelaide and started stealing pushbikes around age ten. He stole his first car at age 12. As it happened, this turned out to be a car that had already been stolen by his older brother. From that age he wanted to prove to his brother and his mates that he could steal cars and make money 'just like the older boys'. Charlie started dealing drugs at 13 years of age and subsequently broke into shops and businesses to support his own drug use. He went on to commit a more serious range of offences through his teen years and early twenties including serious criminal trespass and armed robbery. He also developed a dependence on heroin.

Charlie's mother – long since separated from his father – tells how (when Charlie was very young) her then husband (intoxicated by 'beer and Serapax') nearly killed two of her other sons in a car accident (one of them flew through the windscreen and has suffered life-long injuries). She says her ex-husband was a violent alcoholic who was bent on killing his children and who spent most of his days in prison or drunk. She finally left him one day and placed 'a note on the table and a carton of beer' saying that the alcohol had won out over her. Charlie has not commented on any accident but he has said that he remembers his father doing '15 years once' and that this 'might have been for attacks on us maybe when we were kids'. The odds were firmly stacked against Charlie desisting from crime – certainly at least while he was a young man. Most youth workers had pegged him as a no-hoper and life-long offender. They tarred him, essentially, with the brush of 'intergenerational criminal' – he was always going to do what his father did and he was going to do it for a long time, they would say. But in fact, the precise opposite occurred.

Charlie, by his own admission, was a prolific car thief. He also broke into more premises than he can recall – all, as mentioned, to fund his drug habit. *But* he always considered his offending 'moral' – as causing no more harm than necessary for him to get his fix (which meant keeping the pain of withdrawal from heroin at bay). He was, in his own mind, 'a good thief' who desired to do right.

> I don't do housebreaks.... What I do is...business[es].... Like, just say, this is a business. [Well], I break in and steal the computers

or the TV .... But they got insurance ... to get it back .... I'm sayin', like, [I] get the money to get drugs. But I'm [also] sayin' it's not right.... It's still wrong to break into someone's business.... But I got, like, morals .... I won't go do some poor person over that can't afford to get all his stuff back.... Once you steal it from him, he'll never get it back again.

Similar to David (see further below), Charlie carried the sense that he was not like the rest of the 'run amoks'[4] he grew up with. They did crime for the wrong reasons – to hurt people, to damage property, to cause unnecessary carnage. Charlie held this view even though he, his two brothers *and* his father were once locked up simultaneously in four different facilities. Charlie probably didn't know it, but he managed to pull off a good degree of cognitive dissonance during and following his peak period of offending. Among his peers – and among custodial staff – he once held the unofficial title of the juvenile who reputedly notched up the most high-speed pursuits in South Australia. He also managed to evade the police the majority of times. There was an undeniable buzz to such activity. Charlie, in short, was also (had also been) a consummate edgeworker (Halsey 2008b).

He was also the first person interviewed for the ten-year project on which this book is based. And from the very first, Charlie presented as a plain-talking, take-it-or-leave-it young man. He never shirked a question. Years later, when he was starting to put his life together, he admitted breaking his parole conditions by 'associating' with a known offender. That offender, as it turned out, was his brother who had escaped from custody and was described by police as armed and dangerous and not to be approached. Charlie – with some help from his father – was the one who eventually talked him around. He could sense his mother's profound anguish that one of her sons might be shot and killed by police. At risk to his own emerging 'good news' story, Charlie did his mother – and the public – a very good deed. Years earlier, he probably would have joined his brother on the run and taken any and all risks to evade capture. But things had changed for Charlie. Such a path no longer presented as an option.

Halfway through his last term of imprisonment, he'd started to reflect on the costs of being locked up. In particular, he greatly feared doing more time:

This is the longest I've had in prison now, you know, 18 months.... And I'm sort of thinkin', 'Well, I've got 18 months [to go] now. If I ever fuck up and get caught again, it's goin' to turn ... into six years, or ten years. And before you know it, I won't have a life, I'll just have a prison life.... I won't be able to have kids or nothing 'cause I'm always in here.

Charlie also took to heart a 'premonition' he had – but which he subsequently ignored and nearly cost him his life.

> P: I said [to my mates] ... one night [that] I didn't want t[o go out, 'No, don't worry about it. I got a feeling, man, that somethin' will happen tonight'. And I thought, 'No, I won't [go out].'... And we crashed that night. Like it was on the news and my Dad seen it. He was like heaps worried. Thought one of us might have been dead or somethin'.
> I: ... Was that a bit of a wake-up call for you, [Charlie]? ...
> P: Yeah, sure it was.

His typical trajectory on release from custody was to hang with mates, do drugs, and reoffend. Speaking in 2010 (a year out from his last release episode) he commented:

> When I lived in Adelaide you get out and meet old friends. Like last time I got out I got out on [the] Drug Court program on home [detention] and I was living at my own house in [names suburb]. Everything was going good for like two, three months, everything was all right, and I wasn't doing crime or anything. Just staying out of trouble. I was using a bit of gear [heroin] every now and then but not full on. And then I got on the bus one day and saw one of my mates – [one of my] good mates.... And I've seen him and I said, 'Where do you live?' And he lived just down the road. [So] me and him started seeing each other and before you know it we started breaking into houses and stealing cars and then before I knew it [I] cut my home D [bracelet] off.... And then we went on the run together for about six months. And then I got caught for the armed robberies [and was given a head sentence of six years].

Absolutely central to Charlie's success was his decision – and the opportunity – to live a long way from his criminal peers (Warr 2002). This geographical knifing-off helped him action the commitment to desistance he'd mentioned prior to his release.

If you're always in [your old] area you see all your mates and you just can't help yourself... [T]here's nothing else to do and so you go have a shot at drugs or whatever and then you go steal a car.... No one knows me... here. Well, they know me. But I've got no mates up here that I used to do crime with or anything.

This, however, was just one factor among several which helped Charlie get on track. Equally important was that he had someone and something to desist *for*:

Meeting her done it. If I hadn't got with [Michele] I would have got back in trouble.... I would have got bored.... Because we used to live in the country doing nothing.... No one wants to give you a job because you're a bad crim and you've got a bad past and no one wants to give you a go. But then when I got with [Michele] it's all just changed everything.... The kids started calling me Dad and if I got locked up it would break their hearts. They'd be shattered .... Me and [Michele], we'll stay together now and we'll get married eventually.

The role of an intimate and rising to the challenges of fatherhood are well documented in desistance studies (Laub and Sampson 2006; Halsey and Deegan 2012). But these are not necessarily sufficient to give up offending. Charlie had another important element in the mix. Specifically, he had a plan for giving up crime that echoed Billy's 'moderated outlook'. We've termed Charlie's strategy the 'bit by bit' approach – one built on quite a detailed model of staged gratification:

I know I won't get my licence for a couple a years. So while I'm with [Michele], I'll get my project car [and fix it up] .... I'll just slowly [get some] work and once I get enough money to buy my car, I'll buy it and then I'll work a bit more, slowly get the parts I want for it, the wheels and stereo, the turbo and that... I'll slowly do it up... and come three years' time, I'm gonna have a real nice car to drive around .... I'll be right,... 'cause we're gonna go live at [Michele's] Mum's when I get out. We're gonna stay there for... a month or so.... Then we'll organize the money, like together, we're gonna go get our own house – a nice house to live in, like me, her and the two kids. And when [the kids] get a bit older, that's when we're gonna get married – when they're old enough to walk down the aisle, you know, with the rings .... By then,... she should be pregnant. We'll have our own baby, and yeah,... lead the good life.

With the exception of getting married, Charlie has remained true to his plans. By any measure, his has been quite a remarkable journey. It is difficult to relay the full extent of the social dysfunction that has enveloped his family for decades. One of his brothers is serving a long prison sentence while the other is in and out of lock-up. His youngest brother – a half-brother – was reputedly fathered by one of the most notorious killers in South Australia. Charlie's mother offers support where she can but remains convinced that it is only a matter of time before he slips back into what he knows best:

> They've had a hard life, the boys.... They've seen a lot of bad things. And all they ever knew was what they were shown, and that's what [their] Dad did, went in and out of gaol, and all the time I was pregnant, like, he'd come out and go back, come out and go back. So that's all they've ever known. And now they're like that.... They're only [doing] what they were taught.

Charlie's father spends much of his time in an alcoholic daze – which is not to say he does not care for his sons. It's just that there is only so much he can do. His economic resources are few and his social capital is low. He's always visited his sons in prison, though, and always been there to take their phone calls – mainly to discuss how their time is progressing. When first interviewed several years ago, he was very sceptical of Charlie's capacity to desist, commenting that the buzz of crime (particularly offending with his brother) and getting high on drugs were still major issues. But in a more recent interview he had moderated his perspective:

> P: I don't think they're going out getting into any more crime or any more trouble.
> I: So, do you think that Charlie is done with [crime] completely?
> P: ...I think, well, hopefully, I can say that it's all finished....
> I: What makes you say that?
> P: Because sometimes you see their attitudes now...and you can see that they're getting a bit older now, they're not as swift and fast as they used to be, so the cops are finally winning their thing with the kids and...the cops [in the town where he lives] keep a close eye on them.

There is one further element underpinning Charlie's desistance process. This relates to him catching a lucky break or two in the context of the law and its *non*-enforcement. The following extended excerpt captures the importance of such:

> [Before I got my driver's licence], I reversed out the driveway and went for a drive around the block and then the cop seen me .... He followed me... but I didn't even see him .... [When I got back to my house] there was cop cars out the front and I thought, 'Here we go,' and I took off.... I [went] to [the local shop] and bought some screwdrivers and I was going to go steal a car and leave [town] because I thought I was going to get locked up. But I didn't. I thought, 'Nah, fuck it' .... I rode to my girlfriend's house and told her what happened and she said, 'Look, just go speak to them'. And so the next day we went and spoke to the [police].... And then I went to court and the judge said, 'Look, because you've been out of trouble for so long, you're doing well, I'll just give you a four hundred dollar fine.' ... I [also] had a good parole officer [who] wrote to the Parole Board and told 'em [what happened]. And they said, 'Look, nah. We'll just give you a warning. We're not gonna lock you up now cos it will just wreck everything'. Cos I reckon if I would have got locked up that would have changed my whole mind frame again. I would have been thinking, 'Fuck this'. I probably would have only done three months, but then I would have got out and thought 'Fuck it, I'm gonna run amok again'. Why not? ... It was my car. I didn't steal it. I bought my own car. I was just fixing it up... to get my licence. Then I thought, 'If I start driving it around I'll get in trouble'. So I thought, 'I'll... do it up and sell it'. And as I was doing it up I thought, 'I'll just take it for a drive just to test the motor out' – cos I'd just... fixed it all up properly [to sell].... And the judge said, 'I'm not gonna lock you up over something so petty cos you've been out of trouble now for something like five years'.

The appropriate use of discretion by various enforcement personnel is a critically important if often underutilized part of maintaining people's commitment toward desisting from crime. In compliance-oriented and retributive climates the tendency is to shut down desistance by pushing the breach button for the smallest of infractions (dirty urine tests, contravention of curfews, associating with the 'wrong people' and the like). In our experience – and as will become clear in later chapters – the overzealous (unwise) use of breach provisions or charge options often makes bad situations much worse. In particular, it is constitutive of what we term the 'fuck it' mentality – a view which stems from parolees' or ex-prisoners' perceptions (often rightly held) that all the good things they had done are about to be entirely discounted by the 'unjust' or overly punitive decision of someone who, in the end, has no real sense of what it is like to have to walk 'in their shoes' (see Chapter 7, 'Points of Unrest'). Charlie very much captures this sentiment above. He makes it clear that there is a social contract attached to desistance – that it requires him to do certain things but it also requires the state to 'cut some slack' where the *overall* trajectory is positive. This of course requires the right police, the right parole officer, the right judge – and all at the right moment. So often it is a game of chance in all these respects. But it is a game with potentially very high stakes – especially where the motivation to desist is (inadvertently) weakened by various actors.

David

David is in his mid-twenties. He grew up in what is generally acknowledged to be a rough part of town and left school at age 12 after being repeatedly suspended for fighting ('I was usually just sticking up for my mates'). His attempts, at age 14, to complete his first year of high school left him feeling humiliated (he was expected to learn alongside 'the little kids'). In any case, David had already commenced thieving at age eight ('chocolate and baseball cards'), by 12 was stealing car stereos, and at 13 was stealing cars. At that time his criminal identity was set ('I viewed myself as a criminal... someone that steals to get something'). He was taken into police custody at 13 years of age and, after successive bonds and suspended sentences, received his first detention order just ahead of turning 15. While incarcerated, he noticed that a friend who 'lived down the road' was also doing time. They would meet up repeatedly over the years to hang out and do crime. By his own reckoning, David was in and out of custody about '25 to 30 times' over a three-year period. His onset of offending coincided with 'smoking dope' from a very young age ('I had my first pipe when I was seven'). Indeed, he commented that dope 'led me up to all this' – namely, to his teenage years being imbued by crime and incarceration. David mentioned marijuana as one of two major things in his life he would change were it possible to start over (he also wished he'd received earlier and much better help controlling his anger). In relation to his drug use, David recalled: 'I used to smoke dope... [e]very second weekend when I went down my Mum's house.... [I]t kept building up and building up and then I'd start wagging school [to] smoke dope. And then it got worse.... [T]hen I started breaking into cars to steal stuff for dope...'.

The escalation of David's offending also coincided with his parents' separation – something that his mother, Carol, laments. She remarked at interview that the family dynamics were such as to eventually push *both* her older boys into crime. Their offending was prolific – mainly car theft and breaking and entering – anything to kill time and perhaps make a bit of money. Throughout David's teenage years, Carol says she was on 'first-name basis' with a judge of the Youth Court. She went to all court proceedings involving David – literally dozens of such events over a six-year period. Carol was a ward of the state – she had no parental script to draw on. She did her best, though. But she was also a chronic alcoholic. As an older teenager, David would often engage in long and heavy drinking sessions with his mother. During these sessions, talk of the past would ensue. Accusations would be hurled. Fights (of the verbal kind) would resume. '[Mum] drinks all day ... so then I drink with her... and that doesn't help.' Typically, David's 'solution' to this drug and alcohol malaise would be to (again) engage in offending – he'd 'go off', 'run amok' – unable to pull back from the destructive effects of too much alcohol. Throughout all this, Carol's devotion to her son(s) did not wane. She described David as 'a very warm, caring, assertive human being'. They just didn't see eye to eye on things.

Looking back, David reflected that juvenile detention was like a school for learning how to do more crime. By the age of 18 (on entering adulthood), he had completed four detention orders of varying lengths (up to nine months each) and had served a total of around 1000 custodial days (including time on remand) from age 13 through 17. According to David, 'Everything was about [the] money'. Carol is adamant that the thing David needed most was a strong male role model. Specifically, he needed his father in his life. But that was not to be. Indeed, David received a Good Behaviour Bond for an attempted assault on his father. And each time he was released, David was at a loss to know exactly which way to turn. He spoke in successive interviews of drifting into town and crossing paths (unintentionally) with old associates. At 17, he offered the following account of his behavior:

> I: So tell me, ... what were the circumstances that led to this offence taking place?
> P: Well, ... for the first week [following my release] I had just hung around with my [older] brother, and he doesn't do crime [anymore].... We were going out to pubs in town ... on Friday and Saturday night having a good time. And then I met up with one of my old associates...

I: On purpose, or just by coincidence?
P: No, by coincidence.... And, yeah, one thing led to another and we stole a car.
I: You stole a car again, right. Okay. And, look, when you say that 'one thing led to another', was it literally as soon as you sort of bumped into each other you just started talking about old times or...?
P: Yeah, and then we started drinking, and then, when we are pissed... we didn't really think.
I: [T]hat's fine.... I don't make any judgment about you .... But tell me,... I guess... a lot of people [would] want to know... why did you go and steal a car, as opposed to go and watch a movie,... or keep drinking, or whatever? I know it seems like a silly question...
P: It's a fair question. Probably, you know, it's a bit to do with boredom [and the need for] adrenalin as well and [the] need [for] money.... You know, like, someone might go and kick the footy every time he's bored.... Someone might go to the movies every time they're bored... Me, well, I was accustomed to doing [crime] when I'm bored.... It's just a habit.

Crime as 'habit' – as something familiar – proved to be a common scenario among the young men. David had long hankered for a different life, but didn't know quite know how to put the pieces in place. As early as 16 years of age he was strongly committed to gaining a trade qualification. He told in interview of his strategy for attaining such: 'I'm going to complete my Year 11 [of schooling] and... get a trade through the Army.... I'm used to a structured life.... I can get up... early in the morning. I can work... It's good money...'. To his credit, David never faltered from this commitment. Following his last release from a juvenile custodial facility, he avoided reincarceration for just over three years. During that time he remained true to his word and gained, against the odds, a trade in the building industry. He made genuine efforts to desist from (serious) crime. His resolve was strengthened by the need to set a good example to his younger brother. Eventually, though, with the threat of having to face court again for driving while disqualified, he fled interstate. A warrant was issued for his arrest. For just on a year he worked legitimately – all the while on the run but having 'a ball' living and working independently (that is to say, supporting himself). Not long after returning to South Australia, he was caught drink driving – the warrant for his arrest was also in the mix as was the fact that he was driving while disqualified. At 23, he was given eight months' imprisonment for these offences as well as long-standing unpaid debts/fines.

Since his release from prison at the end of 2012, David has stayed out of trouble. He has continued working in the building industry, pays rent, is saving to buy his own home, is drug free ('I don't do drugs') and has significantly curtailed his consumption of alcohol. Most importantly, though, he is in a relationship with a woman he cares deeply about. She, too, cares deeply for him. They 'get' each other. By David's own admission, Kristie has given him every reason not to do 'anything stupid' and to steer down the path of a conventional life. Through it all, though, David admits to still driving while disqualified. It is a risk he simply has to take in order to work to pay bills, to *become* 'legit', and to consolidate the process of desistance. Like many ex-prisoners, therefore, *David felt he had little option but to persist at a particular type of offending in order to desist, eventually, at all types of offending.* As he put it, 'I've come to terms with the fact that I'm going to drive...whether I'm allowed to or not'. This paradox is something we will return to later (see Chapter 7).

As with Billy and Charlie, there are multiple factors that contributed to David's success. At 15 – in his first interview – he was genuinely worried about the example he was setting (or not setting) for his little brother. This was a major 'pull' element:

> I: What do you think about most frequently when you're in here?...
> P: Probably, ah, my little brother, I reckon. I think about him a lot.... I just think, 'Oh, I hope he doesn't rock up here.'... He's a smart little kid and he doesn't like me coming here.

In the same interview, David offered further insight into the weight of this situation:

> I: [I]f you could change anything about your life so far, what would it be?
> P: I wouldn't have done crime.... Because, I mean, I got my older brother into it. I mean, one time my little brother... drew me and my brother a picture of us in a stolen car and a cop car chasing us.... I was in [a juvenile detention facility] at the time.... He brang it in and showed me....
> I: What did you think when you saw that?
> P: Jesus, look at the impression I've left on him.

Over the years, David mentioned his little brother on many occasions. When asked, at 16, to name something that makes him happy, he responded, 'seeing... my little brother happy [and] doing the right thing'. In his final interview, aged 25, David again referenced his little brother as playing a major part in his desistance process.

> I: ... Do you have people other than [your girlfriend who] actually say positive things to you and just sort of, you know, just say, 'Yeah, well done,' or, 'You're doing well,' or 'Good to see you', or whatever?...
> P: I have my little brother. He sees all the changes and he does say things like that. 'You're doing pretty good', you know.

At 17, David was consciously reflecting on the costs of being locked up. When asked what he'd lost through incarceration, he commented: 'Friends. Girlfriends.... My youth.... Education. Like, I've lost a hell of a lot. I know I've lost the [chance to have] fun.' Key to his commitment toward desistance was the pain of these losses. But along with this came David's eventual determination to deny his 'associates' the opportunity to engage him in criminal conduct. '[I]t's just about... finding good people to hang around with and staying with them,' he remarked. In the same interview, at 16, he also acknowledged that 'my best mate is the person I go stealing with every day'. A year later, David (while locked up for separate new offences) told how he had called his mate to establish the rules of any future relationship: 'I said: "Look, I'm not doing no more crime. So if you want to hang around with me just to be a mate, fine. If you want to piss off, I don't care".' In his final interview – some eight years later – David confirmed that he had more or less adhered to that strategy.

> [A] lot of the time with friends... you've got to break them ties.... [T]hey may be good blokes, like [Steve], you know, top bloke... [But] I had to break the tie.... Top bloke, great mate to have, he'd have your back anytime, but... I told him, 'Oh look man, [I've had enough] ....' He got locked back up and we sort of just lost contact.

A critically important part of being able to action the process of 'managing mates' was keeping one's home address under wraps. As David recalled: '[T]he good thing that helped me was having a house. They [Offender Aid and Rehabilitation Services – 'OARS'] got me a joint [a home] and no one knew where I lived except who I wanted to know. And I already had that mindset where I didn't want to go back to crime, so that mindset helped me. And no one knew where I lived [so] they couldn't come around and harass me. So that worked out quite well.' Being gainfully employed also mattered – a lot. It brought structure, routine, and, importantly, exhaustion – a tiredness which meant David had literally no energy left (let alone the inclination) to do crime.

> I used to have to get up at 4.30 in the morning, ride to the train station because the train gets into work at six after two trains. Didn't get home until bloody half seven at night and then I was straight to sleep to get back up to go to work. But... if you've got to pay bills [and] you've got to pay rent, you've got to do it.

In terms of work, David was extremely fortunate. His uncle owned a small business and knew all about his past (the crime, the time locked up and the like). More fortuitously, David's uncle had also served time in prison so he was especially fit to empathize with his nephew's plight. This meant no résumé, no interview and no background checks: 'I was lucky with my uncle. He was the one that taught me [my trade]. But... he's been in and out of gaol himself.' Social, familial and economic capital converged, in rare and fortuitous fashion, into one scenario for David. Still, even without this serendipitous state of affairs, David spoke of the way in which his chosen industry is more conducive than others to finding employment – especially when you're an ex-prisoner.

> [T]he trick is, I've never looked for advertisements in the paper or anything for plasterers. I just pull up the phone book. That's what I had to do in Western Australia [while on the run]. You get a job within a week no worries. You just ring up all the plastering companies, 'Got any fixing work?' you know, 'Got any flushing work?' and... they pretty much ask you, 'How much experience have you got and what have you done?' and, you know, 'I've worked for this and that' and... they just give me a go. I mean, if you don't put up the board right or, you know, you can't flush, well, obviously you're not getting another job.

As with Billy and Charlie, settling into a steady relationship proved decisive in cementing David's change process. He spoke specifically of the stability that Kristie afforded his life: 'She's put some stability in my life.... Yeah, she's been really good, she's been really helpful, yeah just put a lot of stability into my life and nagged me into doing things right.... She nags me a lot but then she tells me I'm good.' Important here is the affirmation David received ('she tells me I'm good'). This tends to be an underestimated dimension in desistance from crime. People need tangible and frequent praise for making progress – and they need encouragement (not just admonishment) when setbacks occur. Partners (girlfriends, wives) play an incredibly important role here. They tend often to be the only people 'left standing' when other family members, friends and acquaintances have faded away (Halsey and Deegan 2014). Kristie also spoke of the way in which David developed another identity beyond that of worker/breadwinner:

> [T]he way he was with my kids straightaway [when I first him] and then the way he is with them now. Like, I'd always freaked out about having someone else around my kids because after I had broke up with their Dad, David was the first person that I had a relationship with. So the way that [the] kids didn't bother him, and previous stuff didn't bother him, and he just came in [and his attitude was], 'You've got kids. Who cares? This is who I am. This is what I'm about'. And then we just worked around it.

Many run from the prospect of 'instant fatherhood'. David, however, seemed to embrace it. It gave him the kind of responsibility he needed. Along with his work and his relationship to Kristie, raising children formed part of the long-held vision which David had: 'I had this sort of dream.... [A] white picket fence sort of thing, ... because I've never had it.... I've always had that sort of dream.... [And now] we're sort of lucky... as [Kristie's] great grandma [recently] passed away. And [so] we're going to buy [her house]'. They knew the silver lining of this event was it enabled them to afford a house – and to afford it in an area which would likely have remained economically out of reach in any other circumstance. Here, the game of life dealt a good hand – something to which David was generally unaccustomed. Of course, being able to service the loan through legitimate means was also a key element. The combination of work, home, 'fatherhood' and intimate relationship helped fortify a path to desistance. But even this does not tell the whole story. In support of Maruna's et al. (2004) work on delabelling, David developed the means to think about himself in a new way. More accurately, he learned to operationalize that which he always knew to be true – that he was never 'just a criminal'.

[M]y mentality when I went to gaol was...'Most of these people in here are no-hopers'....I try to say to my friends...in there, 'Fucking just stay away from this shit man, you don't want to come back here'....It's not that you're above people. It's just that there's no point making friends with these people because you're never going to see them again....Their gaol stories,...most of it's...bullshit....I suppose I just thought to myself, you know,...'You don't need to be mates with everyone'.

Even when incarcerated, David had a strong sense of self – he was different from 'all the others'. He held this view not to be pompous, but to keep definitively connected to a better (imagined) future. The mire of prison life – although he spent considerable time in it – was not David's 'real' world. For many years he always remarked in interview that it was the little things which tripped him up – that his vice was too much alcohol and his need to drive while disqualified for the sake of his job. Meeting Kristie enabled him to largely eliminate his problems with alcohol. As she remarked: 'I don't want to see him become who he used to be, because I can see him changing, and I can see where he wants to go with everything. I want to be there to see him get there.' The fact that a significant other sees and affirms the change in David has proved of immeasurable value. Above all, perhaps, it has permitted David to see and articulate the change in himself. In his final interview he commented: 'I don't consider myself as a, you know, ex-crim, or anything like that....I just consider myself, you know, a bloke, a tradie [tradesperson]...who gets up and goes to work every day...'. This capacity to comfortably inhabit the present in spite of the past is something many offenders struggle with during the desistance process. Some – more likely, many – are simply unable to fully transition from the primary to secondary stage of that process.

David seems to be someone who has managed to approach giving up crime from a fairly simple perspective. He had a good understanding of why he commenced offending and why he kept on offending. He knew, in psychological parlance, his 'triggers'. He knew the things he could work on (dynamic factors) and the things he could not change (static factors). So he decided to work on the things he had some limited degree of control over. Certainly, David repeated in interview that he had grown utterly 'sick of gaol'. He'd had enough. He wanted out. But coupled to this was that he had a very strong work ethic. David liked to be busy. It was just that until an opportunity to be legitimately busy came along, he was going to be busy in illegitimate ways. It is, ultimately, the suitable lapse of time that is connected to 'proving' and cementing a legitimate identity. Whereas one can attain a criminal identity in an instant, claiming a non-criminal identity tends to be a much lengthier affair. For David, his key strategy was to weigh the years spent working against the years spent offending and/or incarcerated. As he put it: 'I've been gyprocking for five years. I can fix, I can flush, I can cornice.... I'm proud to be a gyprocker .... I've got a trade .... I'm proud of it ... and that's something [people like me] need, is the pride of doing it, the pride, because it makes you proud.' This feeling of pride – a deeply personal thing for David – is the glue that holds his desistance together. This is not to say things won't come unstuck. But this strong sense of (legitimate) self – coupled to his role as partner and father figure – indicates someone who is 'on track'.

Postscript

Shortly after completing the draft of this book, we got word that David was to appear in court on charges of 'aggravated assault against child/spouse'. This news arrived literally within three weeks of us texting him to check how things were going – whether he was still 'on track'. David responded with this: 'Yeah, going good thanks mate. Hope all is well for you too. Book almost done? Can't wait. Should be good. When it's released, [we] should catch up for dinner and [have] a few [drinks] to celebrate'. As with Billy's situation, this turn of events again illustrates the fragility of the desistance process – especially in the early years of trying to hold things together. It demonstrates also the incapacity to predict when and under what circumstances things might take a downward turn – David had *never* shown any proclivity for violence against women or children, let alone been charged with it. As it happened, the charges, in David's words, were eventually 'thrown out' of court. Again, we gave considerable thought to David's story – about where, in light of such events, to place it in the book. On balance we thought it best to let things stand as they are. Desistance is a conditional project. There are no certainties. Besides, it would be remiss of us to cast all David's previous efforts as entirely negated or undone by the charge. The white picket fence is hopefully still within reach.

In sum

For Charlie and David, life seems broadly headed in the right direction. Even Billy's apparent relapse can be interpreted as part of the complex process whereby (alleged) offending emerges as the *exception* rather than the rule over lengthy periods of time. These young men are on track, meaning that they are 'moving toward' desistance as opposed to having more fully 'cemented' that process. Being on track implies, in other words, that while one might be cognitively done with crime, criminal conduct might reemerge in one's life course. In a sense, *each* of the three young men (not just Billy) inhabits a stage where successive moves toward desistance (durable progress) might at any time turn out to be prolonged lulls in offending broken by the resumption of (more serious) crime. Nothing is certain. Life is not a fully predicable project. This is especially so for those trying to work their way of out years of offending. Perhaps Billy will ultimately be proved to have been in the midst of a prolonged lull. On that count, there is something to be said for studies that only try to 'assess' desistance at or near the end of people's lives. We know there are analytical risks associated with trying to examine desistance earlier in the life-course – but those risks (chiefly, the risk of wrongly 'judging' the position of someone on the persistence–desistance continuum) do not negate the importance of undertaking such work. If anything, they make us more attentive to the precariousness of people's situations.

For Billy, it is perfectly possible that the shock of being remanded to custody after doing well for so long might make for a renewed and stronger commitment toward desistance from crime. Certainly, all three young men spoke of prison as something they had grown 'sick and tired' of. They also, though, caught some lucky breaks and these no doubt helped to paint the prospect of reincarceration in a new light. When new responsibilities arose – steady employment, stable relationships, fatherhood – they (unlike many of their peers) embraced these roles. This, of course, makes it all sound easy and 'linear'. But that wasn't so for Charlie and David, and it isn't so for Billy in particular. Each literally had to learn to be a partner, a worker, a parent, a provider – in short, a *citizen*. And each had to do so in milieus where role models for achieving these 'personas' were in short supply. They were also provoked and tested in all sorts of ways and there was certainly (even for Charlie and David) oscillation between offending and non-offending before each finally moved toward a more consolidated form of desistance. Whereas each of these young men would once have probably laughed at having 'duped' a member of the police force, an employer or someone in their family into giving them a second chance, they were now deeply grateful for this. Billy, especially, hopes to learn the full meaning of being given another chance to reside with his wife and children.

The better Charlie and David did at conventional life, the more this 'new' life began to overshadow the 'thrills' of the previous one. Crime became too risky – it meant the probable loss of various bourgeoning positive identities. For David, he knew he couldn't enhance his skills as a tradesperson from a prison cell. There was no pride in that. Similarly, Charlie couldn't do fatherhood from prison. And none of the three could be loving and reliable partners/husbands while doing time. Ironically, for Billy, it was the prospect of *losing* the burgeoning identities of economic provider, father and husband that appears to have underpinned his alleged reengagement in crime. He in no way desired to reassemble a criminal identity and to ruin the other subjectivities he had worked so hard and for so long to develop. Instead, he encountered an impasse concerning how, in the face of adversity, to keep his legitimate selves intact. Still, Billy has an impressive record of moving toward desistance which cannot and should not be overlooked – the longest of any of the young men in our study. He might, with some luck – and perhaps even on the evidence to hand – get to reengage and extend that track record sooner than later.

4
Recurring Breakdown

The four stories in this chapter revolve around degrees of success and frequent setbacks in the struggle to desist from crime. In contrast to the more or less continuous break with offending evinced by Charlie, Billy and David, the following accounts tell of factors that, for Joel, Paul, Reggie and Ben, persistently and frequently undermine their attempts to walk a different path. Between them, and excluding transfers between facilities, they have accumulated well over 100 admission and release episodes during their juvenile and early adult years. Importantly though, each has experienced significant periods in the community between incarceration events. These 'interludes' range from a few months (Joel, Reggie) to more than two years (Paul, Ben) and they involve, by all accounts, periods where offending had ceased (not just periods where each was continuing to offend but avoided arrest). Different factors, at different times, have caused them to 'relapse'. But what they share, in our view, is the inability to latch onto a hook that might produce a more permanent change. In criminological parlance, these young men are *intermittent desisters* – people who 'cyclically or temporarily desist from crime' (Piquero 2004: 105) only to reoffend in some fashion. Joel, Paul, Reggie and Ben are certainly not alone. In fact, they arguably form part of a much larger group of (ex)prisoners who bounce back and forth between custody and community. Such people commit crime at significantly lower rates than their teenage years, but their needs seem never to be properly met either within prison or beyond. We think that the four stories below bring to light many of the key problems facing those who cycle in and out of custody. These include, to name the more pertinent issues, the struggle to shrug off the stigma of criminality, the struggle to secure accommodation and employment, the struggle to deal with ongoing mental health issues and the struggle to establish and maintain familial and/or intimate relationships. In order to understand desistance, it is essential to know how this population do 'well' for a time only to fall back into crime. To this liminal period – 'somewhere between persistence and desistance' (Piquero 2004) – we now turn.

Joel

Joel is 25. He was born in Melbourne, Victoria, and raised by his mother Pam. He never met his biological father and never so much as mentioned him at interview. He has two younger half-sisters resulting from subsequent relationships of his mother. In recent years, an extremely hostile relationship developed with one sister, Melissa, to whom Joel cheerfully refers as a 'junkie' and a 'slut'. As he bluntly implies, Melissa has significant problems of her own – namely prostituting herself to fund a serious drug habit. Each of her three children, one with considerable disability, was placed under the Guardianship of the Minister ('GOM') shortly after birth. They were eventually placed in the care of Pam where they remain today. By contrast, Joel's relationship with Emma, the family's 'model' child, is less strained but also problematic: 'I guess I always felt over-shadowed by my sister for some reason...that she's a bit better – you know, like Mum likes her a bit better than all of us.' Today, Joel conceives of his family in the following terms: 'I'd like to be very close to my family but our family's pear-shaped.... Our family is fucked.... My sister can't even look after her kids. They live with my Mum. My Mum's done...hard yards with us, with [her own] kids,...and now she's got [her] kids' kids.... Yeah, it's not good.' When Joel was a young child, Pam moved the family to Adelaide and then to a town several hours' drive north. There she met and married Robert who raised her three children as his own. Pam and Robert also had a son together. There has never been any suggestion of substance abuse or violence in the family home.

In primary school Joel was diagnosed with Attention Deficit Hyperactivity Disorder ('ADHD') and prescribed the usual amphetamine-based medication. This had unpleasant side effects for him. He often resisted taking that medication and was punished for it. Additionally, he suffered the embarrassment of being called to the school office over the public announcement system for the purposes of administering it. This caused him to be bullied and ostracized by other students. Defiant and with considerable learning difficulties, he was treated as handicapped by teachers, further compounding his miserable early learning experience:

P: Didn't do too well at school.
I: What didn't you like about it?
P: Just mainly...all the...teasing and that that used to go on.... Because I'm AD[H]D they had me on pills.... And all the kids used to go, 'Oh, take your mental pills. Take your mental pills'.... And then I'd be like, 'All right, fair enough, mate, let's go...'
I: Right. And so you'd have a fight?
P: Yeah...
I: Did you ever have a fight with the teachers or was it mainly with students?
P: I belted one of the teachers with a stick...
I: Yeah. How old were you, roughly, then, [Joel]?
P: Probably about 12, 13.

Problems continued at high school. Regularly suspended for 'fighting, swearing and throwing rocks', Joel ultimately found refuge with a group of people who similarly did not respect authority. This was, by all accounts, his first experience of group acceptance. As Joel explained, his early offending was, in part, an attempt to cement an identity with his new associates: 'What made me do crime?'... Not fitting in.... Wanting to look good.... And look where it got me. Now I'm a fucking criminal.' Crime also served as an opportunity to demonstrate his self-professed 'hatred towards the 'richie-rich' and the[ir] community'. In Joel's eyes, 'It's mainly them rich boys that get bashed or the fucking boys that flaunt their money and fucking have flash cars and live in flash houses. Shit I never had'. He felt, in other words, the strain of being poor from the get go. Participating in the robbery of a small shop at age 13 proved a defining moment for Joel: 'I ran away from home and I was looking to fit in with these kids...and we went and done an armed robbery and I fitted right in. I went to gaol.' That was his first juvenile detention order. 'Bang! Got in there. First day I had a big fight. Yeah, just to prove myself, to say, "Look, I'm not a fucking bitch, let's go, mate".' When Joel completed the order, he tried, briefly, to return to school. Only this time, it wasn't just ADHD jokes he had to contend with: 'They had the impression of '[If] you go to gaol you get your ass fucked'. [They kept asking], 'You get fucked in the ass, [Joel]? You get fucked in the ass? [And I'd say], Come here cunt and I'll fucking show you mate'. He dropped out of school before completing Year 8.

By this time, Joel was drinking alcohol excessively and experimenting with a number of hard drugs. He began recording convictions for arson, armed robbery, aggravated serious criminal trespass, larceny and assault occasioning actual bodily harm. He served significant periods of time in detention. Joel would later describe this antecedent report in terms of 'a shameful history' of offending. However, from custody in his teens, Joel remarked that time in juvenile detention crystallized his 'inner-strength' and resolve to retaliate against his antagonists:

> It's taught me how to be mentally strong. Like before I went to lockup, people could be sitting there, fucking [saying], 'You're a bitch'. I'd be getting tears [in my eyes].... Now it's, 'You're a bitch...and...I'm gonna whack you, dog. Come on, step up, mate, let's go'...I love it now 'cause I've got the upper hand now when I get out. Like all them people that teased me about my pills, mate, fuck youse. It's my turn now [to] watch you...cunts run scared.

In a small country town like Joel's, there was little chance his antisocial behavior would go unnoticed and, thereby, unpunished. He loved the kudos associated with his name being code for 'a walking crime wave'. For his mother, Pam, things were very different. Blame for Joel's behaviour arose from a variety of intra- and extra-familial sources and served largely to entrench the sense of disdain experienced by her family. Indeed, blame was a key theme arising from all of our interviews with female NSOs. Underpinning these 'attacks' was the implied (but sometimes explicit) message that inadequate or bad mothering was the key correlate to the anti-social and offending behaviour of their offspring (Condry 2007 in Codd 2008: 17–18; Gavazzi et al. 2003). The take-home message for Pam was that she was fighting Joel's emerging criminality *on her own*. Successive crisis points failed to yield practical assistance, especially from agencies whose specific remit was to offer support. She was left to flounder: '[Parents] have nobody [to turn to].... And the parent help-line ... they're not really much [help]. I mean they're more for, you know, "My kid's got a runny nose, what do I do?" [Well], [y]ou know, "*My* kid's trying to set fire to his bedroom, what do *I* do?"' Robert was similarly at a loss to know what to do. Working as a security guard in town, he was able to see and hear exactly what Joel was getting up to. He was deeply concerned. In fact, things got so dire that Robert had a 'meltdown' in the welfare office as he tried to avert inevitable disaster. It was a hopeless situation:

> I went to seek help from them [the Department for Families and Communities] one day.... The person I spoke to in the office believed I had anger management issues, and as I told him, 'I know what makes me angry mate, it's my son,' I said, 'and he pisses me right off'. And he got the conclusion that I had anger management issues and I was told, 'We can't help you until he offends'. You know how devastating that is to hear someone say, 'I can't help you at all. This office cannot help you until he offends'. And what happens? They offend. At 13 years old, he commits one of the hardest crimes and you think, 'Wow, man. Now you've got all the help you want'.

It's difficult to say whether Joel received 'help' as promised. When we met him at 16, he was serving a sentence for committing robbery with violence and assault causing grievous bodily harm. Child's play it was not. He recounted the incidents enthusiastically and spoke at length about the damage he was prepared to cause over a mobile phone and idle threats to a 'mate':

> I was with my... mate and we were wandering around and I was drinking with him for a bit and he gave me... a whack, like, he chucked me a needle full of Kapanol. A full needle. And I whacked it up and I'm sitting there and my fucking head's feeling like it's going to like, bang, explode.... I was really fucked.... I ended up getting to this dude's house... and... I was looking at him and he's fucking there, flashing around his wicked phone, telling everyone, 'Yeah, I'm getting paid tonight'.... It's like fucking don't tell me that mate, you're gonna get rolled. And bang! Me and my mate we walked off and waited for that fat fuck and his mate to come round the corner and we grabbed them.... I had a blade and I put it up against his neck and I'm like, 'You ever had your head fucking cut off, mate?'.... I kept saying, 'Give me your phone, cunt'. And then I said, 'No, fuck him', and pushed him away. And then we kept walking and... my mate looked at me and he's like, 'Are you going to let this fucking bitch get the better of you, mate?' And he ran back and he grabbed him, slung him around, flipped him on the ground and I ran up, fucking boot! Kicked him in the back of the head. And then when he was on the ground, I just grabbed him and lifted him up and did a couple of big king hits... into the head and he was out like a light.... I got a

phone and a wallet.... I didn't even know that a chick had called the coppers.... After that, got locked up, and here I am.

Joel continued:

> That robbery happened after the grievous bodily harm [incident].... I'd back my mate up with my life, man, like I mean I'd fucking back him up till the day I die. This dude was sending death threats to him... and my mate's found him and he's grabbed him and he's got him by his shirt, 'Right, cunt, what you fucking bringing on, are you going to kill me? You're going to kill me?' And then he pushed him away and I said, 'Come on, man, ... hit him, kick his fucking head in...'. And I fucking ripped my mate out of the way and I jumped in front of him and I'm like, 'What, you got a problem with my mate, cunt?' And he seen me gettin' real wild and he's like, 'No man, no, I don't, man, I don't have a problem'. I said, 'You got a problem with me, cunt?' Fucking, smash! 'Now you do, you dog'. And I fucking... broke... part of his jaw. They reckon I broke the mandible.... Yeah they reckon I broke both sides of the mandible, smashed out five teeth. I only did the one punch, man. I was so proud of that.

For the two incidents, a sentence of ten months' detention was imposed. Despite the severity of his crimes, Joel denied they placed him 'at the top of the tree' in terms of social standing at the juvenile facility: 'There's a pecking order in here.... I'm about in the middle.' At the same time he was also quite possibly the only participant to remain unconvinced by the relative 'luxury' or 'holiday camp' atmosphere of juvenile lock-up:

> I put it this way. You like playing [video] games?... Would you like sharing that game with someone you don't like?... Do you like food? Do you like your favourite foods and that? Would you like having that taken off your plate by a dude that's bigger than you?... If you say 'No' to all of [those questions], [then] simple, fucking don't come here. It's not a good place. It may look good, all spiffy and that, but behind the walls, it's not good.... I don't want to grow up here.

As he suggests, even from the 'deep end' of his offence history, Joel felt his attitude towards his lifestyle had begun to shift. It simply wasn't worth it. It was a degrading and humiliating way to live. He became aware that the anger and hatred from his unhappy childhood – and his way of dealing with it – were pushing him further and further from leading 'a good life':

> I know... it's there somewhere. I've just got to fucking dig it out.... I've got to chuck out all the fucking shit, like wanting to kill people.... I want to chuck all that out.... I don't need to be carrying that excess baggage.... I want to see myself in a good job. That's what I really want to see. I want to see myself with a family, not in the crime shit. Won't have to resort to a gun. One girlfriend. Fucking respect that comes from a higher level, not this fucking bash people respect shit. I want respect from working.... I want a good life.

Things didn't go to plan. Joel would 'celebrate' every birthday from his 14th to 18th behind bars. It was hard to avoid this situation when establishing a reputation for violence was the means for surviving disadvantage and years of humiliation: 'My [main] crime, really, is robbery.... You've got to get a bit of respect, man. Show people you're not fucking around. [Imagine] me and my mates walking into this drug dealer's house with fucking shotguns – can you imagine how much respect we got for that?... We weren't fucking around... [If he'd] smacked me in the fucking face, I would've shot him.' Drug dealing was a natural progression for Joel since in that milieu a 'crazy,' 'wild' or 'killer' social identity is held in particularly high regard (Fagan and Wilkinson 1998: 151; Wilkinson 2001: 246). As a teenager, Joel estimated he could earn up to $5000 a day selling 'pills and powders' to local 'druggies'. When the ice epidemic hit some time later, Joel was in seventh heaven. In his words, 'It's a mug's game.... You can sell a junkie absolute shit for top dollar'. He spoke about the dangers of his own stake in the underground economy and the lengths he was prepared to go to, to protect it: 'I have to carry a gun on me because I'm the dealer.... When I do have a gun... I feel safer.... I don't want to tell you that I have [shot someone] but I guess you... get the picture.... [I]t's not good'.

It wasn't good. Serious assaults kept returning Joel to custody. Another drug debt, another 'bashing' and all the while maintaining he wanted 'out' of the lifestyle but being 'too far in it' to make it happen: 'I want to get out of crime but it's hard.... I'm stuck in the crime web... cause I've got a name for myself.... In [this town], [the] cop[s] all know me.' As he suggests, living in a small town was a double bind. The police constantly harassed him and Joel was desperately aware he needed a fresh start away from his home town, away from his family and away from the 'names' he was called at primary school: 'I just want a fucking chalkboard and [to] wipe it [all] off – "Catch you later"...'. Who could say if Adelaide would be any better? He needed time to work things out: 'I don't know how yet but I'll figure out a way. I'll overcome.' At 17, though, Joel was back in custody serving another sentence for assault. This time he was 'coming off Valium' when he took exception to a 'look' received from a member of the public. 'The stiff' got his 'temple split open' for his troubles. Joel later conceded maybe it was his *own* drug paranoia that led to the attack: 'I let myself down hardcore.' He was more or less a fixture at the juvenile training centre and he would go to any and all lengths to command the respect of other residents. On one occasion, Joel and several others attempted to escape. It was classed a major incident. Staff were injured, but that, for Joel, was no 'biggie': 'They don't mean fuck all to us, like, they're just a bunch of dicks that come and work here while us, we're the lads that are locked in.' According to him, the STAR (Special Tasks and Rescue) Group as well as 50 to 60 regular police converged on the scene. The incident, in Joel's mind, was a resounding success: 'We're on fire with the other residents. We're on fire...Cause they'd be thinking, "Oh fuck, legends, they got STAR [Group] and all called in here". Fucking hell, you know...and it was just for trashing the shit out of a room and fucking smashing through bulletproof glass with a steel bar. Like, it's nothing that much.' But then came the consequences. And, for the first time, it was serious. Joel served the remainder of his sentence, almost four months, in solitary confinement – 'locked down' with no power and no running water. Even a self-described 'hardass' like Joel was broken:

> The stress in my mind was just so full on.... I started losing it a little bit while I was in my cell.... I stopped eating.... There was a stage in there [where] I was, like, hearing a bit of shit in my head.... They had me on these tablets... antidepressants... it helped me a bit.... [I]t was about 22 hours a day [lockdown]... for about... three to four months I reckon. I was just in total lockdown. It broke me.... I broke.... I cried in there heaps of times.... [J]ust the silence for so long sometimes gets to you. You know, being on your own in a room with no TV, no radio, you've only got one sheet, a bar of soap and a cup. That's all you've got in your room.... It's hard to say what I learned from it... because I'm locked up again.

Following his release, Joel again took up where he left off. From the ages of 18 to 20 he was convicted of non-aggravated serious criminal trespass, theft, assault, aggravated assault, aggravated throw missile, aggravated causing harm with intent and breach of suspended sentence bonds. However, during these years there were also significant developments or 'points of light' in his personal circumstances. At 19, Joel got his first real job cleaning public housing stock so new tenants could move in. At the time, Joel was on a 12-month Good Behaviour Bond and was thankful for the structure, money and physicality associated with the position. He knew more than anyone that boredom and a small town didn't mix. Joel remarked he 'didn't need' to do crime during this period as he 'was too built up with stuff to do'. He also entered his first semi-stable relationship with Carlie, who would ultimately have two daughters by him. Brief but repeat experience of prison also motivated Joel to avoid further serious offending: 'You've got no kid shit in here. It's like you're doing time.... You're not sitting in a games room playing fucking X-Box, playing computer games, or running amok around the unit and shit.... You're sitting in your cell most of the day, thinking hard on what you've done.' And then there were the 'screws'. As Joel saw it, they made the juvenile custodial facility youth workers look *good*: 'They're over-assertive, big time.... They think they run shit...'.

When next released to the community, things went better for Joel. For seven months he lived with Carlie, went to work, and experienced the first Christmas day with his family in five years. For his mother Pam it was 'The only time I've known him to be anywhere close to normal'. When Joel found out Carlie was pregnant, he was ecstatic: 'It's killer. I'm happy as'. Then, seemingly without warning, his 'progress' hit a snag. As Joel recalled: 'I left work and [then] I [got] up to... trouble'. 'Trouble' equated to drug dealing. And drug dealing, for Joel, meant violence. There was also the issue of his personal use: 'I just got... back on the drugs – speed.' That's when the next major incident occurred. As Joel put it: 'I got done for bashing this fuck head'. The 'fuck head,' as it turned out, was beaten with the DVD player he had previously offered Joel in part payment of a drug debt. Robert, Joel's stepfather, instantly blamed himself for the turn of events. In essence, he had, just previous to that event, inadvertently 'trivialized' Joel's employment. His comments were well intended, but they led to Joel eventually walking away from the job:

> I said to him when we were drinking one night, ... I said, 'I always see [you] as better than that. I see [you] in a job better than that'.... He could be a mechanic, [he] could do something way better than cleaning yards. 'Man, who'd want to clean yards for a living?' And that's what I said to him that night. And he was like, 'I love it, it's wicked'. And afterwards I realized that [I should] be happy for him, if that's

what he chooses to do and he loves doing it, then I'm happy for him to do that.... [But then], yeah, you know [he] miss[ed] one day, then missed the next day and the next day and then it was just, 'Oh, well I don't have a job to go to'.

Joel told the court he didn't want a suspended sentence or a non-parole period because of difficulties he anticipated with supervision. He was sentenced to 18 months' imprisonment and his Good Behaviour Bond was revoked. He missed the birth of his daughter, Maddie, and spoke of deep regret and shame that he had deprived his child the support and guidance of a father in much the same way that he was deprived of such. This was seen to prompt a renewed commitment to a future beyond crime and punishment:

> All I know is I don't want to come back here. I just want to get on with my life.... I'm 20 and... I should be out with my little girl, bringing up my little girl,... not sitting in a fucking cell... talking with... my cellie all night... I should be out. I should be with my girlfriend. I should be hugging her.... [But] I kept coming back and forth.... It's not good. It's ridiculous. I'm ashamed of it. I feel disgusted with myself because... I wasn't there for [my daughter's] birth.... That's not any way of teaching them to grow up, you know, not knowing where their Dad is.

Despite his wishes to the contrary, Joel, aged 21, was released on parole. Slowly, he began to settle into family life with Carlie and Maddie. Before long, Carlie was pregnant again. He also learned his old boss was prepared to have him back at work. Things looked as if they might fall into place. However, the demands of parole ultimately prevented Joel from accepting the position. Understandably, he was incensed: 'It's ridiculous.... They expect [you to become] rehabilitat[ed].... [But] [y]ou're gonna get fired from most of your jobs for going to see a fucking parole [officer]. And then you've got to tell [your employer] what your day leave is for.... You can't say, "Look, I'm sick". What if they're at the fucking shops and you're walking through to go to parole? It's hard. It's really hard.' Being placed on home detention a short time later proved the final straw: 'It was worse on home D because I couldn't do nothing.... The reason [I came back]... was because of my girlfriend. We argued and... I've just walked out the front, took the fucking bracelet off and just walked off.... I just needed that breathing space from her because it's hard when you're in someone's face 24/7.' In the space of two years, Joel was returned to custody four times for breaching parole.

His missed the birth of his second daughter, Ella. The difference between his two 'realities' (prison and family) was stark: '[Y]ou put on a gaol face. You can't let nothing bother you in here. You can't cry here. You can't... have no emotions in here, basically. If you beat someone up with a frozen water bottle, you can't say, "Sorry", you know. You just get it over and done with, jump in the shower, and wipe the blood off and start the day.' Each time he went to prison Joel refused to let Carlie bring his daughters to visit him: 'Everyone wants to see their babies... but... I've just got a feeling that if I bring my girls into here then it's going to reflect bad on them. And they're going to see me in a place like this and think it's all right.... I don't want that to happen.' He spoke of this period in prison in the following terms:

> The main thing I miss [is] hugging my girlfriend when I go to sleep, you know. It's shattering. And it's basically the little things in life that you miss.... Big things like drugs, money, cars, you don't miss that in here. You think of family. You think of your kids and your girlfriend – whether she's being faithful or not, you think of that sort of stuff. When I've come to gaol, I said to my girlfriend, 'Listen, I'm still with you but, if you feel the need, you know, you may as well do it'. And that's a hard thing for a criminal to say... the fact that you're telling your girlfriend to go out and fuck anyone she wants.

The 'screws' continued to 'push his buttons': 'They just call you a dickhead, wanker, crim, scumbag... [like] they've never done a thing wrong in their life.... The only reason they're screws is because they can't be a copper because they've got a fucking criminal record.... So they come here and try [it on] with their fake cop bullshit. You know, rent-a-cops. It's stupid. They're idiots.' Joel had a similarly dim view of the Parole Board: 'They talk at you. They try and make you feel small...'.

When we saw Joel in mid-2011, he was back in prison after eight months 'on the run'. Following two days performing community service (roadside rubbish collection) Joel had 'taken off' and travelled from Adelaide and Sydney. There had been several key events in his life since his last interview. His relationship with Carlie had dissolved and they were no longer on speaking terms. He was briefly in a relationship with Kelly, which produced a son, Lenny, but that relationship had also soured. Both Carlie and Kelly made it difficult for him to have contact with his children and Joel felt that, with his violent history, applying for a court order would be an exercise in futility. He was offered another chance on parole but instantly declined it: 'I just wrote them a letter saying, 'Look I don't want my parole back.... Don't let me let out early'. The written response from the Parole Board acceded to his request but did nothing to inspire confidence: 'They just said I'm a repeat offender and that... I'm pretty much no good to be in society.' With regard to the future, Joel commented: 'I've looked at it now and I think at the end of the day I'm the one that sits in gaol. None of them little fuckwits [the drug users]... come to gaol, and I always seem to be the one that cops the... raw end of the stick.' His next release, at age 23, was the first time in ten years he was free of all sanctions.

Joel Jnr. was born the year after he got out. His relationship with Louise, the child's mother, ended three months later. Apparently, she remains hopeful reunification will occur although Joel has had several girlfriends in quick succession since then. For a time he was subject to a domestic violence restraining order but Louise had the matter withdrawn. While Joel has not been convicted of any major indictable or 'felony' offending over the last five years, he has found it incredibly difficult to avoid return to prison. He was remanded in custody once in 2012, once in 2013 and once in 2014. Clearly, part of the problem lies in his ongoing refusal to cope with home detention bail:

> I wouldn't come out on home D, no way. [Gaol] is easier, it's a lot easier.... I done home D before and... I didn't like it. My house got really small in the space of two months. Yeah, I got sick of that [and] ended up ripping me home D bracelet off and going back to gaol. And I liked it. I didn't care because at least I could walk in space, you know, I wasn't confined in one confined part.... There was no bullshit... ringing up, 'Can I go to the shops and get a litre of milk?' 'No you can't. 'Well, fuck this breakfast idea', you know, 'There goes the breakfast plan'. Ring them back, 'I've got no toast, I've got no bread, I need milk... Can I fucking give youse petrol money to go pick me up some?' 'Nah, we're not a taxi service'. I'm like, 'Well I wouldn't be using a taxi service anyway, I'm on home D'. 'Oh, this isn't our problem, [Joel]. You should sort this out'. Hang up on me. For fuck sake.

With that kind of 'support', it's little wonder that young men like Joel view prison as a form of respite. He continues to battle drug 'issues' which remain constant in and outside of custody: '[M]ost of the time I go to gaol I manage to have a drug supply where I earn myself money. You're fucking stupid if you don't.' Recently, Joel conceived of his 'progress' as follows: 'I have done longer [in the community] but... [that was when I was] on the run. I haven't done longer out like this before.' It is true that he still has a considerable way to go prior to 'earning' something akin to the desister label: 'I've got to do something instead of just sitting on my ass on Facebook [or] selling [drugs] from my phone.... [I've] [g]ot to go out and actually work.' But Joel has received at least some affirmation for his efforts: 'It made me smile the [other] day [when] I went into [the community correctional office and] she said to me, ... "Oh we've noticed a marked improvement in your behavior.... [Y]ou've been fucking pulling your head in". And I'm like, "Fucking oath I have". [Well], I have, but I haven't. I mean... as far as I can [push things], I have.... But [I've also] been good.' In Joel's view, prison has changed a lot over the past decade or so and is no longer compatible with his understanding of 'loyalty' and 'respect': 'It's about who's got the drugs, who's got the money, that's it. It's not [about] respect these days. It isn't [about] knowing someone for fucking years.' Joel is realistic about the fact that the future is likely to hold more prison time for him. But he hopes it won't come to that:

> If I go back,... like I said, it's just another bump in the road really. It's bullshit... I'm close to it, I'm close to it. I thought I was close last time. That's just because I was making so much money and then it just went to shit [and I] fucked up. But... I reckon I'll be able to get myself out of it. I reckon. It's not going to be long.... Yeah, I don't want to go back there. It's boring as now. It's boring as. [It's] fucking shit....

In his final interview, aged in his mid-twenties, we asked Joel what his 'ideal' life would look like. He didn't blink: 'If I could have one wish it'd be [to have] my kids, a fucking big killer house, the fuck away from [my home town] on a massive grassy hill somewhere and that's it. Done.' He's currently on bail for aggravated assault and some minor traffic matters and to that extent, his struggle for desistance is still very much a work in progress.

Paul

Paul is 27. He is the eldest of three children to Karl and Vicky who divorced when he was seven. Both subsequently remarried and had families of their own. Regarding his father, Paul simply states: 'I don't know where he is [or] what the go is.' The little he knows isn't particularly endearing. Karl, a former air force man, was greatly disappointed by

Paul's early learning difficulties and psychological issues. Paul also knows his father is well aware of his ongoing battles with homelessness and incarceration. But these too, by all accounts, have become a source of further embarrassment to him. His father has never once managed so much as a 'Happy Birthday' greeting over the past 20 years: 'Every birthday he would just leave money or something at my Nanna's. Like I'm 25 years old now, I'm pretty sure he did it last year for my birthday still. Why didn't he come and see me and say "Happy Birthday?"... Seems a bit pathetic now.' Paul estimates they have met on no more than four occasions. As with Ben (see below), Paul periodically wondered how a positive father figure might have impacted the onset and continuation of his offending: 'I've spent most of my life without my Dad.... [A]t times I [wonder] if that's... affected me.... It's just something that I've thought about.' One of Paul's very few supporters is his paternal grandmother Danuta, who migrated to Australia when Karl was just a boy. Living through the occupation by Nazi Germany, Danuta knows the extent of human misery and suffering like no other on our project. Perhaps this is why she was so appalled that her son, with a life of relative luxury, continued to shirk all responsibilities as a father: 'I don't know where they [Karl and his wife] live. I'm – I'm not interested. I'm so hurt, you know, about what's happened to [Paul].... [He] wants his father so bad.... [I once said to his father], "Look after your children. They don't ask to be born. They need you".' To date, these words have fallen on deaf ears.

Vicky – Paul's mother – was also far from the ideal parent. Consequently, Paul missed out on the love and affection or 'reciprocal positive feedback loop' (Perry 2001: 3) critical for normative social and emotional development. He was often berated for his shortcomings without practical assistance on how to address them. As Danuta recalled at interview:

> He had problems... when he was little... [and] when [Vicky] was mad she [would] call him a loser. And [Paul] [couldn't] stand [to hear] it, 'You're a loser'. And I would say to her, you know, 'Don't talk to your son like that.... Give him something. Make him happy, even if maybe he doesn't do something properly.... You know, be a mother.... Don't put him down.' He can't stand the [label] 'loser' and [being told] 'You are nothing. You are lazy. You are this [and that]'.

Paul left school shortly after completing Year 8. For some time he had been walking a fine line: smoking 'dope', swearing and getting into fights with other students. When, at age 13, he assaulted a teacher, he was given his marching orders. Around this time, problems at home really began to boil over. Vicky could be cruel and Paul's mental health difficulties – most notably depression, anxiety and bipolar symptoms – only exacerbated her frustrations. On and off medication since his early teens, Paul remarked that without it: 'I just lose my patience, I lose my cool.... It...makes me feel like a good person.' Regularly thrown out of the house, Paul would often wreak havoc on his way out the door. He would bounce between maternal and paternal grandmothers until they were unable or unwilling to deal with him. On one occasion, aged 14, Paul found himself wandering the streets for days: 'that was one of the worst situations I got into. I had nowhere to go.' Foster care was short lived but Paul lasted long enough to learn how to steal a car from a 'foster brother'. With that, a passion for stolen cars was born: 'it came to the point where I did do it again and again and again. I started liking it.' Between the ages of 15 and 17, Paul was arrested 'countless' times and served two significant detention orders of six months each for illegal use and assault.

By the time he was given his last conditional release from a juvenile facility (to his mother's address), Paul was 18. His court fines, fees and levies were sizeable at that point – well in excess of $2000. With no realistic prospect of making payment, Paul agreed to perform community service. It was a non-issue for him, until, that is, he arrived at the work site. Day one involved 'shovelling shit' at the horse stables. By day three, Paul had had enough: 'I just threw my shovel and walked home.' He was fully prepared to wear the consequences. We note that many of the young males took exception to the range of belittling tasks community service served up to them. For Paul, the sense of hopelessness was overpowering: 'Just going to community service and seeing those sorts of people makes me want to start walking backwards.' Some tasks were unpleasant, others downright humiliating, others utterly meaningless. Sorting through buttons and cutting up T-shirts for rags were two tasks mentioned by participants. Paul learned from the experience that: 'There's a lot of different buttons and a lot of choices of rags.' However, the soul-destroying nature of community service was, for Paul, just one of many hurdles standing between him and desistance. The second, more predictable obstacle concerned his relationship with his mother: 'It broke down again [and] [j]ust got to the point where she didn't want me there. So I left.' Within two weeks Paul was back at his grandmother's. But this time there was a serious complication. Danuta's adult son from her second marriage was also living with her. And he was no fan of Paul's. 'Scared' of the consequences further participation might have for her, Danuta had to withdraw from our study after her first and only interview. She implied that Paul's uncle had significant mental health problems of his own saying, simply, 'He's sick'. After he intentionally cut the power supply to the 'shed' where Paul was staying, there was a violent confrontation. At this time, Danuta had no choice but to call the Crisis Care line and drive Paul to emergency accommodation. It was a new low for the 18-year-old. It took just three days for an older and more 'experienced' resident to stand over him for money. After a brief fracas Paul was arrested and charged with assault. He spoke of his predicament in the following terms: 'Placement's my main issue.... Fuck, I don't know, it's just all mentally hurting and just making me do stupid things, slip ups...'.

Paul was unravelling. He wanted better for himself but could see no substantive means for getting there. He lacked, in short, both the 'will and the ways' (Snyder et al. 1991) to avoid imprisonment. In fact, against this backdrop, Paul actually embraced the prospect of being locked up as a springboard to a future that remained out of reach while in the community. He literally had to go back to go forward. In answer to breaches of his conditional release, Paul was direct: 'I [don't] want my bail. Just give me a detention order to help myself.' The judge, according to him, was stunned. No one had opposed his release. But Paul was resolute: 'I've always had mental problems.... I wanted to deal with them but I didn't know how to go about it.... I'm just having trouble helping myself.' When he became eligible for conditional release, Paul refused that too. He wanted, in his words: to 'get on with getting as much help as I can, just so I [can] make sure... I'm ready, good and ready, for the outside [next] time.'

This, unfortunately, was not the only occasion Paul 'chose' custody over release. At age 19 he was broke and homeless yet again. Months earlier, a serious incident occurred in which two offenders used a broken bottle to rob an establishment of cash and other items. They stole a car and escaped with one being arrested. Paul knew about the robbery and decided that perhaps he could use it to get some stability in his life. In the context of speaking to police about a much less serious matter, he falsely confessed to the crime and put the police off the trail of the actual co-offender. On remand, Paul spent a total of 12 months in custody and 'two weeks' on Home Detention Bail. Home D was an ordeal he never wanted to repeat: 'I basically just felt that I was set up to fail really.... Having to ring up someone just to organize my life every five minutes. I couldn't cope with that. People that can do it for like a year or so on home D with a band around their leg, I don't know how they do it.' He was swiftly returned to prison. For his troubles, Paul was charged and convicted of making a false report to police – a major indictable offence. Describing the matter as 'strange', a judge released him without further penalty.

When we next spoke with Paul he was 22 and nearing completion of a 12-month Good Behaviour Bond. He had been in the community for two years: 'I didn't think I could have gone a month without getting locked up. This is my biggest free stretch yet.... [I'm] just concentrating on myself and not worrying about what's around me and what other people are doing.' At that stage he was 'loving life' with his partner Allison and their two young daughters, Lily and Briony. Meeting Allison three years earlier was a story in itself. While locked up, Paul placed a call to a friend and she picked up the phone. The rest, as they say, is 'history'. By all accounts, the girls were his 'pride and joy'. Paul singlehandedly attributed his recent successes to them. It was clear he walked a little taller just knowing they were in his life. Things, however, continued to weigh on his mind. He described, with great sadness and regret, how he missed both births due to incarceration. It was his fault and he readily accepted blame for it. Still, he was forced to wait 12 months before meeting Briony for the first time. As it turned out, Allison was disinclined to bring the baby into the prison for a visit. Paul went to great lengths to try and catch a glimpse of his newborn child:

> It ruined me a bit...what I had to miss out on. It was something I really wanted, the simplest of things, but she took it away.... I think I spent like five [dollars] or whatever ...on pens and papers and stamps and envelopes and sent it all off to [Allison]. I sent her everything [needed] to write me a letter, and she still didn't send a letter back.... I just wanted something back from her.... [E]ven if she just sent it back empty I would have been happy, knowing that she sent me something.... I asked for a photo [of my child.] I begged for them.

Paul did his best to put it behind him. There was already enough friction with his mother who had kicked them out following a dispute over 'boarding' money. There was little ambiguity in her directive: 'Pack your bags and fuck off', she said. The young family moved in with Allison's brother. Paul continued to enjoy the positive influence of his grandmothers: 'They've done a lot for me. Sadly to say, more than my Mum. It doesn't really bother me. I'm standing strong on my own two feet, doing well.' And he was doing well. Paul had his driver's licence and was making modest attempts to comply with what seemed like a never-ending community service order. Indeed, the only court matter 'hanging over' him was in relation to outstanding community service hours. Paul was resigned to his fate: 'No doubt they'll probably try to put me on another order. What's the point? I've had that many. I'll probably do a little bit and then I'll end up giving up on it because I'm sick of it.... It's just the same routine over and over.' What Paul desperately wanted was a steady job and independent housing. Both continued to elude him. As he commented: 'There's too many judgmental people out there... not giving me a fair go, and maybe just looking at me and judging me by what I look like, or because of something [they've] heard I've done.... It's two different things – who you are, and what you do.'

Breaking up with Allison just six months later, Paul's old battles with homelessness rematerialized. In reference to the split, he was quite matter-of-fact: 'The fire just died down between us. I wanted to get out, so I got out.' Like Ben, Joel and Reggie (see elsewhere in this chapter), Paul had a tendency to throw himself 'head first' into intense relationships that 'burned out' or 'blew up' following each release from custody. All four referred to their need for autonomy and space as a way of combatting the effects of incarceration. In Paul's words: 'I like to spend time with myself... Even in the community I don't have my own place to run back [to] and hide... Wherever I go I've got to share that house with someone... I'm going out with someone the majority of the time so I can never get away from people on my own – get away and just have my own break.' Arguably, terms such as 'run', 'hide', 'getaway' and 'break' don't augur well for a lasting relationship. And as Paul discovered, they don't necessarily make for a 'clean' separation either. Unhappy about the way things ended, Allison confronted Paul and a major fight erupted. Paul was subsequently arrested and charged with assault. An Apprehended Violence Order ('AVO') ensued and he was prevented from having any contact or communication with her. Adding insult to injury, Allison and the kids packed up and moved back in with Vicky (Paul's mother) where they stayed for several years. Once again, Paul felt his mum had 'picked a side' and, once again, it wasn't in his favour. A faint hope that Vicky might at least facilitate visits with his daughters proved groundless. Paul couldn't help but think that history was repeating itself: 'My Dad took off on... my brother and I when we were younger.... And I just feel like, in a way, that my Mum's sort of trying to make me out to be my Dad. Which I'm not. I want something to do with my girls.... Basically I feel she's stopping me from being the Dad I want to be.'

Paul reverted back to crashing on couches while he waited for public housing to become available. In many ways he was thankful his daughters couldn't visit him: 'I wouldn't want my kids seeing me in this position.' Arrested from time to time on minor matters, Paul suffered few serious consequences (and no custodial time). He found casual work at car yards and in mechanics' garages but often found his employers to be, in his words, 'shonky as all fuck'. He would leave soon after. Although directionless, he was, somehow, keeping his head above water. Over a year later, at age 25, Paul had still not secured permanent accommodation and this in spite of long being assigned as 'priority one' for housing. He eventually moved in with a new partner, Brooke, and began to prepare for the birth of his third child. An outstanding community service balance continued to be his only point of contact with the law. This proved a confounding state of affairs for Paul. He knew that prisons were at capacity, that so-called 'real criminals' were walking the streets, and yet police were chasing him over some unshovelled 'horse shit' and unsorted 'rags and coloured buttons'. Warrants for his arrest were issued and executed: 'All I wanted to do was hug my missus goodbye.... [They said], "Alright you can do that, [but] we've just got to put the handcuffs on first." I'm like, "Well, how the fuck am I going to do that with handcuffs on?"' Shortly thereafter, allegations of domestic violence again began to surface, this time with respect to Brooke. A knife was involved and both suffered minor injury. Paul was arrested and spent three months in custody. When the matter was ultimately withdrawn, he was left with AVOs relating to both his current and former partner. Moving in with his maternal grandmother, things slowly began to calm down again. He and Brooke reconciled but continued to live apart. Lucas was born and, this time, Paul was present at the birth. He was even advised by OARS that a residence would be available for him. It sounded promising. But as Paul explained to us, his new 'home' was probably worse than no home at all: 'I was just surrounded by a lot of dickheads... so I sort of threw the house in. I was in a block of units but everyone [there had been] released from prison and... I didn't really want to surround myself and my kids [with] that so I gave the house in.... Shit went south and I ended up here.'

Paul was back in prison. As he explained to us, his 'housing situation' had too many temptations. Drugs were freely available and the music played until the early hours. The whole complex of residents literally didn't sleep. Paul began to dabble in amphetamines, as did Brooke. When he ultimately 'threw the house in' three months later, Paul took a renewed taste for 'speed' with him. Living at a motel, he and Brooke (pregnant for a second time) went on a 'bender' and ended up attacking each other. He was again promptly arrested and bailed but, unfortunately for him, there would be no reconciliation this time around. Instead, things with Brooke became increasingly hostile as attempts to see his children were continually rejected. Paul was beside himself. He was 26 and, excepting the moral encouragement from two elderly women (his grandmothers), had nothing in the world to show for it. No house, no job, no money, no partner, no kids. As Paul put it: 'I just lost my shit.' He picked up the telephone and made a series of 'vile' and 'disturbing' threats towards Brooke and her son from a previous relationship. Graphic pictures accompanied several of the text messages. Paul was convicted of eight major indictable offences including aggravated threatening life. Sentenced to two years' imprisonment, he was recently released on parole. Deeply ashamed of his behaviour, he identified a pressing need to access support systems that would help him avoid returning to prison in the future: 'I've never really known who [to see] or where to go to [get help].' Paul was arrested less than a month later and remanded in custody. We wonder whether this, again, was a 'choice' he made in the hope of finding help.

Reggie

Reggie is 27 and serving a sentence for illegal use of a motor vehicle and assaulting police. He is also liable to serve the balance of unexpired parole for previous offending. Reggie hopes to apply for parole again in the near future but remains realistic about his chances. He has been criticized by authorities for failing to respond to such opportunities in the past. By all accounts, his childhood was an unhappy one. His biological parents had an on/off relationship with his father, Michael, regularly in and out of prison – one of a disproportionate number of Aboriginal men to encounter that fate. Although Reggie's mother is Caucasian, he proudly identifies as Aboriginal. When Reggie was two years of age, his mother formed a relationship with his stepfather who turned out to be an extremely strict disciplinarian. He took an instant dislike to Reggie and used daily corporal punishment to enforce his authority. Both parents were alcohol-dependent and the home served as a 'doss-house' to friends and associates. There were regular, violent fights between his mother and stepfather at the address. Michael's (adoptive) mother, Shirley, describes the wretched circumstances of Reggie's formative years:

> [Tina] would be drinking.... [T]hey had lots of people ... that were drinkers coming into the house.... [Reggie] was put out in a

sleep-out.... He was wetting the bed at the time and [Tina] used to leave it. He's get back into the same wet bed that he got out of in the morning.... Yeah, he had... [it] tough.

It got tougher. Reggie ran away from home at age nine to escape regular 'punch-ups' with his stepfather. A ward of the state by 12, he has since remarked that his mother can 'get fucked' for abandoning him in this way. Reunification never occurred. In foster care, Reggie mixed primarily with 'Potheads. Everyone that does breaks and steals cars'. Asked from where he developed a sense of right and wrong, the 16-year-old was blunt: 'Probably from the fuckin' gutter.' Despite claims he was 'only...caught for one...out of [every] hundred [offences he committed]', juvenile detention was a regular feature of Reggie's life throughout his childhood. Most often he served time for stealing cars, doing ram-raids[1], leading high-speed police pursuits and theft. In his own words: 'There's not much than can beat the adrenalin of getting a stolen car, breaking into a shop [and] driving through a window.' This is more than bravado. Reggie became notorious for destroying two police cars in a head-on collision that resulted in an officer being put in hospital for several weeks. Understandably, friends in the police force were hard to come by after that: 'If the coppers see me, "Bang! Hey, come here". They all [know] my date of birth, my name and all my addresses off by heart.' Reggie is disqualified from holding or obtaining a driver's licence until further order of the court for a period of no fewer than 13 years. All things going well, the earliest he will obtain a licence is 2021. An order for restitution in the amount of $30,000 has also been made against him in respect of the damaged vehicles.

Reggie put considerable effort into his offending. As he remarked: 'Sometimes I wouldn't sleep for three days. I would be planning ... [and] driving around in a stolen car looking for shops that haven't got poles[2] in front of them.' But, by the same token, he conceded he'd 'done over a few delis [i.e. local drug stores] just for a drink of Coke because I was thirsty'. From age 12 to 16 Reggie spent a total of just four months in the community. While the idea of 'three hots [i.e. meals] and a cot [i.e. a bed]' had some appeal, Reggie regarded juvenile detention as a poor substitute for 'home'. By his mid-teens, Reggie began to express desire to break away from the 'custodial crowd' and forge a 'normal' life in a quiet regional town several hours drive from Adelaide. This is where his paternal grandparents, Shirley and John, adopted and raised five abandoned Aboriginal children, one of whom was Reggie's father,

Michael. Outside prison, theirs was the only door that never slammed in Reggie's face. As Shirley remarked, with no biological children of their own, dedication to 'at-risk' youth remains a life-long passion for the couple:

> My dream was to help with Aboriginal kids, and it just happened that we didn't have our own family and we adopted the five kids.... It's been hard, but the thing is we've still got them. You know, they're still around us so that's the main thing. It doesn't matter whether they've been in gaol, what they've done, or anything like that.... You know, they're ours. They're still here.

Life threw Shirley and John a variety of 'curveballs' generally involving cycles of addiction and incarceration – something four of the five children battled extensively. Michael, now approaching 50, was in and out of custody from the age of fourteen, most notably serving what Reggie refers to as 'two bricks' – that is, two separate sentences of ten years apiece. Michael remarked that when he drinks, 'I'm one of the most dangerous pricks you could ever come across'. His sister Jane served a life sentence and remains on parole. Shirley and John coped as best they could, always comforting themselves with the knowledge that 'they're ours' and 'they're still here'. They dug in and stood firm where most others would have given up. During a particularly difficult period around Jane's incarceration they also ran a local 'House of Care', offering temporary accommodation and meals to men transitioning out of prison. For Reggie, these two 'senior citizens' are as real as it gets. On that count, Reggie would frequently travel to his grandparents between custodial events. From there, he would attempt to secure accommodation, find work and start to settle in. Not that he could expect much outside help along the way. In fact, as Reggie soon discovered, navigating government agencies from outside of Adelaide created a raft of issues that threatened to undermine his progress before it could start in earnest:

> Apparently if you move away from town, you've got to wait three months before your file can be [transferred].... It's ridiculous.... I couldn't see a social worker. I didn't have any clothes. I couldn't do nothing.... I just walked in there one time [and said], 'I'm [Reggie]. I've just moved down here. I'm on conditional release'. [I gave] them all my details [and said]... 'I've been told that I can come in here for support', and, yeah, they just [said], 'Well, we haven't got your file mate, so we can't really do much about it'.

Reggie took a pragmatic view of the situation: 'And they call *us* dickheads...'. Unable to secure more than intermittent seasonal work, he rarely lasted beyond three months in the community. In almost clockwork fashion, Reggie would succumb to a lengthy history of drug abuse involving marijuana, amphetamines and heroin. At such points, it was only a matter of time before being locked up: 'I might need something and it's 12 o'clock at night and no shops are open. I got no cash so, yeah, I just go and put a car through the front window [of a shop] and steal all the clothes or bottles or whatever.' In the beginning, as Reggie explained, he congratulated himself for staying out of lock-up for only a few months: 'That's where I think a lot of us young blokes... slip up... We think, "Yeah, three months is good enough". Whereas now, I'm starting to think, that's nowhere near good enough. I want to be out for the rest of my life.'

That didn't happen. Over the next four years, Reggie cycled in and out of juvenile and adult custodial facilities. He'd stopped doing ram-raids and similar serious car-related crime. But he remained regularly swept up in the criminal exploits of relatives and acquaintances: ' "Mate, do you want to come for a walk?" "Where are we going?" "You know, just to get some clothes".... Before you know it, they're chucking a brick through the window [and] you're running in and grabbing an armful of clothes and then running back down the street.' On another occasion, Reggie was evicted from his government-assisted accommodation after extended family moved in and trashed the place. With nowhere to go, Reggie called on a long-lost cousin who happened to be in the business of stealing copper wiring from 'abandoned' businesses. But the premises were very much occupied. He was arrested and given six months' imprisonment for theft of $20 worth of copper. By any measure, it wasn't a sound investment.

At 19, Reggie found himself at a crossroads. After just nine days in the community he was locked up for running a policeman off his motorcycle in an attempt to avoid arrest. Moments earlier he and a co-offender had stolen a car to get alcohol and cigarettes from a drive-through liquor store. Reggie had always made it plain in interview, 'If I ever own a legit car, I will pull over [i.e. for police] but in a stolen car, I'm not going to pull over to come back here [i.e. to prison]. I'd prefer to get high-speed chased and get rid of them, and then just jump out the car and take off.' He explained at interview, the theft was motivated by an escalating heroin habit costing in the vicinity of $800 to $1200 per day. He was sentenced to four years' imprisonment with a non-parole period of two years. By this stage Reggie had four children by four different mothers and no contact with any of them. His girlfriend of two years, Tara, was waiting for him on the outside but Reggie found it difficult to maintain regular contact with her as one phone call cost around a third of a prisoner's weekly state-funded allowance (about $12.50). It was a depressing picture. Things had to change. Reggie vowed to make amends: 'She's wasted two years of her life on me.... I want to make the time back up to her really.'

Instead, 21-year-old Reggie 'moved on' from the relationship just one week after being released. He claims to have discovered Tara was 'playing up' with other men during his imprisonment, something she strongly denies. Perhaps he was simply looking for an 'easy out'. It wouldn't be the first time a girlfriend was cast off when no longer required by their man to source visits and commissary items. In any event, Reggie was out on parole, and with a new girl. He hesitated to use the word 'free' because 'I'm free when I have no...gaol time or nothing hanging over...my head.... I don't think free is...just [being] out of gaol'. Immediately, and to his credit, he found part-time work with an events-hire company, erecting temporary stalls for large functions. The work was hard on the body and Reggie tells, like Joel, of being literally too exhausted to get up to his old ways: 'Like I come home from work on the first day and I was fucked. I couldn't do nothing so I just went to bed.' According to him, this was the best he had ever done, he was changing his ways and resisting temptation to 'thieve' – something he was yet to accomplish during previous periods in the community. Just one month later, though, Reggie was caught driving to the local shops to buy cigarettes for his brother's girlfriend: 'It would have been quicker to walk there...than take the car.' He was promptly returned to custody. Pleading guilty, Reggie hoped the magistrate would note his contrition and legitimate attempts to reform. No such luck. Reggie was handed an immediate custodial sentence of eight months. He was, to put it mildly, disappointed with the result:

> For someone who's been a career criminal up to this point, [but who's now] got a job, he's doing the right thing, he hasn't offended since he's been out, he wasn't taking drugs, he wasn't doing bugger all, he's working. [Well], they didn't even ask how I was going. I think it's just a bit of a kick in the ass.... The judge didn't want to hear [any of the good things I'd done]...Cocksucker.

He ended up serving the full eight months before, yet again, being released on parole – a collective period of around three and a half years.

Still smarting from his latest rebuke, Reggie was defiant: 'It's not going to change my mind.... If I have to I'll still drive.' As with many of the young males we interviewed, Reggie had an almost pathological aversion to public transport. First and foremost, was deep-seated belief that his prisoner status was 'on show' for the captive audience to enjoy. As he remarked at 19: 'I don't like catching public transport. I get paranoid that people are looking at me, watching me, you know, "Why are they looking at me?" I find it easier to steal a car and go there on my own two feet, as you say.' At 25, the impact of further custodial time did little to diminish his attitude:

> I don't really like catching public transport because when you get on the bus you have to pay for your ticket and whatnot and I don't know why but I don't like doing that. It's like, why should I have to buy a ticket?... [S]o [the driver] can... drive me from here to there? I can do that myself.... Say I haven't got my concession card, he's going to quiz me about [that] ... it's like... 'I don't have to justify myself to you, you're not a fucking... cop[...]'.

During his eight-month stint, Reggie spent ten days in solitary confinement after officers found a syringe during a routine 'ramp' of his cell. He concedes the bust may have assisted his application to join the 'Bupe' (buprenorphine) program, which took, in any event, over two months to process the paperwork. He walked from prison shortly after. But not without a significant hitch. Reggie's release was scheduled for Tuesday with his next 'report' scheduled to occur a week from then. This in itself was unproblematic. But between those dates, Shirley and John had made arrangements for Reggie to travel to them to celebrate his birthday. It had been almost four years since they had last seen each other. But there were delays at the prison and Reggie's paperwork wasn't ready. His release was held back three days. No one thought to advise the Parole Board he was in fact released on a Friday. Predictably, Reggie failed to attend the office four days later. Detectives from Operation Mandrake[3] were waiting to arrest him when he arrived home a week later. This was Reggie after all – and for the police, opportunities like this didn't come along every day. Back in prison, Reggie was first to admit that responsibility for the breach ultimately rested with him. This didn't negate the crushing effect of yet another 'pointless' return to custody:

> Look, I did muck up. I didn't report in but this is the reason I didn't, I was up there for my birthday.... [Now] I'm sitting in gaol for the

next ten weeks.... Over the last three years when I've been out, I've committed no crimes. But I always seem to end up in gaol.... It just doesn't make sense.... It's fucking ridiculous.

There was one small silver lining. Michael, his biological father, came unexpectedly to the prison for a visit. Reggie had seen him only a handful of times in his entire life – the last time being when he was just nine years old. There was no sign of resentment and no grudges. Again, Reggie's pragmatism came to the fore: 'It's not his fault he's a fucking idiot.' Having his father briefly in his life 'made me feel like a million dollars'. Released weeks later, the two quickly became inseparable. But Michael had his own demons – something which stemmed from spending more than two decades behind bars: '[After] all the years in gaol, you lose love. You don't know what love is, so you come out... filled with hate and go [on] another rampage and all that shit.... [T]here's just no feeling whatsoever, nothing.' It took more than two decades to get to the point where he was 'ready' to assume some sort of role in Reggie's life. He expressed regret this was ground he might never be able to make up: 'Everyone... talks... about [Reggie] in high regard. And the way they yarn about him sort of makes me, I don't know, like a little bit jealous, not envious, but jealous sometimes that they know him better than I do.' They shared, however, mutual experience of parental abandonment, foster care, imprisonment and ongoing battles with drug and alcohol abuse. Michael saw their relationship in terms of being 'mates' as opposed to 'father and son'. Sometimes Michael gave pause to consider how this new relationship might play out for Reggie in the long term: 'If [my girlfriend] wasn't in my life, I shit you not, me and [Reggie], we'd be shooting cunts. We'd be fucking robbing – left, right and centre – doing armed robs.' Things didn't go well. An unsettled score reared its head. Specifically, years before, Reggie had reportedly stabbed Michael during a heated argument driven by drugs and alcohol. 'Fortunately', Reggie was in custody on an unrelated matter before Michael got the chance to catch up with him again. But when he does, Michael says that 'retribution' will occur:

I don't hold it against him but I'm still going to... sort it out.... He knows that.... We know that we're going to get out the back yard and punch on.... Mothers and fathers from yesterday are all fucking bound and tied by [law] and order. You can't hit your kids no more, [give them a] good flogging. Fucking hell, I used to get flogged. My old man used to flog me and I used to think at the time, 'What did I do wrong?' But looking back now, fuck, I done a lot of things wrong. I should have got a few more floggings and you know it never fucking damaged me, it taught me respect. My word.

The next time we saw Reggie, he'd been remanded on new charges of driving disqualified, resisting arrest and assaulting police. The obligatory parole warrant was in there too. Reggie had been six months in the community – the longest period he'd had out of custody since entering juvenile detention over 12 years ago. In his terms, work was the key to his success. He described the money as 'brilliant' and the structured day helped keep him (briefly) on track. Ultimately, it was a 'dirty urine' that proved his undoing. Indeed, two weeks before his arrest, Reggie returned a positive sample for marijuana, leading to increased parole obligations. One weekly report became two reports, a phone call, and attendance at two courses per week. Without a driver's licence, just getting there was an ordeal. Maintaining work was impossible. Reggie showed appropriate initiative in speaking with his parole officer: 'I said, "I'm working, how am I going to do this course... this Ending Offending program you want me to do?" And I sort of thought, "Well, I am ending my offending. I haven't stolen anything.... I've been working, doing all right and now you want to jack me up with this", you know what I mean?' His parole officer was unmoved. Reggie bought a video console and began to 'play the days away' at home. But he was seriously pissed off. The 'breaking point' came when permission to travel interstate for the funeral of a family member was refused. For someone cut off from his Aboriginal heritage for much of his life, these were crucial moments to 'reconnect' with his people and develop an emerging sense of cultural identity. As Reggie observed: 'They flatly denied it... That's another reason why I sort of [thought], "Well, I'm [over] doing the right thing".' And with that, he made the decision to attend the funeral by any means. He stole a car. From there, things just snowballed. When police caught up with him they 'capsicum sprayed' and punched him in the face. As Reggie remarked: 'I wasn't going to cop that.' He put up a fight. That meant 'resisting arrest' and 'assaulting a police officer'. Despair set in. Up to that point, Reggie had whittled his parole balance to a year and a half. Now it would be 'jacked up' to about four years at least. He had a message for the parole officer: 'If we're doing well, leave us alone. If we're not offending, leave us alone. If we are offending, then no worries, [go after us].'

Six months later, Reggie was released through the Drug Court initiative. At 24, he enjoyed his first Christmas dinner with his father and brother. Drugs were still an issue, marijuana, mostly, but occasionally 'meth' and 'speed'. He put this down to boredom and frustration over the ongoing inability to work because of court/parole commitments. While a degree of tolerance is extended to participants of the Drug Court, slowly but surely, Reggie found himself mentally preparing for an inevitable return to prison. Literally on his last warning, Reggie was looking for a reason to take off. When his girlfriend, Hannah, was arrested and remanded in custody, he was on the next bus to Sydney. Reflecting on this decision, Reggie remains philosophical: 'It was either go back to gaol now and stay in gaol for the next two or three years or go and fucking see a bit of Australia before [I] get locked up again.' In Sydney, Reggie lived 'rough' – sleeping in tents stolen from backyards and thieving 'cooked chickens' from supermarkets for food. He was back to where he started as a 10-year-old, running the streets to survive. After two months, 'heat' from police prompted Reggie to flee north to Queensland. It wasn't long before he was arrested in a stolen car, again with the allegation he tried to run over the arresting officer. Following eight months' imprisonment, Reggie was extradited back to South Australia. Like Joel and Paul, he'd decided it was going to be easier 'to stay inside and serve time rather than do parole... I'm going to tell them to jam it, [to] stick their parole up their ass'.

Reggie is currently serving a head sentence of four years in respect of illegal use of a motor vehicle and assaulting police. These are the offences for which he entered Drug Court some years earlier. He has since indicated he will apply for parole when he becomes eligible at the end of the year. In his words:

> I've been sick of [things] for the last ten years.... My crimes are not getting worser. If anything, it's staying the same.... They want us to be... good pillars of the community but... they won't give us a leg to stand on. I've just lost my licence again for three years. That's before I can apply to get it back.... Back then I would have... been driving a car through a shop window and doing all them stupid things. Now, [I steal cars] just to get from A to B.

And that's the thing. How does one reconcile a sense of progress with being repeatedly returned to prison? Reggie can't seem to find a fitting answer to that question.

Ben

Ben is 29. He grew up in the outer southern suburbs of Adelaide as the second eldest of six children. He shares a biological father with an older sister, and his mother has three sons and a daughter from subsequent relationships. His early childhood was traumatic and has much to do with the parlous state in which he would later find himself. His father was a violent alcoholic who moved interstate shortly after Ben's first birthday. He has not been heard from since. With only a few old photographs, Ben understandably has no memory of him to speak of. His sense of 'loss', however, is as raw today as when we first met him in juvenile detention a decade ago. Back then he would often speculate on how his life trajectory might be altered with some semblance of a father-son relationship. More recently, as evident in the second excerpt below, Ben blames his mother for not doing more to preserve what 'might have been':

> I never had my Dad in my life at all, ever. And it's left me confused and wondering if I had a Dad would I have gone to the Boys' Home? Would I have gone to gaol if I had that guidance?
>
> [S]ometimes there's a bit of anger there... towards my Mum that she didn't keep in touch with him.... I just find it selfish.... She left him, she had her reasons but there's a child involved that... needs to know their father. There was no reason behind cutting him off from me. I've got a couple of photos of him [from] when I was one. I was on his lap eating a birthday cake, my first birthday cake, having a bath with him, yeah. From those couple of photos he seemed like a loving Dad.... I don't know why she didn't keep his details or organize for me to have visitation with him or something.... [I]t's a massive hole in my life.

Ben might be in partial denial about his father's actual character and capacity to be the role model he yearns for. But everyone deserves a fair hearing and a second chance. Of all people, Ben feels qualified to speak to that. It's why he continues to hold out hope a reunification might occur – if only as a means to 'make up' or 'move on':

> Most people would say, 'Oh I've never met my Dad, apparently he was, you know, an asshole. If I ever see him I'll bash him.' I'm not like that. I'd probably embrace him.... I reckon all that anger would be gone and I can... speak to him and see what I get back and then make my own judgment [as to] whether he wants to see me or whether he is an asshole and I'm wasting my time.

Ben didn't get to make this judgment. Instead, he was introduced to an assortment of stepfathers, all of whom mistreated him to varying degrees. He regularly ran away from home and was 'belted' for it. As a result, he continues to nominate the poor 'choices' of his mother as standout features of a lonely and unhappy childhood: '[I wish] that my mother would have changed, that...she didn't move from bloke to bloke to bloke....It messed with my head for a few years...seeing all that stuff'. Notwithstanding his home life, Ben reports a relatively typical educational experience up until age 12. He made friends easily and was, by all accounts, a talented musician and athlete. Around this time, however, his two-year-old brother was struck and killed in a motor vehicle accident. For Ben, the immediate casualties were two-fold. Not only was his little brother dead, but whatever trace of a mother he had vanished deep into amphetamine addiction. It became routine for her to pawn Ben's electrical equipment to purchase heroin and speed. Consequently, the quality of 'boyfriends' at the house hit rock bottom and has remained at that level ever since. Ben even described being kicked out over his attempt to intervene following domestic violence incidents at the house:

> I remember one night...one of [Mum's] boyfriends attacked her with a knife and beat her up pretty bad...[but] she didn't want to charge him....I ran into him the next day at my Mum's house and pretty much told him I didn't appreciate it and to put his clothes on and get out – [to] never talk to my Mum again. And, yeah, he had an argument with her about me. I was only sticking up for my mother and she ended up kicking me out about it....[Like], 'Get out of my house...Don't talk to my boyfriend like that'....She's always...put the man figure before her kids.

Arguably, few 12-year-olds possess emotional reserves sufficient to cope with pain and suffering of this magnitude, especially when the prospect of homelessness enters the mix. It is unclear how these events affected the other children at the house. We do know, however, that Ben's mother eventually lost custody of her three youngest sons, something she has never managed to regain. In Ben's case, consecutive psychiatrists were unable to make inroads into the extreme anger and aggression he began to funnel into crime. By the age of 13 he was excluded from school by reason of poor attendance. At that time he was frequently in and out of custody. Ben reflects on this period in the following terms:

> The first time I got in trouble with the law was when my little brother died. He got hit by a car at the age of two and I just, you

know, went downhill from there and haven't been able to turn it around since.... I was pretty angry...a bit immature as well, selfish, you know, just cared about myself. Like, I thought that crime was fun. It took me six years to notice that it wasn't.... It's not getting me nowhere. Yeah...I was pretty angry since my brother died.... Grief and loss. That's what made me angry. I just kept it all inside.

Still aged 12, Ben experienced juvenile detention for the first time after he was caught stealing a pushbike from his local area. Petty at best, the offence was unlikely to result in either conviction or custodial sentence. Bail was a *fait accompli*. However, because his mother was unwilling to offer 'placement' (a residence and guarantee), Ben was remanded in custody until arrangements could be made through community welfare services: 'She didn't want to hear anything about it when I came into police stations, so the only option was to put me in custody.... I [eventually] got put into a foster home 'cause my Mum said she didn't... want anything to do with me.... And the area I went into was the area where people in custody used to live and so...[crime] was all around me.' 'Official' rejection by his mother continues to weigh heavily on Ben: 'I felt unwanted...the first time I got locked up.... Yeah, she gave up on me heaps.' The experience of foster care, combined with the physical and emotional abuse of stepfathers past, threw Ben's life into disarray. As he reflected, 'It's easy to be brought down if everyone's yelling at you, "You're good for nothing. You're not going anywhere. You're not going to be nothing", and stuff like that. That's what I put up with as a kid, as a teenager, and I'd always run away from foster homes and get locked back up [for] stealing cars...'. Ben (and others) described the 'soothing' effect of racing around in a stolen vehicle, irrespective of whether police were in pursuit: 'There's something about stealing cars that calms me down.' And on those occasions where a police chase ensued, there was always a hot meal and a bed waiting for him at the juvenile training centre. This was the best 'care' Ben experienced at that time: '[T]he residents treated you as friends. The staff respected you.... [They didn't mind] giving you time, talking to you, caring for you.... Something you never got on the outside.'

For a kid battling abject poverty and homelessness, there was, understandably, little if any hesitation regarding better access to basic things such as food, health care, television, video games and recreational facilities. From this vantage point it was impossible for Ben to appreciate how far removed he was from the reality of prison ('the big house').

And prison, as he approached 18 years of age, was inching ever closer. Some years later he remarked:

> The problem with Boy's Home [juvenile detention] when I was there [was] it was all a bit too easy. It was like a holiday camp.... My average outside time... was about two weeks. I'd get out for two weeks and I would breach my bail and go back in and I wouldn't care that I was going back in. I would have a smile on my face.... I was hanging out to get back to [the custodial facility] so I could see all the people and jump in the pool and go for a swim, you know... go... ride a motorbike.

Against this backdrop, Ben estimates he stole about 50 to 60 cars before reaching his mid-teens. What began as 'joy-riding' to experience the thrill of an expensive car soon became a 'hustle' in which he was engaged to steal and 'rebirth' cars for the black market. In this way, achieving the 'master status' of a proficient and respected car thief not only guaranteed money but also enhanced his sense of purpose and identity on the street:

> All my mates were older than me and they were like professional car thieves and I used to look up to them.... I was thinking it was cool or something.... [And] as I was getting older ... more younger people starting going through the [crime] zone [and] they started looking up to me.... I liked the respect. So I just kept doing what I was doing, you know, showing them how to do it and stuff.

All this, though, began to change at age 16 when he met Jade during a brief stint in the community. For some time he had toyed with the idea of stopping crime, but now he felt well placed to action it: 'I feel down about all the time that I've wasted but confident about what I'm going to do with the time I've got left.' To Jade, Ben impressed as genuine, well-spoken and considerate. There was nothing to indicate he was, in fact, a 'frequent flyer' of the criminal justice system. Nothing, that is, until he was literally arrested on her doorstep:

> I was just doing the dishes and my brother's like, 'Oh, come and have a look at all the cops out the front'.... [W]e were just sitting on the step laughing about it and watching this kid get locked up.... Yeah, I was sitting there for, like, ten minutes before I realized who it was.

They slammed him on the bonnet and he looked at me, and I was like, 'Oh, my God.'

If Ben was worried, he had no reason to be. Jade was in for the long haul – through nine years and two children to be exact. It was the longest lasting relationship of any of the young males in our study. Their eldest child, a daughter Lucy, was born when Ben was 17 and locked up. Missing her birth as well as first birthday hit him particularly hard. His own father had managed a better start and Ben knew how that turned out. For the first time, he felt the pull of a 'real' family on the outside – of two individuals that needed him and, more to the point, actually *wanted* him in their lives. This circumstance was considered by Ben to be a 'game-changer': 'Secure care didn't really bother me.... [B]ut since I met my girlfriend and... I got my daughter... I see her as a whole different... ball game'. Despite her commitment to Ben, Jade moved interstate soon after their daughter's birth. At 16 years old she was struggling to hold it together with only limited family connections and a partner in lock-up. Ben was disappointed but accepted Lucy's interests were best served in Victoria with the assistance of her maternal grandparents. For him, the plan was to get out, get a job and then raise the funds to move to Victoria where he could reunite with his girls.

Things didn't play out that way. Released from prison at 18, Ben discovered just how difficult it was without the resources of the juvenile system behind him. With only a few dollars and no housing, he was again staring down the barrel of homelessness. He was also suffering from a major depressive illness. For a time, he managed to tread water, couch-surfing at the homes of his friends. He even got a job for two months but left after confronting his boss over the latter's harassment of female employees. With Ben's record, obtaining gainful employment was always going to be a formidable task. Slowly, he exhausted all his options and did what he always did. He stole a car and went for a cruise. This decision, as Ben later observed, set in motion a chain of events that would lead to 'full-on offending again'. Out of sheer desperation, Ben convinced his mother to bail him out of the cells. To raise the funds, she sold all of his possessions to a second-hand dealership frequently used by addicts to hock stolen goods. Predictably, Ben lost his cool and his accommodation in one fell swoop. At this juncture, stolen cars promised more than a quick thrill or a ticket to somewhere else. Now they provided a warm, safe place to lay his head at night. Ben described his 'slippery slope' in the following way: 'So I was ... using cars as bedrooms and after a while it just escalated to going back to making money by doing shop breaks and stuff like that...just to live, [to get] survival money.'

Following his arrest, Ben received a head sentence of four years' imprisonment but was paroled after serving 12 months. This time – with full approval from DCS – he was on the first bus to Victoria. He noted though, that things at that time were tough: 'I breached my parole almost straightaway.' As it turned out, Ben didn't get the fairytale homecoming he had hoped for. Lucy regarded him as a stranger and objected to his very presence at the house. He became highly suspicious that Jade had been 'cheating' on him with another man. Ben felt pressure to get a job so he could provide for his 'family' but was continually frustrated by a lack of opportunity and the obligations of his parole agreement:

> I found it pretty hard over there. My goal was getting a job. [But I] [c]ouldn't get a job. I had several other commitments. I had to see my parole officer twice a week, go to counselling once a week, community service once a week. So there was no time for getting a job. So I was stuffed for money and slowly but surely I fell into my old ways again.

Ben began taking 'short-cuts' to make ends meet. He engaged in recreational drug use. He took liberties with his parole attendance. The tide was coming in. Then, talk of Jade's infidelity began to do the rounds again. Ben just let it take him under. He found himself in the Victorian prison system before he knew what hit him. That's what stealing a car in order to go and assault someone does. But Ben caught a lucky break when the judge determined to release him ('time served') without further penalty. He was free to continue his parole, to get on with his life. His response was noteworthy:

> I thought it was...a chance of a lifetime that I got released after all that....I started doing good. I joined the football team, going to training Tuesday and Thursday nights, playing on Saturday....I was the leading goal kicker....I pulled my head in. Had a 100 per cent reporting record with my parole officer. I was going to all my programs. I...made a few friends, [was] doing all right. Settling in, and then it was all taken away from me again.

According to Ben he remained 'crime free' for ten months. Things were finally looking up. Jade was pregnant again and he had earned a position in an A grade football team. Competitive sport, as Ben discovered, was a fine metaphor for life. As golfing great Lee Trevino once remarked, 'The more I practice, the luckier I get'. But just as things were getting on track, Ben's luck ran out:

> Four police officers [arrived] at my door with an extradition warrant.... My parole officer didn't even know [it was coming].... They say because I spent time in a Victorian prison, that [that] cancels my parole [back in South Australia] straightaway. But then I don't see why they let me out in the first place.... It gave me false belief... that I was given a second chance. I was shattered. I felt that it was all for nothing. Waste of time. You know, why bother, if this is just going to happen to me all the time? They come and got me a month before my son arrived, so I missed out on his birth.

Madness. Speaking from custody in South Australia, Ben was left to rue the devastation of his latest setback. The situation was incomprehensible even to a seasoned campaigner like him. In the community he was slowly but surely learning to be a partner, a father, a team player. These were the best indications yet he had what it took to become a responsible citizen. Now, for three years, he was consigned to 'smoke weed and just watch fights [or] get into fights'. He'd missed the birth of his son, and with that, another opportunity to distinguish himself from his own father went begging. Ben became more and more depressed. As long as he could remember he'd battled difficulties with his mental health and this time he needed more support than ever. Jade was still in the frame but a world away in Victoria. In juvenile detention, there had always been a glut of counsellors, therapists and social workers on hand to pick him up again. But this time, in the adult custodial context, Ben was abruptly reminded how differently things operated:

> They put me on suicide risk [after] I told them I had problems. But I told them I wasn't suicidal. I wouldn't do that to myself. And they went ahead and did it anyway.... They come around every five minutes or so and flash a torch on you.... I was in with all different cellmates. I wasn't allowed to be on my own, so I had no privacy at all. I got a bit upset about it. I told the officer that I was upset about it and next thing I know, my head is in the brick wall 'cause I was complaining.... And then I retaliated. I grabbed his arm and pulled it off me. Then he pressed his [duress] button and a lot of [officers]

ran in, and they took me to this punishment unit, and they made me put my head on the window and not look back. If I looked back, they'd hit me and stuff. And yeah, they were kicking me, stuff like that. [They] [l]eft me in that room in a canvas skirt for two days and then they put me in another punishment unit. All over just asking about my suicide risk.

Ben kept asking himself how he could have been so stupid – so trusting. Part of the prisoner code is *never* admit to being vulnerable. Never seek help from an officer – particularly not from those stationed at the prison with the worst reputation in the State. Years earlier, Ben had occasion to learn of what officers were capable of when he tried to come to the aid of a fellow prisoner:

Last time I was here, 2004, there was this Palestinian guy, and the officers were yelling in his face, and when they were yelling, they were spitting at the same time and he was wiping it off his face with his hands by his side. And they kept yelling at him and he kept wiping their spit off his face. [Well], he wiped the spit off his face one too many times and they dragged him in the room and roughed him up a bit. [So] I went in there and I said, 'You just can't do that'. And then they put me up against the wall and [one officer] had his fist like that [clenched and raised to Ben's head], and said, 'I'll shatter your jaw with one hit'.... Yeah. There's just too much hatred.

Even Ben's dedication to Jade and the kids came under fire in prison: 'They said if I cared about my family, I wouldn't be here.' Jade had, in fact, relocated their young family back to South Australia so they could be ready to start their lives from scratch again. Officers did not hold back in telling Ben that she should have kept running while she had the chance. Two years later Ben was again released on parole. He acknowledges the transition was a harrowing one, not least for Jade, Lucy and baby Adam. With the words of his antagonists ringing in his ears, he was far from the 'model' partner and father he wanted to be. This only served to intensify his anger over issues that had plagued him since childhood:

My time in prison... I didn't know what effect that had had on me [until I got out]. I got out and I wasn't the same person. I wasn't violent towards my partner and my children, but I was angry towards them. I threw a coffee cup into the wall, put holes in the wall, and stuff like that. Things that I'd never really do. But yeah, my time in gaol changed my outlook on life. [It] [m]ade me an angrier person.

To his credit, Ben somehow found full-time employment – hard, physical labour in the vineyards of South Australian wine country. On parole and disqualified from obtaining a driver's licence, Ben risked freedom with every commute. But, as he reasoned, he actually owned a car that was not only registered but also insured. He'd never felt more 'legitimate'. As he put it, 'I was doing the wrong thing [by driving while disqualified], but at the end of the day I was feeding my kids. Better than going out stealing like I used to. I was going to the vineyard and working for my money'. It took six months before he was arrested for driving without a licence. Ben received a date with the Parole Board but was confident he could avoid serious action over the breach. But after again being caught in the same circumstance, he was reincarcerated. Following ten months in prison, Ben was philosophical about the latest events and drew a sharp distinction between his past offending behaviour as against his more 'responsible' offending of recent times:

> [Jade and I] took it [my parole] for granted. I didn't think it'd go to the lengths it went to....Yeah, we were just enjoying each other's time too much...and next thing I'm just snatched away.... [I] kind of couldn't believe it was happening.... I was out getting hot chips. I drove to the fish and chip shop to get hot chips for the kids for dinner, and that's when the police got me again for driving. [And this time] I wasn't getting out of [it].

It seemed such a waste of court time and public resources – like putting Reggie back in prison for driving down the road to get a pack of cigarettes. Eventually, Ben was released from custody and the subsequent interview was the first of several with him to be completed in the community – the first of such occurring at the home he shared with Jade and the kids. He was 24 years old. Like so many young men, Ben had always struggled to avoid prison when a lengthy parole order hung over his head. The struggle was always exponentially harder when he was homeless and broke. As he commented, there is often 'so much pressure, so much anger' that 'normal' people just don't understand the thin line one is walking. But, this time – even though he was on parole – things were looking up. He was setting goals and getting serious about music again: 'I'm very comfortable where I am.... I feel like I've been here for years, and it's only been two weeks.... I've got all this new energy that

I've never had before. [A new kind of] motivation now I'm out.... I used to get sick and tired of things, and angry.... [But] now life's too short [for thinking like that].' In hindsight, though, Ben reflected that he had never really gotten to 'know' Jade. They'd been a couple for nearly ten years. He was always the one in crisis. But this time he was getting things together and he wanted to do things with his life. He didn't want to be constrained – parole was constraint enough. After all the effort he put in to mending their relationship, Ben slowly but surely began to feel suffocated by Jade. It wasn't her fault, as he explicitly noted. But the more he tried to carve an identity for himself, to set things right, the more Jade sought to 'push back' against him and the life he was creating:

> I spent over half of our relationship in gaol. So every time I got out it was like a fresh start, getting to know each other again, and she's always wanted to be the number one in my life. Like, my Mum sent me 20 dollars one year in gaol, and [Jade] didn't like it because she was the one who was there. When other people started caring she didn't like it because she was the only one in my life that cared [for so long].... [When] I found my music group and they started to care and I found friends who started to show an interest, she didn't like it and she tried to stop me going to my music group, tried to stop me seeing my Mum again, and seeing my friends. She basically just wanted me home all the time, and yeah, we've both gone different directions with our lives.

Ben was facing the breakdown of his relationship. His mother said he could live with her. He expected some level of resistance from Jade regarding this, but he wasn't ready for what actually occurred. Jade felt, quite rightly, she had given Ben almost a decade of her blood, sweat and tears, but that *he* had called time on the relationship. She became enraged to the point of punching Ben's mother in the face and was duly arrested for this. But more devastatingly, Jade refused Ben contact with his children – the one thing he cherished above all else. This was a common scenario for the young men in our study. Indeed, James, Lee, Joel, Matt, Reggie and Greg have very minimal contact with their kids. To our knowledge, Ben was the only participant (excepting Billy) willing to take the fight for custody through the courts. Not that it has come to anything. Despite several decisions in his favour, Ben has yet to spend any quality time with his children. It has now been over four years since last contact with them.

After what, for Ben, seemed like an eternity, he completed his parole. He was 'free' for the first time in 12 years. And for the next two years or so, his interviews with us again took place in the community. He was actively looking for work, performing 'gigs' with his group, and playing some good footy. Money was tight but he was getting by and resisting temptation for 'one last job':

> I still get criminal urges... while I'm out there.... It's just my old ways of making money kick back in. Like, I'll be short on money, have no money, and then I'm thinking of ways to get money. And instead of thinking of legitimate ways, I'm thinking of breaking the law and it's just the first thing that comes to my mind. And then I have to talk myself out of it.... But the way I changed my mindset was just, like I said, thinking about the little things that I've missed out on.... So I've kind of trained my mind into thinking about... being outside instead of inside and just enjoying life.

But life for Ben was far from being easy. Jade took every opportunity to be, in his eyes, a 'bitch'. And his relationship with his mother would, Ben realized, always be a volatile one. As he described it, he was either paying her rent or funding her drug habit, whichever way you wanted to look at it. Like Paul, he had long been rated 'priority one' for public housing – something he desperately needed if he was to ever get the kids for a visit. No one, least of all Jade, would ever allow them at his mother's 'drug-den'. During this period, Ben was arrested from time to time for minor things like public drunkenness. He also narrowly escaped prosecution for driving disqualified. He had to cop some breaks. But there were seriously dark times too. A close friend was shot and killed, plunging Ben back into a major depressive state. On another occasion, Ben was jumped by three ex-associates over a drug debt, leaving him with a fractured eye socket and nose. He estimates he was hit over 200 times. He never reported it. It was, after all, street justice (Jacobs and Wright 2006). A new relationship produced a baby boy, but ended shortly thereafter. Another child he would never see. Ben's life was again becoming directionless. It was just a matter of time before things fell apart:

> I had a bit of a weed and [a] gambling problem and I ran [up] nearly a $1000 debt. I didn't have the cash. I got given an option to re-birth a car for this dude. I went to do it, got the car, [and] as I was driving it got pulled up [by police] and I really thought about a high speed

chase. [But] then... I thought, 'Nah, I'm sick of this shit', and I pulled over and got arrested straight away.

It's difficult to know what to make of this. One could view it as a 'failure' because a car was stolen. But one could also say it equates to a 'success' because Ben resisted engaging in a police pursuit. By all accounts, he wouldn't have hesitated to flee in times past. Regardless, things were about to unravel in more serious fashion. In the midst of a debilitating depressive episode, he failed to attend court in answer of his bail. Realizing the oversight, Ben handed himself in to police the very same afternoon. Ordinarily, that would be end of the matter. Bail would simply resume. The magistrate, however, thought it prudent to require a guarantor – a standard condition that would have major adverse consequences for Ben (see Chapter 7). Unable to contact his guarantor, he ended up in prison in segregation after a suicide attempt. After six days of 'hell', he was released. But the trauma of this last return to prison continued to hurt him:

> I still feel institutionalized.... I still feel like I'm going back there even though I'm not doing anything.... I'm hard working and stuff but I think [prison is] my second home or something.... [I've] done way too long. My average time for staying out used to be like four weeks and I'd be back in. Now I've been out for two and a half years it still hasn't settled me yet. It feels like two and a half months.

But beyond the pain of incarceration, Ben's real angst came from being without his kids. A positive record as a father is the only record that really matters to Ben. He can live with the 'criminal' label, but he cannot abide the tag 'dead-beat dad'. That, to him, is an indefensible identity: 'It's ripping me apart. Like, I just want to see them... grow up. I want to be there for them.... Not every kid gets a dad that wants to be there all the time and that's what I want. But [their mothers are] pissed off with me over our relationship[s].... That's pretty much the only thing that gets to me at the moment'. To this day, Ben is unsure whether he will be able to 'get there' without the support of his kids. As he recently remarked:

> When I'm with them... I'm on the right track. The longest I've ever stayed out of gaol was three years and that's when they were in my life, and [I was] doing everything for them. [But] as soon as they get

taken out of my life... I've got... nothing sort of going for me. [And then] I tend to slip up a bit.

He continues, however, to make progress by finding employment, seeking assistance for his mental health, performing music and playing football. But Ben knows only too well how quickly fortunes can change – especially when your 'reality' depends on someone with worse drug problems than your own:

I was out working and I got a message saying that she [his mother] wanted money and I knew what it was for. I told her, 'No'. She goes, 'If you're not here by [such and such] time with this amount of money I'm going to give your stuff away'. And she pretty much would have just swapped it to a dealer all my electrical goods and stuff like that.... I didn't cope too well. I started smoking amphetamines and, yeah, just let the lows take over me basically.

Ben has been returned to custody on several occasions in the last two years, generally for offences involving motor vehicles, breaches of parole and petty dishonesty – always in the context of settling drug debts acquired in moments of crisis. In fact, we note that Ben is one of only two young men in our study without conviction for any major indictable offending (David being the other). The last time we saw Ben (in mid-2013) he was preparing to leave custody again, hopefully for the last time. He is disqualified from holding or obtaining a driver's licence until 2018. This must certainly present as a risky situation for him: 'I need to get my licence, that's what I need to do, that's the main thing since [I was] 13 [years old]. So to nail that, you know, driving gets me into a lot of trouble.' He was also still trying to secure permanent accommodation. Ben knows the future holds much uncertainty but takes heart in the fact he was able to put at least 'runs on the board'.

I can get that feeling back again... but I've [got to have] a new approach to it.... I need to do it myself, stand on my own two feet.... [Over] the years I've... pretty much felt sorry for myself and [I've been] looking for those support networks.... [But] most of the time they break down and I lose them and so, yeah, I need to learn to stop... reaching out for that support or the wrong support networks that kind of breakaway and... try and stand on my own two feet.

We view that as an entirely admirable approach. Very recently, we received advice that Ben was arrested in late 2013 for driving while disqualified, driving in a manner dangerous and engaging in a police pursuit. He was for a period on home detention bail but subsequently remanded into custody for a breach.

In Sum

The experiences of Joel, Paul, Reggie and Ben resonate through the juvenile and criminal justice systems. Their accounts of relapse in the desistance journey are not particularly dramatic or out of the ordinary – especially when compared with those evinced by, as shall be seen, Lee, Matt, Sam, James and Chris (Chapters 5 and 6). There are no 'shoot-outs', no 'hijackings', no 'glitz and glamour' and little or no media coverage. Instead, these four young men wage 'silent' and chronic battles with homelessness, drug addiction, personal trauma and relationship problems – typical of those encountered by hundreds of thousands of ex-prisoners the world over returning annually to various communities (and, thereafter, to various prisons). As their stories demonstrate, wanting to change, needing to change, and 'knowing that change is necessary' (Haigh, 2009: 314) is not, of itself, enough to sustain long-term movement away from crime. To be fair, it is not even crime per se that periodically unravels fledgling attempts to forge a 'conventional' or 'pro-social' lifestyle. These young men felt they were 'set up to fail' time and time again. To this we would add they felt stigmatized and disheartened by the way their criminal records followed them. Perhaps the one exception to this was Joel who, undeniably for a time, was drawn to a 'ghettocentric' (Hagedorn 2008) and 'toxic' version of masculinity (Kupers 2005). For the other three young men, though, missing an appointment, leaving a designated address, returning a positive drug test or being arrested for minor 'street' offending all routinely exposed them to breach action. So often, they were confronted with the choice to 'stay' and face the music (the Parole Board) or to 'flee' – to literally go on the run or put the 'pedal to the metal'. How each responds to being breached (or the mere threat of) goes directly to whether they transition to being 'on track' or suffer further breakdown or possibly 'major derailment'. Whatever the case, these four young men – like so many others – consistently fall through the cracks of post-release support. For all their faults, they cannot be accused of lacking the motivation to desist from crime. But when desistance seems to be successively and senselessly interrupted by disproportionate or irrational monitoring and enforcement, it is little wonder that Joel, Paul, Reggie and Ben present as repeat customers of the penal estate.

5
Major Derailment

In this chapter, we focus on the stories of Lee and Matt. Between them they have been released from serving time in juvenile and adult facilities on over 40 occasions and collectively have been incarcerated for more than 17 years. Unlike the young men mentioned in previous chapters, Lee and Matt have engaged in repeat serious criminal activity which goes well beyond motor vehicle theft, thieving from houses and businesses, assault or the like. Armed robbery, major stakes in the heroin trade, facing a charge of attempted murder – to give several examples – put these stories on another level. Still, both young men have told for several years how they want out of the crime and incarceration game. Both, as shall become clear, had very different starts to life, and both were drawn into offending through very different avenues. To our minds, though, what they share is an ongoing struggle between the seductive elements of crime (Katz 1988) as against its destructive power – the way it curtails their futures, hurts their families, and victimizes innocent bystanders. Both know the pain crime causes, but this has not prevented them from transitioning from 'small'-time offending to 'big' crime (Haigh 2009: 312). By any measure, desistance has been a rare commodity in their lives. Their attempts to head down a different path have generally come to naught. Again, different factors have derailed such attempts. One possible way of framing their trajectories would be to suggest they are in the midst of 'ramping up' before 'settling down' – that each is engaged in a criminal purge prior to really committing to desistance. Whether this is in fact so, remains an open question.

Lee

> I reckon if you can't help or change the boys going through juvenile, it's going to be too late. Because once they reach here, it's

too late. We've already made up our minds. We already think we know everything...so that's the road that we walk straight away.

Lee is in his late twenties. In August 2013 he was returned to custody after ten months on parole for the offence of causing serious harm with intent. Previous to this, he had been acquitted of attempted murder after he shot someone with a double-barrelled shotgun in broad daylight in front of dozens of witnesses. Lee concedes he was 'lucky' the bullet struck where it did. At the end of the day, centimetres stood between him and a prospective life sentence. Whilst this offending was a dramatic escalation in the severity of his crimes, Lee was first convicted of common assault at the age of 14. However, he received sanctions (formal cautions and/or family conferences) for assaulting other children from age 11. As a juvenile, he was dealt with for common assaults, a robbery and multiple offences of dishonesty and carrying offensive weapons. In view of his 'ongoing disrespect for the law', a sentence of eight years' imprisonment was imposed in respect of the shooting. He is currently charged with trafficking in a controlled drug, possessing a prescribed firearm without a licence, possessing a silencer and assaulting police. In January 2014, Lee called to let us know he was released on Home Detention Bail pending trial. His parole continues.

Migrating to Australia from Asia when he was three years old, Lee's family are hard-working people with a business on the rural outskirts of Adelaide. The family home was situated at the heart of one of the most deprived communities in the region. Despite their reported care and concern for him, Lee's parents were unable to protect him from negative influences. As Lee put it: 'The area I was living in, it's a pretty bad area and we all just got together and got ideas in our heads.' At interview, he consistently described cultural and language barriers between himself and his parents as strengthening his pathway into crime. At age nine, Lee gravitated toward an anti-social peer group, and began to spend most of his time (and from age 12 lived permanently) at the home of a neighbourhood friend. The father of that friend was a drug dealer. And that turned out to be a fateful moment in Lee's life. At that house, he was encouraged to become involved in crime (including stealing cars to work on them) and was exposed to and participated in drug abuse and violence. As McCarthy and Hagan (1995: 68) note, car theft generally requires elements of 'initiation and instruction' and serves 'as a prelude to more advanced criminal activities'. When locked up, Lee used his time to learn more tricks of the trade:

> These fellas, they all tell me bigger and better things. And I learn to do that... [w]hen I didn't even know nothing before.
> When I was going to juvie [juvenile prison]... I always thought about different crimes... what I really wanted to do and that.... Like, as in, which crimes I'm going to do, ... which one's going to pay off.

With that, Lee's embeddedness in criminal networks developed steadily to the extent that he was selling heroin with Asian associates by age 15. As he explained, the original motivation for, and attraction to, participating in high-level street crime was rooted in social and economic gains:

> We were a group together, and... without money we couldn't do nothing, couldn't get nothing, couldn't have anything, you know?... So we just put our heads together.
> We couldn't have fun if we didn't have any money... and we were kind of slack and that so we wanted to have it the easy way.... We started selling heroin because we were all, like, Asians.... It's easier for us to do that stuff.... [The] Australians out there mainly sell speed.

Preoccupied with image and status, Lee saw the achievement of material possessions as attainable only (or perhaps most readily) through crime. In his ethnographic study *Street Corner Society*, Whyte (1943: 273) illustrates impediments young men from deprived communities face to 'get on the ladder, even at the bottom rung'. Lee, though, had no interest in starting at the bottom rung. Were he inclined to do that, as he explained, he would have engaged in 'menial labor' in his parents' business – something he had tried but wholly detested. The work, to his mind, was backbreaking. But more to the point, there was no money in it. Instead, as Lee would remark, he was drawn to the 'hedonistic, glitz and glamour' lifestyle provided by the illicit drug trade. Even he could see the irony. Australia was a world away from the harsh realities of life in Asia, and yet here he was, peddling drugs on the street corner:

> I had good parents, they gave me everything and... guided me down the right [path]... but I just didn't want to do what they wanted me to do.... I wanted to rebel against them for some reason. I just

wanted to have fun and live on the streets where it was hard...like, for no reason, when I had everything at home.... [I] just chose to do things that [more unfortunate] people have to [do] everyday.... I wanted that.... I just went that way.

Lee specifically recognized his will to offend prevailed over the capacity of his parents to put a stop to his anti-social behaviour:

[My parents] were always on my back and that because they'd know that I'm up to something.... But I'd always deny it to them because I never wanted them to see what I'd done. There [were] times that the police...would come [and then] they would kind of get the picture.... One day I got enough...courage to say, 'Yeah, this is what I do and you can't stop me'.

As he discovered, the heroin trade was highly lucrative. Such was his talent for selling drugs, Lee estimates his dealing totalled around $20,000 per week, spent largely on 'cars...because that's all we wanted.... We wanted to go out and have nice cars, nice jewellery, stuff like that'. Pearson and Hobbs (2003: 344) note the tendency for those involved in mid-tier drug brokerage to 'develop a sense of exaggerated personal power and invulnerability' and 'to spend money with abandon, in an "easy come, easy go" manner of "fast lane" conspicuous consumption'. Lee's juvenile status only amplified this situation. Certainly, we observed his love of designer labels and luxury vehicles firsthand. However, as Lee became further ensconced in organized crime, his propensity for violence also increased – either as a means for retaliating against perceived transgressions within the trade and/or to intimidate and threaten in the course of his dealing activities. As he reflected: 'Gangs started happening and then our group was fighting against other groups', and 'we couldn't go out without getting into trouble.... Every time we went out there was always run-ins with people.'

From the outset, Lee enjoyed the status, identity and emotional gratification conferred by gang membership. This was in addition to obvious material gains generated by his increasing success in the drug milieu. Authors argue a criminal 'working identity remains a locus of commitment as long as it is thought to be successful, or, more specifically, as long as, on average it nets more benefits than costs' (Paternoster and Bushway 2009: 1105). Put simply, crime 'worked' for Lee. He was respected, he was feared and he was (becoming) rich – heady circumstance for a 15-year-old. That being said, he refuted the suggestion that crime formed part of a permanent long-term agenda: 'I want to...settle down ... [but] this is not the time for it yet'. Aged 17, and speaking from juvenile detention, Lee consistently earmarked age 18 as the point from which he would desist from crime. For him, the perceived costs of adult imprisonment outweighed the excitement of the drug trade:

> I've always said to myself, '18's the line.... Like, I'm not going to Yatala [Labour Prison][1].... Even if I'm making millions, even if I'm hooked on it.... That was my rule... 18, stop. No more, no more nothing... because I feel like that's a new start for me.... Whatever I do from then on is how my life's gonna be. So [if] I do crime, then, that's how my life's gonna be.

In this way, Lee saw desistance from crime as a natural progression in his maturity and as a way to circumvent the adult system before sustaining 'real' damage to his future prospects. Meanwhile, juvenile detention was an occupational hazard made more or less tolerable by access to food, health care, television, video games and recreational facilities. Similar sentiments were echoed throughout the wider sample of young men. Still, Lee was a participant in serious organized crime. He also had a raging heroin habit. And so did those in his inner circle. It was this that ultimately destroyed the syndicate from within: 'We were smoking [our own drug supply] and we [got] addicted and that's why we couldn't walk away... [T]hat's why it didn't work out no more.... We were our own best customers.' Barry (2013: 58) notes that while drugs are 'not usually an issue (in terms of addiction) when young people start offending... substance misuse can rapidly become an issue during the course of an offending career.' Certainly for Lee, drug use and violence escalated in tandem with brief, yet frequent, periods of incarceration. His continued use of (illicit) drugs in custody was the worst among our participants. To this end, Lee has been particularly vocal about the futility of standardized programmatic responses in custodial settings. He 'graduated' multiple times from drug and alcohol programs – only to relapse on release. His 'review' of community-based interventions was equally disparaging. At best, 'CBT' (cognitive behavioural therapy) was patronizing and completely divorced from reality. At worst, individuals felt such programs 'distracted' from things more likely to be of benefit. Things like work, training and education. For Lee, intense 'concentration' on his 'traps and triggers' during conditional release had a particularly destabilizing effect:

> They kept sending me to [drug and alcohol] counseling.... So that made me keep thinking about drugs... [But after] 12 months [in juvenile detention] there [were] no drugs in my system.... It wasn't a problem. It [was] gone, right... [But] I [still] had to do [counselling] or else I'd get breached. And... that means I [was] worried... [about] get[ting] locked up and shit. That was the only thing that was on my mind: drugs, drugs, drugs.... And cos I just kept thinking of drugs, I fucking went and did it... to cool me down... because you get so tense. I got so intensely scared that [I was] gonna get locked up if I don't go through [with] this counseling drugs shit.... [What I] needed [was] time on my own. [But it was] just drugs, drugs, drugs. [They] were... in my head all the time.

This is not to say that counselling *made* Lee relapse into drug use and further offending. Nor did he attempt to discount the importance of having some kind of plan to get desistance going. Rather, in the community Lee spoke of being constantly monitored and evaluated all against the backdrop of the omnipresent threat of a return to custody. He became, understandably, highly agitated and paranoid – a perilous state for a heroin user. For Lee (and others) simple attendance at a combination of police stations, community corrections offices and various medical and treatment outlets proved incredibly onerous. This was made especially so for Lee who, again like all the young men, lacked a driver's licence and access to reliable (public) transport. Fear of failure, loss of control and the significant personal investment required to 'go straight' inclined him to revert to offending, where, ironically, risk and reward could be more clearly evaluated. Lee talked about achieving 'expert' status in his criminal milieu and elevating his status among his hometown community. It was impossible not to pick up where he left off: 'What if you've been working for the last six months and all that money is just nothing compared to what you can make in a night, do you know what I mean? And your mate rings you and [says], "Mate, there's $50,000 on the table for you".' By his late teens, crime had become an enduring and integral component of Lee's identity to the exclusion of other potential (and legitimate) identities. He was fatalistic regarding earlier hopes that offending would be limited to the juvenile sphere: 'When I [got] out of [juvenile] I tried to get back into society... and tried to get a job but it... wasn't for me.' Perhaps Lee was trying to disguise disappointment over his repeated rejection or failure. On the other hand, we don't doubt the sincerity of his belief that: '[Crime] is all we're really good at. Like, that's all we've known all these years and we've put our heart...and our soul into it.'

At age 22, Lee committed and was arrested for his most serious offence to date. There is some vagueness about the precise motive for the shooting but it related to the victim's attempt to regain a mobile phone that he suspected Lee had in his possession. In any event, Lee and his victim were known to each other and were known players in the heroin scene. Evidence provided in court suggested Lee was travelling in a vehicle armed with a loaded shotgun. He did not give evidence at his own trial for fear of being labeled a 'dog'. However, Lee has provided us with a detailed account of the circumstances of the offence that differ considerably from that described in Court. He admitted shooting the victim (who he described as a 'middle man' with regard to drug dealing) but denied taking a gun to the scene and denied the shooting was premeditated. Lee himself sustained a gunshot wound to the right ankle. He spent seven weeks at large and neglected to seek medical attention for fear of apprehension. The gunshot wound, though, became badly infected and he eventually attended hospital for treatment, leading to his arrest.

By the time sentencing came around, Lee and his partner, Holly, had two very young boys. His 'fast' lifestyle, unreliability and desire for social acceptance from anti-social peers was (and continues to this day to be) a source of aggravation for Holly and her family. By his own admission, Lee was, at that point, ill-prepared to be a father and unwilling to change his lifestyle to accommodate two children: 'When I come in [to prison] I wasn't ready to have kids...[So when] she said to me she's pregnant...I wasn't agreeing with that...and I said, "Look I've got to go in here, I'm sorry,"...I said to her, "I won't be able to be any help".' The enormity of these circumstances continues to impress heavily on Lee. At 22 he was facing substantial prison time, had a significant heroin addiction, was dealing with continual threats of reprisal from his victim (also incarcerated on unrelated matters) and had an 'instant family'. As time passed, shame and regret led to a greater commitment to his children: 'I've been punished...but...it was wrong for them to be punished as well...[for] my selfish mistakes. And I've only learnt that now.' Lee's absence during his children's formative years and their gradual awareness of his situation made this sentence the most difficult to date. He spoke of the pains of imprisonment in the following terms:

> I didn't see the bigger picture back then as I do now,...missing out on all these vital years of my kids' [lives]. Like, one to seven...they're the most vital years...to support them...help teach them, give them the

things I never got.... And I'm only missing out now through my stupidity and my mistakes.... My heart really melts... when I hear them say things like... 'Why weren't you there?'... [or] 'We don't want our present anymore. We just want you at our birthday Dad.'

Lee consistently identified desire to be a good father and a role model to his children as the primary motivation to change his life and desist from crime. He fully understood a positive father–son relationship to be a privilege and not a right, which he would have to *earn* over time: 'I haven't even earned that right to say they're my kids, you know what I mean? Because I haven't been there.... They might call me Daddy and say, "Hey Daddy, I love you Daddy"... but I see it, like, I haven't earned that yet.' Lee was also anxious to rebuild relationships within the Asian community that had suffered as a result of his offending.

[When I] get released I'm taking it as... a rebirth.... It's my time to start fresh.... All my bad stuff's behind me, I've stuffed up... I've paid for it and now it's my time to correct things.... It's going to be... [hard] to make [things] up [to] my own community ... the Asian community. Not only because I've lost face in my parents' [eyes] but I've lost face... [in terms of] their [good] name.... I've made them look bad... [and] the Asian community is pretty small and they all talk.... So that's just something I know that I'm going to have to dig a lot deeper to earn their respect and their name back.

Certainly, these were 'lofty' goals for someone who knew only intimidation and coercion as a means for achieving desired outcomes. But Lee knew it was going to take more than wanting to change: 'I'm not going to sit here and bullshit.... I'm going to do my best and see if I can provide for my kids and that, but... I could be out at the shop or whatever and someone could just start on me, or this and that, and you don't know. Like, I can't really predict that.' While commitment to his children was clear, Lee's relationship with Holly was decidedly more 'fluid' throughout his sentence. At interview, he was repeatedly unable or unwilling to define the status of their relationship, to others, or, as he suggests, to Holly herself: '[I said to her] "Well, look, what if I just [do] my thing and then when I get out, if everything works out, it works out, and if it doesn't, it doesn't", you know what I mean? "But I'd be there for the boys".... And [so] I put my cards on the table...'. By the time he was released on parole in 2012, it was clear reunification with Holly would not occur. We suspect the relationship had been broken for some time and that Lee had kept up appearances to enhance his application for early release. In any event, his last year in prison failed to provide the smooth transition to community living he had hoped for. A departmental error – in fact a case of mistaken identity (mentioned more fully in Chapter 7) – prevented Lee's placement at the low-security prerelease cottages. By the time the error was resolved, he said he'd 'already thrown... my hopes and dreams out the [window]'. His motivation to do well went into immediate and sharp decline. The 'fuck it' mentality had kicked in and Lee soon returned a dirty urine test.

Hope: 'An individual's overall perception that personal goals can be achieved' (Burnett and Maruna 2004: 395) Despair: 'a loss of hope; hopelessness' (Pocket Macquarie Dictionary 1995: 278). In prison, Lee was perpetually caught between the two. When things went well, he took his 'tramadol' (a narcotic-like pain reliever for his gunshot wound) and kept a low profile, worked as a meal server, contacted his kids, and lifted weights. When things went 'to shit', Lee caused trouble, injected heroin, and did 'deals'. Indeed, his record of drug 'incidents' somewhat perplexed the Parole Board. How could someone fare so poorly in such a 'controlled' environment? But that was just the point. Lee was out of control, literally. He had recently gotten word (again) that there was a 'hit' on his head. Protective custody was quickly ruled out as an option. Only 'dogs' (informants) and 'tamps' (paedophiles) went there. To his mind, Lee was better off dead. He would just have to sit tight hoping that forewarned was forearmed. At that time, he knew too that Holly was probably going to leave him. Again, he just had to survive until being paroled. Then he could sort things out. The catch, though, was that Lee was going nowhere until he had completed the Violence Prevention Program ('VPP'.) His sentence plan made that much clear. But after five years of petitioning staff for a position in that course, Lee was still no closer to getting a place. As he remarked at interview:

> I've been putting my hand up to do the course.... Every place... I go... I put my hand up and [I've] volunteered every single time.... I've [even] written a letter... to the Manager of the Rehabilitation Branch [to] let him know my circumstance[s].... And now [I fear] they [will] want me to do it [in prison] after my release date.... [People may think], 'Oh you've done... six years, what's another nine, ten months.' [But] that nine, ten months could break the ice with my family.... [It] might mean the whole world to me... even if they [have] noticed little [signs] that I have matured

and [I] have changed.... [What if] they're still in doubt because they haven't seen it in action [yet?].... That little bit... could be... [my] whole life... in nine, ten months [I could] lose everything.

Lee's growing sense of despondency proved to be one of the more salient themes to emerge from interviews with him. As de Viggiani (2007: 123) argues, prisons often oversee flawed rehabilitative strategies where 'prisoners [are forced] to become subservient or to rebel'. Without hope, Lee felt 'free' to rebel and to engage in drug use and violence. In fact, he was eventually ambushed and stabbed by a small group of prisoners. His take on the situation goes to the heart of prison life: 'There's hyenas here, there and everywhere, and they hunt in packs and they only feel tough when they're in numbers.... [T]hey all want to mark their territory and want to earn their keep and they think doing something to somebody might take that person's title.' It was a close call and one he couldn't again afford. Lee decided, at this time, to pursue an affiliation with high-profile motorcycle gang members who offered him the solidarity, respect and protection to which he had grown accustomed. Lee's reputation for acting-out made him a particularly attractive recruit. The net effect of this alliance led him to observe: 'I was fighting both sides. I was fighting... [the] inmates and I was fighting against [correctional services].... At the end of the day I wasn't winning nothing, I was getting shafted, that's what I felt like.... And the Parole [Board] didn't know.... [T]hey were sitting miles away.... They've got the key to my freedom and they don't even know what's going on.'

To his astonishment, Lee's application for parole was approved in late 2012 only weeks after commencing the elusive 'VPP'. However, Holly's own drug history (including an early attempt to smuggle narcotics into prison at Lee's request) and mental health issues inclined the Parole Board to grant a non-contact condition as part of his parole agreement. The upshot was that Lee would need a third party to facilitate access to his children. He was furious. Couldn't the Board understand that Holly's family already hated him enough? Now, though, he was expected to 'grovel' in order to see his *own* children. Lee's relationship with Holly quickly spiralled down and access to his sons became, again, intermittent. Presumably, Holly took exception to the 'tall blonde' girlfriend already on the scene. For Lee, he became overwhelmed by the realities of everyday life and was struggling from the outset to adapt without a structured regime. It was not uncommon for him to sleep until 3pm every day. This proved sharply at odds with twice-weekly reporting and urinalysis, telephone monitoring, as well as attendance at welfare and psychological appointments required of a 'high-risk' parolee. Lee spoke of his first days in the community in the following terms:

> [My parole officer] introduced herself to me and I introduced myself to her and she said, 'You're a high-risk offender, so you're going to have to sign in twice a week. You're also going to have to ring up during that week. Also you're going to have to provide urine whenever we ask you to... because you've had drug incidents in gaol.' Fair enough.... 'And we're going to make you see us each week... once a week, right, to see the psychiatrist.'... And then I had this other course I had to do and then I had to see the drug counsellor.... So all my time was [taken] up [with appointments].... [T]hen Centrelink made me jump through hoops.... [They were all] just making me chase my tail. Like I wasn't gaining anything. I was getting no [ID] cards, I wasn't getting no licence. All those little things I had to do myself.

Transport issues aside, without a Tax File Number,[2] a bank account or a driver's licence, Lee was unable to claim an immediate 'crisis' payment from welfare, on which (ex)prisoners generally rely. As he notes, 'I was just lucky that I had people [who were] willing to give me their time to take me to the places [I needed to go] and people that knew the things I had to do.... [Otherwise] I would have had no hope.' Even arranging to meet in a café for a research interview created unexpected problems, inadvertently exposing him to breach action: 'Is this a licensed premises?... See, I'm not even meant to be here'. Socializing proved even harder. For New Years Eve, 'friends' wanted to leave the State to party in Western Australia. Presumably this was beyond the watchful eye of South Australian police (all were on varying degrees of bail/bond obligations at the time). Lee knew the Parole Board would never let him go so he didn't bother asking. He just bought a plane ticket. But at the last minute he decided to watch fireworks in his home State with his sons instead. He was proud of the decision, not least because he didn't spend the entire night looking over his shoulder.

The last time we saw Lee before his arrest on current matters, it was clear his life was headed out of control. He had become increasingly unreliable and difficult to engage and there were strong indicators he was once again heavily involved in serious organized crime. On this occasion, he drove a luxury vehicle and had a wallet brimming with hundred dollar bills. A 'gym junkie' in prison, Lee estimated his weight had dropped by 25kg. He admitted to being armed. Of particular note, continued affiliation with outlaw motorcycle gangs was regularly bringing him back into police focus. There had been peripheral roles in drug raids by the Australian Federal Police and questions asked in relation to an ongoing murder inquiry. Nevertheless, Lee was undeterred and continued to associate with underworld figures out of a (misplaced) sense of loyalty and solidarity. Indeed, he had long clung to these concepts, referring to them often throughout his incarceration. As time passed, Lee grew more paranoid that his phone calls were being monitored. He changed his number, literally, on a weekly basis. He carried six phones. He was ever more reluctant to meet in open spaces during daylight hours although it is unclear whether it was police or other 'gangsters' he was anxious to avoid. He referenced a shootout with a rival 'sergeant-at-arms'[3] only weeks after making parole. Alarmingly, Lee appeared to completely 'gloss over' the seriousness of such events: 'I was outnumbered and I just defended myself and tried to be a gentleman and talk about something and it escalated and went a different way.... I tried to go there and I tried to talk and tried to sort it out.'

In late 2013 we learned of Lee's arrest after receiving an anonymous text message. He and his brother had gone out for a drive and not returned: 'Could we find out which prison they were at?' Lee later told us police had located a large sum of cash, firearms, passports and gold bars in a vehicle he was driving. He wanted to flee at high speed but couldn't because his two young nieces were in the car. Lee saw fit to assault the arresting officer. After a trip to hospital he went straight to the police cells. From custody Lee sounded almost relieved to be back inside. He was withdrawing 'bad' from heroin but still made the effort to keep in touch. Looking back through his many interviews, we were struck by a comment he made several years ago: 'I've just got to stay on the same track.... Most of the times when I got out... it was straight off the rails. It didn't take long.' Not much, it seems, had changed.

Matt

> 'Fucking wake up son,' you know? 'You're going to waste your life. You're going to waste it, your youth... being a gangster.' (Rick, Matt's dad)

Matt is 24 – and with the exception of Sean, is the youngest of the males in our study. His parents separated before he was born with his father, Rick, regularly in and out of prison. Matt would have little to do with him until reaching his late teens. His mother, Stacey, had (and continues to have) significant problems of her own. In particular, alcoholism and drug use compounded her extensive history of mental health issues. As Stacey remarked: '[Life] doesn't get easier for me...I class myself as an alcoholic....I may have one, I might have two [or] I might knock myself out...every day'. At one point, things got so bad Stacey made genuine attempts to suicide, in front of Matt. It happened on numerous occasions. Years later she would lose custody of Matt's stepbrothers who remain outside her 'care'. For Stacey and Matt, 'home' was the suburbs of northern Adelaide. Matt described it as 'The Bronx. You know, like in the movies...junkies and all'. At interview, Stacey confirmed theirs as the 'worst street in the worst neighbourhood'. Unfortunately, living in a poor community was the least of Matt's worries. Still in primary school, his 'first' stepfather abused him verbally and physically. When his mother and stepfather had their first child together, Matt essentially became a 'punching bag'. More than that, his stepfather utilized the property as a 'grow house' for the commercial production of cannabis.

As a possible site for positive stimuli or refuge, school in fact turned out to be place of abject failure. Diagnosed at an early age with ADHD, Matt was repeatedly suspended and excluded for 'throwing chairs' and 'fighting' with staff and students. As he recalled, more punishment was awaiting him at home: 'I was being suspended from school all the time. So I used to get beaten up for that.' After attending seven different primary schools, Matt was finally expelled, 'no ifs, no buts', during Year 9. By this stage he was consuming alcohol and marijuana on a regular basis, presumably sourced from abundant stocks at the house. Life was starting to take a bad turn:

> I just started running amok...taking off everywhere...[because] I thought I had a fucked-up life. My stepdad used to treat me like shit...beat me up every day and probably like three times a week he'd smash me....My Mum walked in the room one day, you know, seen it and then they broke up and since then I've just had [bad] memories...and that's what got me into [crime].

Matt, aged 13, had found his escape, literally and metaphorically speaking. A stolen car was the best way to put 'distance' between him and the next round of domestic abuse. It was also a 'break' from the disadvantage, monotony and unhappiness that was his reality. For young people fully engaged in the moment, car theft has been described as 'an intense, quick thrill that often climaxes in a ritualized destruction of the vehicle' (Ozanne et al. 1998: 188). Reflecting on his first detention order for illegal use of a motor vehicle, Matt commented: 'I just like driving... [to] get the need for speed out of my system.... It blows you away, because of the adrenalin rush.' It made him pretty popular too. For Matt (and many other young men) it was customary to bring stolen cars back to their neighbourhood to show them off by 'hooning' around the streets and doing 'burnouts' in front of the homes of their friends. A high-speed chase with police always garnered maximum bragging rights. On the fringes, 'girls' also provided incentive for young males to live 'fast and furiously', Matt later remarking that 'she always wanted to be in stolen cars, ... the mother of my kid'. He viewed juvenile detention as a cakewalk. Why wouldn't he? If he could take a 'belting' from a grown man twice his size, he could surely match it with kids of his own stature. As it turned out, Matt found lock-up a far less violent place than his own home: 'I just fitted in well.' He spent much of his time marvelling at the 'luxury' of his new digs:

> When I've come here [to juvenile detention] it's like: 'Fuck, you've got a TV sitting in your room, you've got a radio, you've got a shower, your own toilet, your own sink'.... Most people are like, 'Yeah, I like this place lots, I want to stay here.... It's good here how they've set it all up, it makes it easier... it makes your time go quicker.... They've made it more homey for us'.

For the next three years juvenile custodial facilities served as regular opportunities to detox, sleep, gain weight and, more pertinently, hone new skills: 'You meet someone in here that you get along with real well and they talk about their crimes as being better than what you can do.... [So you] meet up on the outside and do it...' It almost sounded like fun. But behind the scenes Matt was suffering. The trauma of his past ran deep. Psychological reports continued to describe ongoing nightmares and intrusive thoughts about the violence to which he had been subjected as a child. As a teenager there were deliberate attempts at self-harm, including an overdose of prescription medication requiring hospitalization, as well as self-mutilation behaviour. At times, he was assessed with extremely severe levels of anxiety and as likely to be suffering from Borderline Personality Disorder. In that context, Matt's offending, upon release, continued unabated. It was mainly car stuff, still trying to 'outrun' or 'outlast' his problems, of which there were many. In those early years there was, as seemed logical, a decidedly juvenile 'flavour' to his offending. He was totally unsophisticated in his modus operandi and was readily apprehended. But when Matt moved to 'hard-core' drug use at age 16, in his words, 'shit changed fast'. His drug of choice was 'ice' (methamphetamine). Aggravated robbery and serious assault began to punctuate his record. 'Joy-riding' gave way to 'jumping [shop] counters'. His rap sheet began to run into many pages rather than one or two. By age 17, Matt had been dealt with in relation to charges of using a motor vehicle without consent, numerous bail breaches, non-aggravated serious criminal trespass in a place of residence, larceny, robbery, aggravated serious criminal trespass in a non-residential building, failure to comply with bond obligations, interfering with a motor vehicle without consent, stating false personal details, assault, aggravated robbery with an offensive weapon, threatening to cause harm, endangering life, driving dangerously to escape police pursuit and driving under disqualification.

At 18, Matt felt the weight of the adult system for the first time. Four years and six months for 'hijacking' someone from their vehicle and 'robbing' another with violence. All just three days into release from juvenile detention where he had just served a ten-month term for robbery and other, less serious, offences. This time, Matt and a companion had approached the driver of a parked vehicle and demanded the keys. Matt said he had a gun and would use it. After stealing the car, the pair then robbed a hotel before taking a carton of alcohol and speeding off. About an hour later, with the same accomplice, Matt entered the front bar of another hotel and threatened the attendant, saying they had weapons and demanding access to the cash register. In the course of those events, Matt struck a patron and said he was not afraid to use a gun and nerve gas spray to get what he wanted. The explanation Matt later gave for this crime spree was that he had met with some friends, that they had commenced drinking, and that he wanted money to buy drugs. Matt intended to use the stolen alcohol to trade at known haunts for drugs or money. This was 'big crime' (Haigh 2009: 312) – a far cry from racing a stolen car and doing 'doughnuts' in a shopping centre car park with a few mates. The second he entered the prison sally port, Matt knew he was out of his depth: 'Juvey [juvenile detention], that was *my* house then.... That was *my* show.... [But] when I came into the adult system, I changed my thinking pattern and my way of words. As soon as I stepped foot in [the adult custodial environment] I knew it [wasn't gonna be] the same.' He hit rock bottom. And at that point there was only one other person that could possibly know what that felt like.

Rick, an ex-ward of the state, had spent well over a decade in various prisons. As a young boy Matt remembered hearing stories about how, in his heyday, his father was one of the most violent and dreaded 'thugs' going around. But musing from his cell in a maximum-security prison,

Matt also knew Rick had 'done good'. Yes, he probably still did drugs. And yes, he may drink to excess. He probably still bragged about all the 'cunts' he'd 'bashed'. But he also now owned his own small business and he worked 9 to 5. He had a family. He wasn't doing crime and he certainly wasn't doing gaol. Matt knew he had to call him. 'Basically, I told [my Dad] straight up, I said, "You want anything to do with me, you clean up your shit, to try and help me clean up my problems."... And he done that.... He did it all for me. He didn't do it for Mum, [but] he done it for his son'. Rick was on board. He was willing to try and overcome his own amphetamine addiction, willing to walk back through the prison gates for the sake of establishing a relationship with his son. It wasn't all 'one-way traffic' though. Rick was doing this for himself too. Something good had to come from all the damage he'd done:

> [While I was in prison] my mates would brag about me to [Matt]: 'Should have seen your dad bash this cunt.' So who does [Matt] want to be like?... I passed that fucking shit onto my son because he was old enough to see what I was doing and I didn't know it at the time because I was proud of what I was doing in my own secret little fucking world.

Clearly, Rick had a lot to make up for. And a lot of work ahead of him. He commented on this during successive interviews:

> He's an adult now.... The crimes he's doing, it just worries me, you know? He's doing full-on bad things. You know, he's not just breaking into houses. He's jumping counters.... He could have got shot. He could be dead. But they're the things I try not to think about every day, otherwise I would fuck up.
>
> I'm trying to feel for my son and tell him that it's all a waste of fucking time. Time you can't get back. And when you get older, all that ego you got, there's another 17 cunts coming through with that mate and you're getting older bruv. So what are you going to do? Start shooting people? Because you're going to have to if you want to stay in the life, because as you get older you fucking can't do what you done and... [not have to] shoot cunts.

It *was* possible to leave the life. Rick, of all people, was testament to that:

> That's another reason I work for myself – to prove to [him] that, yeah, I can get somewhere in my life. It might have taken me a long time, but I'm doing something about it now, and that's what I expect [him]

to do.... [Prison's] hard. It'd be the hardest place to better yourself, because cunts will give you a hard time. But if you can do it in gaol, you can do it out here, and that's what I try and tell him.

As it turned out, Matt didn't get a 'hard time'. In fact, it was he who robbed and beat an older prisoner (allegedly for cigarettes). He pled guilty and his non-parole period was extended by a year. It was back to basics for Matt. He put his head down and committed, in his terms, to do no more 'stupid shit'. Six months prior to his scheduled release, he made it to the State's low-security prison. Then, Matt's fortunes changed again. He'd received news that Stacey (his mother) had been hurt. Information was scant but what he heard wasn't good. Her boyfriend had 'bashed' her within an inch of her life and she was in the hospital. Matt was desperate to see her. He was refused permission to do so. So he simply walked off the prison grounds and did what he always did in the midst of a crisis. He stole a car. For all her failings and abusive partners, Stacey was still his mother. As Matt explained: 'I flipped out.... I feared for her life, really... and I'd just had enough. I thought, "Fuck this". I needed to protect her and I wanted to hurt him.... I just wasn't thinking right.... I was going to hand myself in [afterwards] ... [but] I wanted to make sure she was alright... because all I got really is my Mum.' He didn't get far. More accurately, *they* didn't get far. On the spur of the moment, Matt linked up with a lifer during his 'escape'. Having a convicted murderer in tow made it impossible to keep a low profile. They barely made it down the road. It was only once he was in the prison van that the long-term consequences of what he'd done came hurtling into view: 'I heard the van rock up [at the prison] and I said to my [co-offender]... "Are you ready for a beating? We're going to get kicked in bad from these cunts".' With that, Matt was back before the superior courts for the third time in five years – a dubious honour of sorts. Of course, he felt fully justified in his behaviour. And he felt aggrieved the system had not seen fit to grant him the capacity to see his mother. Nonetheless, Matt pled guilty at the first opportunity and provided no indication he perceived the extension of his sentence to be unfair. He hoped – just as Ben had – that the judge might distinguish this latest 'compassionate' form of offending from his 'senseless' criminal exploits of times past:

> She had to get plastic surgery on her face and her nose. Her fingers got broken. A whole heap of stuff, which was all in the medical records saying what she'd gone through.... And I wanted the judge to see

that so they could understand, 'Well, he hasn't just done it for no reason. Obviously, it's built up and he wanted to go and make sure she's okay'.

Matt caught a break. The judge considered a sentence of 12 months appropriate by virtue of the 'little planning and no property damage' involved. Stacey's injuries, though, didn't so much as rate a mention in the sentencing remarks. For Matt, it was the ultimate insult from 'on high'. Another old 'fucker' that didn't understand the way his life worked. In fact, despite a resounding lack of success, preserving and improving a relationship with Stacey was often at the heart of Matt's intermittent interest in building a conventional, non-criminal lifestyle. At 18 he remarked: 'I've got to stop for my Mum.... She's worried, and she thinks [my offending is] her fault.... [S]he thinks that I don't love her.' More recently, the concept of family – especially the experiences he'd forfeited over the years – began to assume greater significance for Matt:

> When I was younger and Mum would say, 'Come to the zoo', I'd make an excuse, 'No, my leg's sore', or something. And then I'd take off and get locked up that day. And I think to myself now, I think, 'I should have went to the zoo that day with my family and spent time with...[them]'. Instead, I wanted to go with these dickhead mates that don't give a fuck about me and get locked up with them....I remember the things I missed...[but] I think I have [changed.] I've calmed down a lot....I used to be aggressive and want to fight all the time....Just sitting in here...for all these years...[I think of the things] that I miss out on with my family and my brothers that I should have done. I can't make up for all of that lost [time].... This life's fucked. And it's taken me so long to realize it. I've said it a lot of times before [but] not like that.... [T]his is it...I'm not coming back.

After serving nearly five years, Matt at 22, was released to a lengthy period on parole: 'People don't understand [that] fucking parole is hard [and] I've got a lot of parole to do.' It is generally accepted that young offenders lead highly unstructured lives (McCarthy and Hagan 1992). But for Matt, the highly restrictive regimes of home detention and/or parole have helped to ensure long-term contact with the criminal justice system: 'The gaol's a revolving door for most people.... [And parole], it's a head-fuck. They set you up. They let you out. You've got no money, nothing when you get out, you know, no support.' Without exception, all the young men in our study consistently cited tougher enforcement of parole provisions as undermining 'global' if fleeting improvements in their offending trajectories. In other words, repeat custodial sentences more often reflected the stringent requirements of community-based corrections rather than increases in the severity of offending (see Barry 2011). Matt can certainly speak to how a parole breach can inflame matters. Having completed just under two months in the community, and fearing imminent arrest, he decided to go 'on the run'. He'd become aware that a breach report had been submitted after curfew checks had failed to locate him at his designated address. He subsequently ceased attending requisite programs. Later, from prison, Matt revealed concerns for his family's welfare were again behind his latest 'non-compliance'. His auntie had recently died from a heroin overdose sending his mother, Stacey, into another downward spiral. With her history of drug use and suicide attempts, Matt wasn't taking any chances: 'I [was] so worried about her so I kept fucking off from my [approved place of residence] to [where my Mum was living] to check on her. And they done a check at my house, a curfew check, and I wasn't there and that's what made me go on the run.'

Absconding (the 'fuck it' mentality), we note, was the default position for many of the young men caught up in breach proceedings. The thought of making contact with a community correctional officer generally failed to register as a possible response in the days and moments before such a response. Perhaps this reflects the limited personal resources and life circumstances of many persistent offenders. Or maybe it reflects a long history with countless departments and workers that lead to a deep-seated lack of confidence in officialdom. So often, young men viewed departmental personnel as patronizing and out of touch. As Matt remarked:

> I've got this stupid bitch [of a parole officer]....I didn't like her from the first day I met her....She's going to me, 'Oh, I'm sorry [Matt] but I've had three wankers and dickheads...[who] breached today, fucking idiots', like, bagging probably people that are my mates....And I said, 'Yes and when I breach, if I do, are you're going to [call] me a dickhead and wanker and fucking idiot?'

With quite alarming regularity, the correctional system seemed to hand Matt obstacle after obstacle. His sense of optimism and commitment toward doing better began to wane. Just learning to take 'directions' from someone else – let alone a stranger – was hard and carried particular psychological baggage for Matt. He revealed something of why this was the case to an older prisoner who had taken him under his wing:

> [This prisoner friend of mine] goes, 'So you know why I growl at you sometimes when you get out of line? Because I love you, you little cunt.' And I said, 'Don't growl at me though. Not in that way. I don't look at it like that. I used to get growled at when I was a kid, and get bashed, so when you growl at me like that and put me on show, I'm not going to cop it, mate.' ... I was getting a hiding every time I'd get growled at, so it makes me feel confronted and I want to fucking fight.... Because I'm used to getting growled at and then punched in a damn fight.

Matt described the weeks after being released from prison as monumentally disappointing. His auntie's death and his mother's subsequent bingeing on alcohol and other drugs led to her losing her house – the place she had long said Matt could stay and from which he (they) could start anew: 'It fucked me off [that my Mum had] done all this. She said to me because I had been in [prison] for so long that I need to get out to a stable environment and everything would run smoothly and then in a week it was just worse than my life's ever been, structure-wise.' As Burnett and Maruna (2004: 398) keenly observe, 'the impact of hope shrinks as the number of problems encountered rises'. In this context, Matt lost all desire to 'stay calm' and work things through. It wasn't his style. He'd not had, in any case, anyone ever show him how to do that. Never one to simply 'capitulate' to authorities, he 'jumped off' his buprenorphine medication and, like his mother, binged on alcohol and amphetamines. Charges for tendering a forged prescription and carrying an offensive weapon followed in quick succession. All thanks to one lousy curfew condition. The Parole Board was *not* going to like this. In Matt's eyes, his position became irretrievable: 'I just got fed up and thought, "Fuck it, I'm not going to just breach my bail, I'm going to do something else".' And so a minor slip-up evolved into more serious crime and an immediate custodial sentence. Of course, in the context of violent offenders, the stakes involved in these 'fuck it' moments are high – and not just for innocent bystanders. From custody, Matt voiced concern (and annoyance) that his relationship with his father might be the next casualty of his ongoing criminal behaviour: 'If I keep going, I'm not going to have a family. Dad's already told me, "You fucking come in here again, that's it, you're not getting any more visits from me, that's it." ... I look at him and think, "You're a bit of a hypocrite", but he's right. That's a risk'.

After serving a further five months in prison, Matt was (again) released on parole with (further) stringent home detention conditions. This proved a particularly turbulent time as he and Stacey struggled to restore equilibrium, both as individuals and as a family: 'I get out [of gaol] and it's like [she's] just given up, like, [she] can't handle me being around and it's always "I'm the reason for the way [she is]".... I found out she's off her med[ication] and all this shit.... I can't handle it.... [S]he'd better change soon because otherwise she's going to lose me.' Notwithstanding these difficulties, Matt successfully completed four months in the community without incident. In his words: 'It's the best I've [ever] done.' However, fearing (again) imminent breach action, Matt cut his electronic monitoring bracelet and fled. As he later acknowledged, the decision was poorly considered and instantly regrettable: 'As soon as that bracelet come off my ankle, it hit, "What did I just do?" and it's too late. I said, "You're a fucking idiot man".... Because I was doing good. I didn't even [reoffend]. I had three breaches [of bail] and I was sitting in the cop shop thinking, "Why am I fucking here? I'm going back to gaol ... for coming home late ... and giving a dirty urine".' Only it wasn't 'just' a broken curfew and a positive drug test. This time, things went seriously wrong. Whereas Joel, Reggie, Ben and Paul slowly came to 'invent' less harmful ways around warrants for their apprehension (contacting a lawyer, surrendering themselves to police, laying low until their court/parole date), Matt did the opposite. Spotted by uniformed police during a daytime patrol, he reverted instantly to 'flight mode' and suddenly was leading police on a high-speed chase through busy suburban streets. In essence, little had changed since he was first admitted to custody at 13 years of age. It was only when Matt eventually crossed on to the wrong side of the road and collided 'head-on' with an oncoming vehicle that he was finally arrested. By sheer luck, the other driver sustained only moderate injury as both cars were 'written off'.

Matt, speaking from custody, was quick to distinguish this from his violent offending of the past. However, it is evident his decision-making remains poor and that he possesses an alarming lack of insight into the seriousness of his behaviour: 'I was a serious criminal when I was younger. You see me coming out now, no robberies. I'm not going around with guns.... [The worst thing now] is crashing into another car.' That might be true, but the risks to the public (in terms of probable injury and/or death) are substantial. This is something that resists computation in Matt's mind. It's a type of cognitive dissonance – a dissonance that requires sustained and sensitive assistance to resolve. Matt recently pled guilty to charges of driving dangerously to escape police pursuit and aggravated causing harm by dangerous driving. He received four years' imprisonment for these offences and was disqualified from holding or obtaining a driver's licence for ten years. It was the fourth time he'd faced sentence for major indictable offences since turning 18. As Rick once noted, sometimes there is little option but to be thankful for the basics: 'As his father, I'm happy he's breathing... simple as that.'

In sum

Few people can lay claim to helping to orchestrate a drug operation that reputedly crosses international borders. Fewer still are charged with attempted murder in the course of such activity. For Lee, 'achieving' both earned him classification as a 'serious violent offender' prior to reaching his mid-twenties. A series of robbery incidents and assaults caught Matt under the same umbrella from a young age. With nearly two decades of custodial time between them, it was highly unlikely they would ever last in the community without a comprehensive program of assistance. To this extent, we observe a fine line between 'assisting' versus 'annoying' (ex)offenders. By all accounts, Lee and Matt were certainly 'busy' trying to fulfil requirements of their parole agreements – reporting, attending programs, giving urine samples and the like. Lee referred to this as 'making me chase my tail'. The State, however, considers this as giving each the chance to get their lives in order. It is therefore parolees' 'choice' as to whether they make the best of things or not. We would argue, though, that while Lee's and Matt's time was 'occupied', nothing of any real significance was changing. 'Jumping through hoops' failed to yield so much as an ID card or bank account. There was literally not enough time in the week to make a *legitimate* dollar and to slowly accumulate the social and economic capital that comes from being gainfully employed. We do not pretend, of course, that either would embrace such an opportunity were it on offer. Certainly, for Lee, the street was 'open' 24/7 with the prospect of 'fast' and 'big' money. His ex-partner (Holly) may not have accepted him, but his 'crew' certainly would. Matt, on the other hand, remained unable to deal in non-violent ways with chronic family issues. He was as quick to say 'fuck it' at age 26 as he was at age 13. The thought of *not* escalating a situation failed to enter his mind at so many junctures. This is where something has to give. More prison time seems only to inflame the sense of (social) injustice that pervades Matt's life – the sense of being born poor, of being beaten as a child, of not having a father-figure, of knowing, essentially, only milieus of violence and dysfunction and returning to these each time after release from custody. In this light, Lee's pathway is all the more interesting as his background was precisely the opposite of this. Of all the young men, Lee is the only participant whose forays into offending seem to stem from actively 'choosing' that type of life. Only in later years has he seriously wrestled with the costs to his family and, especially, to his children.

Given this, it is deeply problematic that the systemic response to Lee's and Matt's respective situations was so similar when their needs and pathways to date were so very different. Desistance does not happen in generic fashion. A package for such can't be pulled off the shelf (a pinch of violence prevention, a dash of drug counselling, a bit of reporting and so on). It needs to be carefully pieced together in ways that deal with the real needs and ongoing nature of relapses in would-be desisters' lives. And it needs to align with people's hopes and aspirations as well. Lee will always privilege the master status of organized criminal/drug dealer over father or partner so long as the latter seem impossibly out of reach. And Matt will always fall back into the role of armed robber so long as the role of son or worker or partner reside way over the horizon. For us, these are the things that tend to be ignored in custodial and post-custodial 'support' arrangements. As Ward and Maruna (2007) argue, dealing with criminogenic needs (issues with impulsivity, drug use and abuse and the like) sometimes has to take a back seat to addressing basic needs (securing loving human relationships, shelter, employment, education and so on). In fact, we would argue that the latter very often underpin the former. In the next chapter, the relative merits of this contention will come starkly to the fore.

6
Catastrophic Turn

This chapter is based on the lives of Sam, James and Chris. Each shares the inability to get any meaningful purchase in the struggle to desist. All aged in their mid-twenties, they have amassed well over 10,000 custodial days between them (nearly 30 years spent incarcerated). Chris's and Sam's offending trajectories have seen them over the years progress steadily in terms of the frequency and seriousness of criminal activity. The offences for which they are currently incarcerated made headline news and caused untold trauma to their victims. James, on the other hand, has struggled with more or less the same types of crime for much of his life. But the offences for which he is currently serving time are of a demonstrably more serious type. These too brought him substantial public notoriety. In an effort to do 'justice' to the complexity of issues revealed during successive interviews with the young men, their stories are told in significant depth (more so than previous chapters). We believe these stories – the catastrophic nature of them – speak not just to the many problems besetting the juvenile and criminal justice systems, but also the social and cultural climates to which people return when released from custody.

Sam

> It seems every time I plan to do good on the outside, I do bad, so I just stopped planning to do good. I just like, let it roll out in front of me.

Sam is in his mid-twenties. One of five children, he grew up in several of the most disadvantaged pockets of northern Adelaide. Both his parents used amphetamines, particularly his mother, Paula. His father, a truck driver, was frequently away interstate for extended periods.

Sam characterized his parental experience as haphazard and permissive. We suspect this underpinned the strong internal locus of control pervading his early interviews: 'I influence myself. If I'm not going to do nothing, I'm not going to do it. It's as simple as that. But if I want to do something, I'll be doing it, if this person says so or not.' During time spent with his mother, Sam was consistently exposed to a culture of drug use and criminal activity. Indeed, paraphernalia or *indicia* of low-level drug dealing were evident at her residence during interview. At age 22, Sam reflected on his home life in the following terms:

> It's a whole lifestyle that you live when you live with my Mum ... the drugs and the going [out] to do crime to get drugs.... [She doesn't send me out to do it] but she does take in the rewards.

By age three, Sam had begun to demonstrate extremely disruptive behaviour causing Paula to seek psychological and psychiatric intervention for him. As a toddler, he was regularly found on the roof or inside the homes of neighbours he had never met. Paula continues to question whether complications during childbirth were the underlying cause of his problematic early childhood behaviour. As she remarked: 'He was born dead.... It took ten minutes before he was actually breathing.... I don't know if there was brain damage done but he had all the symptoms of being ADHD.' Sam's unpredictable behaviour led to his attendance and removal from five primary schools. At one of them, Paula even became a classroom volunteer as a means to bypass daily phone calls advising he was up a tree or inside the roof space. She knew this strategy was only ever buying time to figure out her next move. Formally diagnosed with ADHD at age eight, dexamphetamine medication offered an immediate, if short-lived, reprieve from Sam's behaviour. Paula remembers this moment vividly: 'When I did eventually get him onto the pills it was like, "Oh my God, I wish I'd done this years ago".' Importantly, clinical diagnoses often provide comfort to parents struggling to come to terms with the behaviour (crimes) of their children. However, maintaining his medication throughout the school day ultimately proved untenable. Paula reports the educational system as largely unsupportive and unhelpful in this regard. She was back to square one.

With possibly two exceptions, all the males in our cohort attended, at some point in their childhood, at least one of two Adelaide schools for behavioural management. Indeed, friendships that spanned both juvenile detention and adult prison settings often had their genesis in these educational settings. By all accounts, Sam's attendance at both only accelerated his emerging criminal proclivities: 'There were other kids [there] just like me. So they put all these misbehaved kids... in one school and they got together and they just made it worse.' He was regularly truant or suspended for fighting with other students. As Sam has remarked, the chaos and dysfunction of his neighbourhood offered up no shortage of anti-social peers to pass his time: 'Where we were living... that area, it's full of shit... and that's where most of my friends came from.' Aged 11, Sam and a friend stole their first car to experience 'adrenalin rush driving' and because he 'used to like impressing people'. From then on, Sam was frequently in trouble with the law and began accumulating what is now an extensive criminal history. Even prior to reaching his teens, Sam was dealt with for numerous serious offences, most often involving motor vehicles and theft with violence. Describing an otherwise aimless existence, he was matter-of-fact about life as a young offender: '[Crime] is kind of like – it's virtually a routine... I'd get out of bed and get dressed, go catch a train... to wherever I want to go and just do whatever I need to do.' This offending went hand-in-hand with significant alcohol, cannabis and amphetamine consumption and Sam suffered drug-induced psychosis on a number of occasions. Already ensconced in the management of serious personal issues, Paula was unable to cope and left the family home with her remaining children.

As we've previously illustrated, the decision by significant females to withdraw support is an agonizing process ultimately requiring choice 'between their own psycho-social health and the emotional stability' of the offender (Halsey and Deegan 2014: 13). For Paula, drawing a line around the limits of care occurred in response to crippling despair and abandonment by family members, most devastatingly her spouse:

> [H]is father and I broke up. I don't blame [Sam] but [he] had a lot to do with it.... It was hard enough with four boys but to have one that was just full on, it was even harder... [So Sam] stayed with his father and I took the other three boys.... I just couldn't deal with it anymore. And then he'd come and stay with me on weekends and I'd literally feel sick knowing that he was coming over to stay.

To this day, Sam is largely unaware of the role he played in the separation of his parents. Following their split he lived primarily with his father but reports intermittent periods with his mother and siblings. He coped poorly with his new circumstances and felt this legitimized engagement in further crime. Leaving school by Year 8, he'd amassed convictions for aggravated robbery, multiple counts of driving a motor vehicle without consent, escaping from custody, attempted theft using force, aggravated serious criminal trespass in a place of residence (that is, burglary break and enter), multiple counts of breaching bail, and much more. Viewed in isolation, this antecedent history inspires little confidence that Sam was ever seriously wrestling with how best to change his life and desist from crime. At interview, however, Sam continued through the years to possess a remarkable degree of self-reflection regarding his situation and what he might do to desist. He was honest about his motivations for offending but also often spoke of the premium he placed (and continues to place) on becoming a law-abiding citizen:

> I think about the past a lot and go through what I've done...[and]...I realize that it wasn't very nice....I'm trying to force myself to change, so I force myself to feel bad....[But] mostly [what] I think about is preventing myself from coming back here....How to change my mindset....Try to get into a new routine....Break the boredom....When I'm doing nothing...I do crime....I gotta break that and look for a good job...and maybe get out of Adelaide.

Sam also touched on his belief that change had to come 'from within' himself since various systems can only do so much to assist people. This does not negate, as he explained, the need for the right kind of assistance for those trying to change:

> Back then I didn't really have any intentions to stop crime...I might have said I did, but...deep down, I knew I was still going to do crime when I'd get out....But these days, I've thought about it....It's not what it used to be. It's just not worth it....When I was young...you would get locked up and you would get out and run amok and you'd get locked up again and get out and get locked up, get out, get locked up again, get out, get locked up, get out. And there was nothing...really there to stop us doing what we wanted to do....We just [did] whatever we wanted – done crime, stole,...But these...days,...it's more within ourselves....The workers we've got, they help us, but they only help us to a certain extent, probably about 10 per cent of what we really need to be helped. The rest...is 90 per cent...and most of that's in us....When you really think about it, that's all they can do is that 10 per cent...and they just hit a brick wall and they can't go no further....The rest [of the] 80 or 90 per cent is up to you.

To his great credit, at age 17, Sam secured permanent full-time employment as a forklift driver at a suburban warehouse. In addition to compulsory training, his commitment to the role was evident by preparedness to wake daily at 5am, ride his pushbike to the train station, catch the train, and then bike out to the work site. One could speculate that, for many, such a prospect might increase the appeal of 'sitting back' on social security benefits. However, in virtually all of our interviews, Sam made it plain that he *needed* the structure, social stimulation and purpose that a job, however modest, could provide him. More to the point, he credited gainful employment with his developing sense of moral agency and emerging 'sense of clarity surrounding past events' (King 2013: 155). As he remarks below, the distinction between legitimate earnings and proceeds of crime impressed heavily with every pay packet he received:

> I'm tired of getting locked up. Just tired of...getting told...what to do....It's been happening to me for the last eight years....[W]hen I was out, I found a better life....Like, when I was doing crime, I didn't have money in my pocket...I couldn't just go down the shop and buy a magazine or I couldn't just go to the shops and get myself a new phone or get what I wanted. I couldn't do that because I didn't...always have money....But when you work and when you live like a normal person, you can do those things because you've got the money there....And it's legitimate. And you feel better about it – that you're reading a book which you've earned – gone out and...like, worked [and] sweat[ed] for....And it feels a lot better than going and...stealing money and then going and buying something with that stolen money...Some people, in theory, who haven't had much – like haven't done it [that is, earned a legitimate income] very often...would say, 'No, it's just the same'...But when you really think about it, it does feel different because you're not watching over your back. You can sit there and read your magazine...and...think, 'They can't take this off me because I've paid...for it with my own money, what I earned...myself, legitimately'.

For three months Sam managed to juggle the demands of his new job with the strict conditions of a six-month suspended sentence bond. Eventually though, he gave in to the lure of a Saturday night spent drinking with friends. The evening culminated with a smashed car windscreen and Sam's arrest. Unable to remember exactly how the glass was broken ('I was pissed. I was drunk'), Sam considered he might have 'fallen through it'. Police disagreed. Sam was charged with illegal interference of the vehicle, something he strongly denies. Despite a grant of bail, his boss was unsympathetic to learn of Sam's ongoing legal troubles and terminated his employment on the spot:

> Out of respect... Monday morning I went to his office and told him... 'I got arrested [and] I got a court date I have to go to'.... And later on that day he called me in to the office... and said, 'There's no more work here for you. You can finish the work off until Wednesday'.

Losing a job – especially one that has significant personal meaning – is generally accepted as an immensely stressful life event. For Sam, it was so much more. He was angry, frustrated and perceived a grave injustice had been done to him. After all, it was only a broken window. He was doing armed robberies and escaping from detention centres not that long ago. As was the case for many of the other young men, without positive reinforcement Sam soon became disenchanted with 'going straight', effectively liberating him to engage in a rush of criminal activity. He told of losing any desire to do the right thing:

> I can see where he's coming from. Like, I wouldn't want my employees to get arrested on the weekends.... But he could at least wait and just see what the outcome from court was because after I lost my job, that's when I went downhill again.... After I got the sack, everything went down at home and I moved out. I went and stayed with my family and just started running amok again.... I thought, 'No, there's no point trying anymore'. So I [breached] my suspended sentence. So then I just thought there's no point in stopping now, and I just kept on going. I didn't go to court the following day. I had a warrant out. I was on the run for another two months.

This is the archetypal scenario of the 'fuck it' mentality. It is an all-too-common event in the lives of the young men in our study and we revisit the issue in the next chapter. 'On the run', Sam committed a string of 'breaks' on residential and commercial premises. On the last occasion, he fell through the roof of a factory he was attempting to 'knock over'. So severe was the impact of the fall that Sam fractured his skull and was forced to wait, incapacitated, for the owner to return and call an ambulance. He was now 18 and was required to serve the remainder of his suspended sentence in prison (that is, an adult custodial facility). Sam, however, seemed totally inured to his new lodgings, commenting that 'the juvenile system moulded me to the gaol life, so it wasn't a shock for me... My generation, when I was in and out, all the boys, they're here [now], every single one of them'. With this in mind, Sam 'sailed' through the six-month term. Paula had been preparing to have him released to her place on home detention. But fate intervened. As she was driving her youngest son home from school, police noticed an old warrant for driving disqualified. She was pulled over and arrested in front of her son and two-year-old daughter. More distressingly, Paula was driven straight to the watch-house[1] as her children were loaded into a taxi and sent to an empty house: '[T]he worst thing was I didn't know where [my daughter] was. I didn't know who was looking after her. [And] I had no money.' The irony was stark. Sam – a persistent serious offender – had just made home detention bail, whilst a mother of five entered prison for a traffic offence. Paula spoke at length about the trauma and 'risk' this generated for her young family:

> Some prick of a judge thought he'd make an example of me after I was picked up driving under disqualification. I got locked up for four weeks then released a few days before Christmas. But because I was on Home D, I couldn't do it at home because [Sam] was there doing his Home D. I didn't even have [the baby] with me. Two days before Christmas I cut the bracelet off so I could go home. They didn't arrest me for a week. And I spent the next month in gaol ... Yeah, [Sam] didn't handle it very well.

To put it bluntly, Sam went 'ballistic'. Sure, his mum had problems – had broken the law – but this, in his eyes, was plain wrong. The system was cruel. It caused people in pain only more pain. It put those on the edge over the edge. Sam felt tremendously guilty. But mostly, he felt enraged. His baby sister, whom he adored, was without her mother, during Christmas no less. He threatened to 'go off the deep end', but his older brothers continually talked him down. He didn't reoffend. But, at the same time, he never gave home detention an honest crack either. After all, why should he? Whatever faith he had in the system had been extinguished. Sam continued to breach his bail and continued to be released on increasingly stringent conditions. In fact, he described a moral victory every time he left court by the front door instead of the back. It was almost like a game, 'a win for the good guys'. However, nine days into his last release to home detention, Sam found out his girlfriend had met someone else while he was incarcerated. And she was leaving him. This was the absolute tipping point. As Sam put it: 'I lost it, yeah...I lost it and I just went on a spree...I was only out for nine days and I just went doing crime and got locked up.'

This description grossly underestimates the magnitude of events that followed. In fact, Sam engaged in what could only be called 'a violent rampage'. Over the course of approximately two hours, he and a co-offender committed no fewer than three distinct and terrifying robbery incidents. Coincidentally, Sam's co-offender had recently fallen out of a relationship and had lost his job. They had been commonly aggrieved. And their collective sense of injustice and rage was going to be released somewhere and/or on someone. Their plan was simple enough. They would binge on drugs and alcohol, abscond from home D, and ultimately deliver a 'beat-down' to one of Sam's long-time 'rivals'. Viewed as a form of street justice, in their eyes no major harm would have been done (Jacobs and Wright 2006). But things didn't go to plan. Armed with a baseball bat, they instead hijacked, chased and rammed successive occupied vehicles. Sam personally confronted each victim and began striking their vehicles with the bat if they failed to acquiesce to his demands. A bus shelter was completely destroyed as one of the vehicles went through it. Victims were traumatized. The damage bill was extensive. It took police only ten minutes to arrest Sam after he abandoned the last of the stolen cars. After a lengthy remand, Sam's 'appalling' history of juvenile offending left the judge to seriously query whether he was 'without hope' of rehabilitation. He was sentenced to seven years' imprisonment.

Clearly, this dramatic escalation in the severity of his offending represents a serious departure from Sam's stated quest to build a more positive future. Indeed, expectation that 'serious offenders engage...in big crime while those either experimenting or attempting to move away from crime engage...in small crime' has a powerful logic and defines much thinking about how desistance should ideally 'look' (Haigh 2009: 312). For Sam's mother Paula, the value of such a distinction is probably moot. As she explained, the sense of singular relief associated with Sam's last incarceration episode far outweighed disappointment or outrage over his behaviour: 'Thank God...they've stopped it. They've put him in gaol....At least I know where he is...I know he's not out doing 160km down [some suburban street] going to kill someone.' In fact, mothers in our study often reached the tragic point where prison as a 'known' quantity afforded an 'immediate means to halt the (escalating) chaos in and around their lives'. As we have previously remarked, 'this kind of deep despair led to *the curious 'embrace' of the correctional system* as the means for short-circuiting cycles of harm' (Halsey and Deegan 2014: 10, emphasis in original).

On several occasions, the young males in our cohort similarly recognized imprisonment as a 'necessary evil' when life got seriously out of hand. As Sam acknowledged from custody: 'I think I needed this [to be incarcerated]...I don't know why I did it. I just did...[D]eep down...I wasn't ready to stop.' We do not suggest that Sam (or others in our study) 'likes' being incarcerated. In fact, prison is generally known to be 'an expensive way of making bad people worse' (Burnett and Maruna 2004: 390). Sam recognizes this and confirms that violence is a 'perfectly acceptable [practice] in th[e] social setting' of prison (Trammell 2012: 94): 'In here you could get into a fight over a toilet roll.... Little stuff that you wouldn't even care about on the outside like a TV and the channel we watch. In gaol it'll start a big fight...[and] all you've really got in gaol is your respect.... If you lose that, you virtually lose everything.' Sam got into several serious physical fights while incarcerated. Paula knew something bad was going on: 'I know he's copped a few beatings in there...[And] the only reason I know is because he took our names off the visitors list...He got a beating and he just didn't want us to see him.' At interview Sam confirmed his victimization. He told of being assaulted and left unconscious with a broken nose and severed artery. It led to him being hospitalized and requiring a blood transfusion.

Comparatively speaking, though, a much worse ordeal lay ahead. Locked down for the night, news coverage of a horrific home invasion and gang rape in his old neighbourhood caught Sam's attention. He watched in horror as images of his childhood home, cordoned by crime scene tape, flashed across the screen. Reportedly, the incident was motivated by the victim's stash of illicit drugs at the premises. The victim, as it turned out, was Paula. It would be the first of many sleepless nights for Sam. As he explained to us, coming to terms with his mother's brutal rape was one thing. But being incarcerated with one of her (alleged) rapists was quite another. Incredibly, of all of the units, in all of the prisons in the State, Sam literally found himself face to face with the prime suspect. For a time, he even found himself listening to the prisoner's protestations about his innocence. However, as Paula reminded him during weekly phone calls, an abundance of DNA evidence left little doubt the police had their man. Sam again became enraged. He had, through being 'absent' in prison, 'allowed' a serial rapist to do unspeakable violence to his mother. The urge to retaliate was overwhelming and offers to arrange a 'hit' came thick and fast. Paula was beside herself with worry: 'I rang the gaol and I said, "Look, this is [happening], what's going on", you know, "Do you care? He shouldn't be in the same Unit.... You know [Sam's] been in there for [four] years. He'll be getting out soon and I don't want him doing anything silly".' As Paula inferred, Sam's eligibility to apply for parole was just around the corner. Maintaining that he and his brothers would 'sort it out' eventually, Sam held his composure and transferred out of the prison to another facility. He has now served five years – all of which has been spent in a high-security regime due to his escape from a custodial facility in his juvenile years. This has dramatically limited his social and vocational opportunities while incarcerated:

> I spoke to the CMC [case management coordinator] the other day.... I thought because I'm of good behaviour and I don't start trouble, maybe they could drop my security rating down. But nah... he just said 'No'.... So what's the point of me keeping my nose clean when I can't even get my security rating dropped so I can work [while I'm locked up]?

As it happened, Sam's application for release on parole was unsuccessful following institutional and psychological reports that he continues to deny his propensity for violence. Like several other young men in our study, Sam prefers to conceive of himself (and most other prisoners) as good people who have, clearly, made some serious errors in their lives: 'Half these guys in [gaol], they've got a good heart.... They're good people like myself... They've just been able to do what they want most of their life and that's what they're doing, that's all they know... They just make stupid decisions.' Despite an offender history spanning over a decade, Sam resists attempts to label him as a criminal:

> I: Do you see yourself as a criminal?
> P: I don't like to put it like that but I done crime so in a way I suppose I do, but I'm kind of in denial as well you know....
> I don't want people looking at me like a crim.

Davis (1961: 120) terms this a process of 'deviance disavowal' involving the 'refusal of those who are viewed as deviant to concur in the verdict'. When they do concur, 'they usually place a very different interpretation on the fact or allegation than their judges'. We are not in a position to confirm or challenge the accuracy of accounts presented at

Sam's parole hearing. Clearly, the Parole Board was sufficiently moved by recommendations contained therein. We have no problem saying, however, that Sam (and others) appear, at times, to entirely underestimate the dim view society takes of particular (repeated types of) behaviour. He once commented from juvenile detention: 'One of the workers reckons I have to prove myself to them. [But] I don't think I have to prove myself to nobody.' This refusal to give much on the culpability or responsibility fronts has made it difficult for Sam to receive even the smallest quantum of support while locked up. In a sense, Sam is holding desperately to the idea that 'deep down' he is a good person who has had to negotiate an endless series of bad situations. But through these situations he has learned to push all manner of people away, further compounding his plight. The more serious his offending becomes, the less people want to 'invest' in him as a candidate for reform and rehabilitation. And the more they distance themselves – the harsher the correctional system acts toward him – the more concrete his perception becomes that he is, in the end, on his own: 'I don't want [help from] people who's got no faith in me or other people. I don't like those kinds of people. I don't want them in my life, because they put bad energy in my situation.'

Despite many major – indeed catastrophic – setbacks, there are some indications stemming from Sam's latest custodial sentence that the desistance journey continues. He has consistently indicated genuine remorse and desire to repair the harm caused through his offending. Recent commentators note increased victim awareness to be strongly associated with development of a desistance narrative (see, for example, King 2013). Although he knows he could never 'undo' the damage sustained by his victims, Sam nevertheless wrote several letters of regret in which he acknowledged the trauma inflicted through their terrifying interface with him. As he explained to us, accusations of duplicity prevented many prisoners from similar undertakings:

> If you're in gaol the community automatically thinks [you're] bad people...that they don't care about anyone. But [we] really do.... I've lost count of how many prisoners I've spoken to where they've said, 'I wish I could apologize to my victims'... or 'I shouldn't have done that'. You know, they've come to think that [what they did] was pretty bad. Like heaps of people [in here] on a daily basis [say that].... And if you write a letter to the judge or something or the families, the courts [are] just thinking, 'Oh yeah, they're just sucking up. What do they want?' Sometimes that is the case. But there's

a lot of people who, like I've said, have got good hearts and sincerely are remorseful for what they've done.

He also commented: 'They think we're criminals and we're just trying to rort the system... so when you actually... do... something [good] they don't believe you.' Sam remains caught, therefore, in the classic Catch-22 situation. Authorities expect prisoners to be remorseful, to reflect on their actions and to change. But when they do show signs in these directions, they are roundly condemned as insincere or as manipulative or only doing such things because they got caught. Most people – let alone prison or community correctional officers, Parole Board members, or other professionals charged with judging the 'truth' of (ex)prisoners' claims – steer away from any chance of 'being hurt, taken in, suckered, abused, put down or in some other way made to seem a less-than-competent player of the social game' (Lofland 1969 in Maruna et al. 2004: 272). The extreme difficulty involved in establishing one's credentials as a reformed person leads Maruna et al. (2004: 272) to speculate that a too hard and fast scepticism might in fact contribute to a 'self-fulfilling prophecy of sorts'. In short, convincing prison and post-release personnel of one's commitment to change is incredibly difficult. Becoming a 'new' person requires access to pro-social contexts where crime and violence are the exception to the rule. That, patently, is an inimical circumstance to becoming and being a prisoner.

As he nears the end of his custodial sentence, we reflect on the issues Sam most recently identifies as critical for successful reintegration in the community – a process that he maintains *is* extremely important to him. In particular, through the unlikely portal of prison, he has actually managed to enhance the quality of relationships with family members: 'The only thing that keeps me going in here is contact with my friends and family. If I didn't have that, I don't know where I'd be.' Whitaker and Garbarino (1983 in Pinkerton and Dolan 2007: 220) observe that support from families remains the 'bread and butter source of help' for those prisoners fortunate enough to have such contact. Despite the difficulties with his family, Sam needs them not only as witnesses to his commitment to change but also as people who can affirm any progress he might make in the struggle to leave the life of crime and violence. He knows the stakes are high:

> I've just missed out on too much with my family... probably nearly half my life I've been in custody... [and] this time... it's been the hardest time ever.... I've just had enough. I miss my family too

much.... I've been through rough patches with my family, but I still love them to death and that will never change.

Not many things scare me...but losing someone close to me...I'd never be able to forgive myself,...I'd be thinking, 'I've lost all this time, you idiot [Sam], you're selfish,...you've wasted all this time you could have spent with them'.

Of more immediate practical concern to Sam is his major dependency on methadone – a synthetic opioid used for pain relief but primarily to flatten the peaks of acute heroin withdrawal. Despite a documented history of poly-substance abuse, Sam told us heroin addiction was merely a pretext to gain access to drugs in custody. As he described, his uptake of methadone was intended as a prison survival strategy, allowing him to do 'easy' time whilst, supposedly, getting high: 'I just thought [when I got to prison], "Yeah, I'll get on the methadone and I'll be smashed, I'll get stoned and rah, rah, rah", and it just went too far.... I wish I didn't get on it.... I kept on putting requests in to go up, up, up and then before I knew it, I was on [the maximum dose] and I thought, "[Sam], what have you done?"' As he discovered, the analgesic effect of methadone, as with all narcotics, diminishes with continued use, requiring increasingly higher doses to maintain desired results. Methadone is taken for its sedative as opposed to stimulant or euphoria-inducing properties. Paula – a one-time prisoner herself – knows of the dangers: 'He's going to have a habit when he comes out...A lot of prisoners take it because it's so easy. They [medical staff working in the prison] offer it to you the day you walk in, you know, and [prisoners] sleep their days away on it.' Prison officers similarly referenced the liberal supply of methadone in prison:

> I would go as far as to say that...close to 100 per cent of people in gaol, they're here either directly or indirectly, because of drugs.... So with that, the gaol's full of it and not just from contraband being smuggled in. The Department supplies it...methadone, Suboxone, buprenorphine...We supply it [all]...to anyone who's coming in and going out and they're encouraged to go on it. (Prison Officer, 20 years' experience)

There is strong evidence suggesting that methadone is merely permitting prisoners to replace one addictive drug with another. This has implications for how people like Sam will cope when released from custody. Speaking from the prison in which Sam is incarcerated, the officer quoted above expressed his dismay over the Department of Correctional Services' ongoing support of methadone in prison. He and his colleagues reported incidences of diversion of medication, 'stand-over' tactics and resale of the drug: 'I went to the nurse and I said, "Why are you keeping these people on the program when they are actively diverting [it] for profit?...You keep giving it to them...[and] I keep catching them red-handed".' Certainly, Lee, Matt and Sam have all recorded disciplinary infractions and police charges for diverting or forging prescriptions for methadone and other opiate/narcotic medication. With a reported street value of around $120 per dose, incentives to do so are high. For Sam, the temptations that lie ahead, especially should he return to live with Paula, will be significant: 'My Mum's a druggie as well. So when I go live there...drugs are all around me...[But] I can't tell people how to live their life...' To this end, Sam plans to live with his father in a major rural centre away from Adelaide. For him, maintaining distance from neighbourhoods and associates of times past are central to the struggle to desist: 'The way I see it, if you put criminals together, they're going to think like criminals again. And then, when they get out, they've made new friends...[and] do a lot worse things than what they were doing, and they get into higher crime and they end up back [in prison] again...[So] I would exclude them from their environment, where they were living and the people they hang around.' By the time he is released, Sam hopes to have received assistance in basic life skills that will enable him to live independently and avoid further offending.

> At the end of the day, if someone wants to be violent, they'll be violent. Nothing with these people [that is, therapists] will prevent us doing violence. What needs to happen...is educating people...[about, for instance,] how to structure a home....[Or] if they can't have such a home with their family, [how to] make their own [home], and just educating [them] how to live on a day-to-day basis.

There are strong similarities here with Chris's needs (see further below). It is the most basic of things that so often go begging. Sam, to our way of thinking, is speaking here of learning how to live in non-violent fashion. But he is also speaking of the building blocks necessary for such – education, a safe place to live, a neighbourhood that isn't riddled by drugs, a job and the like. Anything less amounts to condemning people like Sam to a life lived *through* rather than beyond crime. He is optimistic: 'I guess I'm changing....I don't want to come back here again....I'm starting to think different and I'm happy about it you know.... I think, "Yeah, I can do alright when I get out... I can stop crime".' We hope this optimism proves well placed.

James

James is in his mid-twenties. He comes from a large family and grew up in a country town about an hour's drive from metropolitan Adelaide. He was bullied incessantly at school and he would end up in endless fights. His parents divorced when he was a small child and due to the instability in his life – as well as being expelled from school – he completed only eight years of schooling. Attempts at living, alternatively, with his mother, then his father, failed – the latter was violent toward James, and their household was a known amphetamine 'hangout'. By age 12 he was placed into foster care: 'I love my family but they haven't done much for me...' he would later comment. From the time he was first locked up at age 13, to his transfer to adult custodial jurisdiction at age 18, he spent roughly half his days incarcerated. In the six years since first being incarcerated as an adult, he has spent just 15 per cent of his days in the community. James has amassed countless court appearances and convictions – mostly for car-related offences but also for successive breaches of bail, and, more recently, for failing to abide by the conditions attached to his Drug Court rehabilitation plan. But, as shall become clear, James's main offences involve stealing cars and evading police. In fact, James could probably lay claim to being an even more notorious car thief than Charlie. He certainly caused the police no end of problems and was well known to officers involved in Operation Mandrake.

James recalled that his offending 'started in primary school' when his parents 'let me walk to and from school'. He came from a poor family and he knew as much: '[We] didn't have much money and stuff, you know, so I used to steal – shoplifting stuff.... Anything that I wanted I'd just go and steal it...' He describes the slow slide into more serious thieving in the following way: '[I started out] [pocket[ing]] something little. You know, [it] starts with a chocolate bar, then a block of chocolate, and then a box of chocolates. And then you start going into bigger shops... [to steal] clothes.' James was doing this out of need, not because he wished for trouble. He defined crime, quite logically, as 'want': 'Crime [is done by people who] want. They want the rush, they want drugs, they want money. Want, want, want, but can't have. So they take.' He would talk in successive interviews about being incredibly aware of what he lacked – good clothes, good shoes, a good home, a bit of money to spend on 'going out'.

It wasn't long before James 'graduated' to stealing from cars and various premises – all for cash or for goods to sell to get cash. He started out riding with mates in stolen cars. Joyriding, though, soon lost its sheen. In his mid-teens James fell in with other kids (all of whom he met while locked up). They were dubbed by the media as the 'Gang of 49' – a group of young offenders who, as mentioned earlier, were targeted by Operation Mandrake for crimes of car theft, ram-raiding, armed robbery and torching of vehicles. The goods obtained through such offending would be consumed by the young men themselves or for exchange in the underground economy:

> [S]omeone teaches you how to steal a car [so] you start stealing cars.... You joyride...for six or seven months and then you start going, 'Oh, this is useless'.... You don't get nothing out of it. So you start doing ram-raids and smash and grabs and...you get into high-speed chases and stuff. And then...you end up getting in big high-speed chases. [Then] you get more time [in lock up] and, you know, helicopters chasing you, and you can never get away.

In fact, years later – living ever so precariously within the general community – James would end up being front and centre in a notorious high-speed pursuit (more on this below). It made national news. As a teenager, James reflected on why he kept offending even though he knew he was putting other lives (and his own) at serious risk:

> P: [T]o this day when [I] look back at them situations, I think, 'I could've died'.... But you always keep on going back.... I've actually had heaps [of] bad car accidents and been arrested and...you're sitting in the cell at the cop shop and you think, 'Far out, I could've died...I could've killed someone else'. But then when you get out six months later, you go back and do the same thing.
> I: ...Why do you think you go back and do the same thing?...
> P: ...I never really did crime for money. I did it for chocolates and clothes. I did it for clothes. I like to look good in stuff, you know, and [I] did smash and grabs and shops and stuff, ram-raids on bottle [shops] and shit. But I never really did it for money. I always did it for something that I wanted.

James learned from a young age that cars helped him to kill the boredom that defined most of his days. He was never comfortable in any of the foster families he was expected to reside with. Cars offered a means of escape – no matter how dangerous this was for him and the public:

> [I]t's not stealing the car.... It's when you start it and you're actually driving away and you're driving around, there's that freedom there.... It's not your car but you don't have to think like that when you're in the car.... You think, 'This is mine'.... And [it's] just that [feeling of] freedom.... [T]he main thing that gets me in trouble, is I like the cars, man. Cars, cars.

He was literally 'addicted' to cars. He remarked that car theft for him was a 'daily' event: 'I was either locked up or frigging stealing cars.' Cars offered James the means to get around, to steal merchandise, to become popular among his peers, and to feel 'free' from the hassles of the street (see Copes 2003). Throughout his teenage years – from the time he first 'watched car races on the weekend' with his Dad and took up playing PlayStation – cars were his drug of choice:

> P: I started [stealing and driving cars] and that's so much of a rush, so much of a feeling, nothing could replace that feeling....
> I: Can you describe the feeling that you get?...
> P: It's just – it's more than adrenaline. You... get an adrenaline rush when you're running from police... and you think, 'Oh, man'. And then you get away and you think, 'That's cool'. There's nothing like it... I've been stealing cars for that many years now that... [i]t's just an everyday thing for me. I go out and steal a car and pull up down the street man. Just a normal thing.

James's first serious police pursuit happened when he was 15. He was with a mate in a stolen car travelling at more than 200km per hour (the needle was off the dial) and spotted a breathalyzer unit up ahead. Knowing he'd be caught for driving without a licence and motor vehicle theft, he put his 'foot flat' and tried to evade the police. Other police joined the pursuit and in a major game of 'chicken' James pulled onto the wrong side of the road to try and get the oncoming police vehicle to call off the chase. Instead, the vehicles collided with a combined impact of around 140km per hour. Remarkably, no one was seriously injured. James and his mate fled on foot but sniffer dogs tracked them down. He ended up in detention for six months. He got out and went to visit his father. The visit was cleared with James' liaison worker on the condition he come back to town 'by Monday'. He failed to do so and was breached and served further time – with some additional days thrown in for unresolved matters. He got out again. This time he was on home detention and required to wear an electronic bracelet. James cut it off after two days and went on a major crime spree:

> P: I cut my bracelet off and I was on the run for about a month and in that one month, man, I done more crime, you know, than in the last year....
> I: I'm guessing there was no school at that stage or anything....
> P: No, no.... During the day I was sleeping, during the night I was stealing cars. Literally, every night, doing crime, you know, here, there and everywhere.... Just cars and ram-raids, smash and grabs.

Eventually, after a month of couch surfing from place to place, going 'clubbing' and 'cruising' with mates each weekend, and using a series of false names to evade capture, the police caught up with him. James, at 16 years of age, was given a lengthy detention order of 18 months for his troubles. At first, this did not bother James. He knew '90 per cent of the boys' serving time with him. But eventually the longer stretch gave him pause to think about some of the near misses he was involved in and the damage he had caused: 'I still have nightmares about... when I hit the cop car.... I think about my mate.... [I]n that car accident [he]... shattered his two kneecaps [and was] in hospital for months and months before he could even walk again.... And I think about that shit all the time.' James also remarked that such thoughts quickly dissipated when back on the street. At interview (part-way through his sentence), James, as a 17-year-old, was adamant that his offending days were over: 'I will stay out of trouble when I turn 18... because I've got control over what I do.... I'll just have to have the willpower to straighten out my life and want to do it.... And I do want to do it.' He spoke of replacing the thrill of stealing cars and driving at high speed with riding motorbikes on a mate's property. At such time, one of the programs run in detention was making some sense to James. He had long thought that because he did not ever directly assault anyone, that his offences were 'victimless'. In lock-up, he learned differently:

> With 'Victim Awareness', you have people coming in... showing you what you do to the victims.... Some [guys are in] for bashing people

and you hear them stories and you think, 'Oh, that's rough. Man, I couldn't bash no one'. You hear [from] the victim, and you think, 'Yeah, I'm alright... I do shops over and steal people's cars. I don't hurt no one'. And then someone comes in and [says], 'I had my car stolen once [and] my kid was sick that night too, just happened to be sick and I couldn't take him to the hospital'. You think, 'Fuck, you know, it does affect me too'.

James has always had a conscience. Even in his teens he would wrestle with feelings of guilt and remorse. He cared about the type of crime he committed. He cared about the person he was and could become. His way of illustrating moral standing was through the small choices he made while doing essentially 'bad things': 'I've never stolen a car with a baby seat. But [even when there is no baby seat I] hop in a car and [I] steal it and [I] think, "Oh, [the owners] could still have kids"....I think about that. But as soon as I'm driving a car...I don't care.' James talked at length about needing a house. He talked about wanting a job – but one where he was shown some respect – not one where he would likely have to deal with 'pricks' being 'rude' to him (such as behind 'the counter' of a fast-food place).

At age 17, James was already talking in quite generative terms. He didn't know quite what kind of job he wanted but he wanted to work with kids in custody – to make a difference to their lives: 'A bit like a counsellor but...not a counsellor....I just want to be someone that comes through and talks to you about your family. I mean,... "I've been through that...but I've straightened out my life"....Like, a cross between a counsellor and youth worker type thing...' It sounded promising. James was adamant he wouldn't be reincarcerated: 'There's no way that I'll reoffend.' Yes, he admitted, he would certainly 'hang around' with his old mates. But he wouldn't get drawn into crime. And yet James also remarked that he trusted no one and that, to date, he lacked any kind of role model for actioning desistance. Asked where he saw himself five years hence, he commented that he wanted to own a car, have a job, and become a father. It sounded relatively straightforward.

He lasted a month. It came down to the struggle over suitable accommodation. 'My main issue [is] with my placements – placements, placements, placements, always placement,' he would say. The public and emergency housing waiting lists were (are) extensive. James would be forced, therefore, to agree to reside at his mother's or his auntie's as a condition of release. But this was a less than ideal situation. James hadn't seen his family in years let alone lived with them. It was, for him, like entering some foreign land:

> I: What else went wrong? [You mentioned] [t]hey sent you back to people that you don't really have any ties with.
> P: Exactly.... Well my auntie, I love my auntie, I've always loved my auntie, but the thing is... when you haven't lived with your family for ten years... it's uncomfortable to go straight back in and have that parent[al] authority figure over you when you haven't had it for so long.... It's very uncomfortable.... You walk in... and they still expect you to live by the same rules that you did when you were 12 years old... [The irony is that they now expect me to live in the same town the police and courts banned me from] until I was 18...
> I: You got banned from the whole of [name of town]?
> P: The whole of [name of town], yes.
> I: And that's your family's area...?
> P: That's my Dad's side of the family, you know what I mean. I've got my Dad lives there, my grandparents, my great grandparents, my aunties, my uncle.
> I: So they cut you off from your family and then expect you now to....
> P: Eight years later to go back there, straight into there like nothing's happened.... Like, I went back in there,... I love my family – but I don't relate to them any more,... I don't feel comfortable with them any more.

James spoke during interview about not being able to adjust to a 'calm' home environment. It was anathema to him. This fact was never understood by authorities – that you can't just expect a young man or his family to pick up where they left off nearly a decade ago: 'My memories of my mother is when she lived with my Dad and... [then] getting divorced and... smashing houses and stuff.... So to come into a house that's calm and perfect... [well], that's not the mother I know.... I could probably go back into her house where my Mum and Dad are arguing and at each other's throats.... I could walk into [a] house like that and feel more comfortable.' James told his liaison worker time and again he didn't want to be released to his family. He wanted to go to a friend's place. They were happy to have him, but there was someone residing there who was on bail. The system wouldn't allow it. It was too 'risky'. The inevitable occurred. James got out but refused to reside at the stipulated address – an immediate breach of his conditions. A warrant was issued for his arrest. He lasted four weeks. And as it turned out, he stayed with his preferred family (the young man bailed there had in any case been returned to prison). He was doing fine. The police finally picked him up when he got into an altercation over a stolen cigarette lighter. Compared with ram-raiding and evading police at high speed, James couldn't understand the fuss. He thought he was making progress. Still, the magistrate gave him another two months in lock-up. He was feeling confident in the weeks prior to release. For the first time he was getting out with 'no strings attached'. His singular commitment was, again, to not be tempted by the criminal offerings of mates. He would associate with them, but he would not do crime with them.

Regrettably, if somewhat predictably, James was wrong about being able to hang with, but resist, the temptations of mates: 'It comes down to willpower for me not to want to hop in a stolen car when someone pulls up out the front... and goes: "Look at this one"... It comes down to willpower for me. I don't want to go to [the adult] system... I've got strong willpower [but] the only weak thing... is my hang-ups about my mates.' His fingerprints on a stolen vehicle quickly landed him back behind bars. After several months James was again released and took up residence with his girlfriend (Mia). He'd known her since he was 13 – she knew all about his trials and tribulations. She fell pregnant. Problems with 'neighbours from hell' saw James try to kick in their door. Adding further pressure to the situation was the omnipresent problem of old ties:

> I moved to [name of rural town] into [my girlfriend's] house... and then all my old crowd comes around that I haven't seen [for years].... [T]his was the crowd... I had to get away [from] when I moved to Adelaide.... [Anyway], I caught up with all of them and [Mia] was a bit snooty and saying, 'Oh, you've got to change all this'.... And I'm telling her I'm not going to sell out my mates.... I kicked a stink at home and then... I've gone out and fucking walked the streets and then I got seen trying to break into a car that happened to be owned by a police officer.

Looking back, James sympathized with Mia. He could see, only in retrospect, that she was right:

> I: At the time of that argument, did [Mia] know she was pregnant?...
> P: Oh, yeah.

I: So do you think she was worried about [your] behaviour... because of the baby?

P: Of course.... She's already got a kid to someone else.... That's what she was thinking [about],... her family and support[ing us] financially and mentally and just, you know, settling down.... She was just thinking about the future.... And honestly, I understand that.... [But] in the heat of the moment I just didn't care.

He again committed to doing better – to being, in particular, a good father:

When I get out of here my main thing is to try and get back with [Mia] and... be a father... be there with my kids.... Like, take my kid to kick a footy and stuff and just take them to the park... I think about it all the time.... When I think about that stuff, [it] makes me not want to be in the shit. [It] makes me think, 'Why do I do stupid shit?'

There were signs, in other words, he was trying to change: 'Now I can talk things out and walk away from problems... I don't have to pull my hair out and [do] bad things [and] hurt other people... I was like that when I was younger... I'm not like that any more... You grow out of it...' He spoke of being positive about the future: 'I'm hopeful... I'm not even worried about reoffending because I don't have the urge for stealing cars any more.' After another six months in prison, James was released on parole. Within ten days he was back in custody and serving another nine months. He was 19 and knew at least '50 per cent of the [people in] gaol'. The circumstances leading to his arrest are worth citing at length:

P: I got out for 10 days and on that 10th day I caught up with an old mate of mine that I hadn't seen for a while.... We caught up, had a few to drink and we decided we were going to meet some girls [in the northern area of town].... I was walking across the main road with a bottle of Jim Beam in each hand and a police officer drove past. The friend that I was with didn't want to stick around so he took off running. I had no need to run... but I ran anyway.... The cops caught up pretty quick.... So I've stopped [and I] get searched. [They] find a screwdriver on me.... Now, I'm on parole.... [T]wo days earlier

I was due to do an Anger Management course and never
showed up... so I just presumed that I was in trouble with
parole.... [They] check up [on things but] no warrant was on
me.... So they arrested me for carrying an offensive weapon,
the screwdriver.... They charged me... and took me to [the]
cop shop.... [They] put me in the cells for a couple of hours,
got me out, and give me bail.... [But] it was 11.30 at night
[and I] didn't know where I was. [I] didn't know how to get
home. Right?... So I said, 'Can you keep me in the cells for
the night... and I'll catch a bus when the buses start up
again in the morning?'... And [the cops] said, 'If you wait
till the morning there's a different sergeant... [and that]
sergeant might not give you bail'. So straight away I thought,
'Fuck that', and got pushed out the door at 11.30 at night.
No buses.... I had $40 of money, right? I live [way down
south of the city... so $40 ain't going to get me back down
[home].... I was just stuffed, so I started walking. Walking and
walking and walking and literally all I had on me was nothing
but $40 and [some] ID... Just coincidently I walked down the
road onto another main road... and a car flies past, you know,
pulls over [at a petrol station].... The car's got all my mates in
it and I... hop in the car.... Anyway, [we] pull out of this
[petrol station] and straight away [the] cops [are onto us and
we're in a] high-speed chase.

I: Straight away?
P: Straight away.
I: Do you think they were pursuing that car anyway or they just
happened to see it, then they...
P: No, no, no, just happened to see it. Just happened to see it. As
we pulled out they were coming out of that street and we
pulled out right in front of them.
I: So... why is that?
P: ... You see a Commodore full of black kids, man, the cops are
going to pull it over.... [T]he car [was] full of black kids... with
all hats sideways.... Of course the police are going to pull them
over.... So we've pulled out in front of them [and] straight
away they chased us – went about two or three suburbs
[and] wrapped around a frigging stobie pole [a metal and
concrete pole supporting electricity wires] exactly where I was
sitting.... I ended up with black eyes... [and a] broke[n] nose.
[I got] arrested.... [O]bviously these boys, before

> I hopped in, had been doing earlier stuff... [house]breaks, particularly.... Now, I get put in the gutter, handcuffed... then they took me back to [the same] cop shop, worked out that I was out for... about 40 minutes or so.... I [then got] nine months.

He was released on parole to a share house. Within a day the guy who managed the place took a dislike to James, and so James took off. Reluctantly, he took up lodgings with his auntie but managed, at least, to find some labouring work – cash-in-hand. He 'saved about $1500' but then the work stopped. James spoke of becoming bored. But instead of doing what he normally did – steal a car – he went and bought one. Within four days he was pulled over by police for doing '97km' per hour in an 80 zone. He was of course unlicensed at the time but he was proud of himself for 'pulling over straight away'. And he was proud the car was his. It was a legitimately registered vehicle (of sorts). Back at the police station, James informs the duty sergeant he's on parole. The car is impounded but he makes bail. It was up to his parole officer whether he would be breached and sent back to prison. Meanwhile, James bought another car that promptly 'blew up' within two days of driving it. With his remaining funds, he managed to buy a third vehicle which he described as a 'Very beautiful car. It was only 650 bucks [dollars] but it wasn't registered.... But I couldn't help myself. Beautiful sound system'. James was very careful to stress he hadn't done any crime even though he'd been out for six weeks. In his mind, that was a significant achievement. But he was flat broke. His solution was to steal 'a couple thousand dollars worth' of cigarettes and sell them at a profit. So, he had a car, he had money, he had his smokes. But again he got pulled over by the police. James knew the gig was up. Nonetheless, he gave them a false name. While the police ran the name, James fled on foot. He was caught, arrested, but made bail. Immediately on leaving the courthouse, the police rearrested him. They'd matched his face to security camera vision taken from where the cigarettes were stolen. This time he didn't make bail. Instead, he got a year on the bottom (that is, non-parole period) with close to three on top (that is, head sentence) for breaching parole, driving while disqualified, exceeding the speed limit and providing a false name and address. He knew that the sentence for the cigarette cache (aggravated serious criminal trespass) would likely result in additional time. And it did. He was 22 years of age when he next walked out of prison. James' son was nearly three years old – roughly equivalent in age to the time his father had been incarcerated.

At 20, and from the confines of prison, James was still talking about his passion for cars. The link between cars and freedom was foremost in his mind: 'It's not the speeding, it's not the stealing it, it's the freedom of sitting in a car going, "I can go anywhere I want right now". You know, "I don't have to worry about this or worry about that",... I can just... go anywhere I want now.' James lacked the personal mobility he needed to break free from the small country town he grew up in and from the city that kept pulling him into its vices. But he knew cars were only the symbol of deeper problems. As he commented:

> I [remember once]... walking down the street to go back to Mum's house and I just turned away... and walked down to the beach... and I end up... steal[ing] a car.... I've only been [out of prison for] 12 hours and I'm driving [a stolen car] and that's when I've clicked and I've realised, 'Fuck, I feel more comfortable getting chased by the cops in a car than sitting at home with my own family'... That's when I realized... 'Fuck man, I've got a real problem'. I feel [more] comfortable... in a dangerous situation than sitting at home... with all my family.

In the same interview, James spoke passionately and emotionally about wanting to connect with his son upon release. It constantly occupied his mind. He played the scene of meeting him over and over in his head:

> I think about the day I get out and all I can think of is getting picked up... and... walking in... and approaching my son for the very first time and like sitting down at his eye level, sitting down and saying, asking, 'Do you know who I am?'... For the last two years I've been thinking about what I'm going to say, how I'm going to say it....

This weighed heavily on James's mind. The longer stretch in prison was also helping him to think about the 'type' of person he was or wanted to be. Like Charlie, he considered himself to be an 'ethical offender':

> I was explaining to a couple of [the other prisoners], I said, 'Do you know what?... I've never done a house-break before. I've never laid a hand on a woman before. I've never stolen a lady's purse before. You know, I'm a car thief. But I would never steal a car with a baby seat in it.... And they've turned around and said to me,... 'I don't think you should be a crim.... You got too much, errr, morals, you've got too

much conscience, you shouldn't be a crim'.... And I think to myself, 'Yeah they're right'.

He was talking again at this time of his 'dream job' of being a youth worker, but knew he had to stay out of trouble for a long time to have any hope of becoming one. In the interim, he was happy to work on building sites or as a 'storeman'. He'd also read the transcripts from his previous interviews with us. What struck James was the way he had 'matured': 'I think about stuff before I say it.' He looked back on his days of high-speed pursuits as 'just fucking stupid'. And whereas he once considered the constant phone calls from his liaison officer as overbearing and intrusive ('this cunt's constantly ringing me'), James now had come to the view that he was 'the perfect youth worker' – just looking out for him. His attitude was changing but he was on edge about whether he'd make parole – potentially only a couple of months away.

James made parole, but he breached within several weeks due to returning a dirty urine test and for not showing up to his assigned community corrections office. He knew the cannabis in his system would be detected and got 'a bit paranoid'. He served a short period in prison and was then again paroled. It didn't get off to the best of starts. James had to again accept being paroled to his auntie. This was not ideal for all the reasons previously remarked upon. But he wanted to get out so he accepted the condition. His auntie, however, was going away on holiday on the very day he was due for release. James informed the authorities of this saying he needed to be discharged in time to reach his stipulated address prior to his auntie leaving for her holiday. They didn't complete the paperwork in time. By the time he got to the house, it was locked. He couldn't get in. James went to a friend's house and subsequently to the place where his new girlfriend was living. The police had already called at his auntie's house and had issued a warrant for his arrest ('failure to reside...'). James was spotted randomly by the police drinking from a Coke bottle. The police assumed it contained alcohol and wanted to breathalyze him. It didn't contain alcohol, but James fled as he knew he was not residing at the stipulated place of residence. He ran through six different yards and when the police caught him they charged with him with six counts of being unlawfully on premises. They also, as it turned out, had vision of him stealing a bottle of alcohol. That was a further count and it meant, potentially, at least another 18 months in prison. All this occurred just as he met his new girlfriend. Tess, in James' eyes, was all he could ever have hoped for.

> She does things for me.... She washes my clothes, she feeds me,... she comes in and says, 'Oh, have a shave', you know. I've never really had a Mum.... Well, she does everything for me.... Don't get me wrong, I'm not a slack person.... She said the best thing about me is when something has to be done I never have to be asked to do it. I see the dishes I do them.... Like, I haven't been with her for that long... but that whole time I was with her I had clean clothes, I was always fed.... She's got two kids of her own, she's an excellent mother, so it's somewhere I can take my son... [and] the mother of my son [can] feel comfortable to let my son go there.... [Mia's] accepted her as a good mother and a safe place for my son to go to.

James described how Tess was fundamentally different to his previous girlfriends, who he said were caught in the midst of a 'Bonnie and Clyde' lifestyle. He felt – and feels to this day – that he has to do all within his power to make things right with Tess:

> This one is... a totally different situation.... She fell in love with me for who I am.... Whatever I do in my life she loves me.... But that doesn't mean she doesn't want me to change.... She said this to me, 'I want you to change. I want you to become a part of my kids' lives'.... I've done a lot of time in gaol [but] even though I've only been in this one week, she's made more of an effort to stick by me than any other girl in my life.... She's made more effort in this one week and in the last few months... than bloody my mother did in [the last] fucking 12 years of my life.

The trope of ethical offender helped James cope with his situation – he had to believe he was different to others around him: 'I like to pride myself on being a reasonable, a decent criminal... I've never broken into someone's house before, I've never hit a girl in my life, I would never stick a gun in a lady's face.' He hoped this would count for something because his fate, at 23, was again in the hands of the Parole Board.

He made parole. But this time he got out to home detention (complete with electronic bracelet) on the Drug Court program. James had long ago developed a dependency on methadone – it was given to him years back as a substitute for the morphine-based medication he was taking for an old injury sustained during a car accident. He couldn't sleep without methadone. But it made him drowsy during waking hours. So on the Drug Court program he signed up for Suboxone – an opiate substitute that produced few if any side-effects for him. James specifically requested to be on the program to try and give himself the maximum chance of staying out. '[Last time] I was out I was on the run from parole [and] met a real good woman,' he said. He was doing it for Tess as much as, if not more than, for himself. For the first time James was able to meet up in the community for interview. It was a good moment. The major problem was that he had to reside in Drug Court housing. This was located in the middle of a run-down suburb on a main road and it meant having to be in a block of units with like persons – some of whom were not as committed to changing their behaviour as James. He wanted to live with Tess. But he was refused that privilege. The travel time between his Drug Court housing and Tess's place was at least an hour and a half. Still, he was committed. For the first time James felt he had something of importance to lose if he mucked up: 'I've got a lot more to lose this time.... I'm getting very close to my kid. I've got two stepsons that love me heaps.... I've got a missus that does everything for me, looks after me,... and I've never really had that before.... She's the reason I don't want to go back to gaol.' That's what he reflected on when thoughts of giving up threatened to overwhelm.

The program was strict: no leave passes from home except to report into the city three times to his Drug Court officer; three urine tests per week; no searching for work until granted 'Phase 2' status (and even then only permitted to be away from the house from 9am until 4pm); participation in various courses (particularly, MRT or moral recognition therapy). Although he had some trouble managing his curfew, even the magistrate acknowledged James's early progress: 'She goes, "I was looking at your history.... This is the best you've done. Keep your good work up".' That was very high praise in James' eyes. It kept him motivated. He'd been in the community for about ten weeks – his longest 'survival' period in years. James' biggest stress was juggling the program and his commitment to family: 'You've got to come into this program putting it first and that's the hardest thing.... I want to put my missus and kids first.' After paying rent, he was living on a government benefit of just over $200 per fortnight. Cigarettes and bus tickets reduced that to about $150. He had few clothes (we ended up sourcing some extra jeans, shorts and underwear for him). There were stresses. But in spite of these, James remarked, 'I've never felt so confident about not going back to gaol'. He was careful to qualify this statement with the fact he knows 'anything can happen'. James also revealed he had debts totalling about $120,000 stemming from an accident he had in his juvenile years. He hit a police car, and the combined costs of fixing the car and the medical bills of the occupants were sheeted home to him. There was little hope of him ever paying it off. But if he was fortunate enough to ever be gainfully employed, a good portion of his income would go to settling this debt.

James also spoke of the pains of re-entry. He repeatedly used the word 'uncomfortable' to describe how he felt. Negotiating public transport – a must for someone whose driver's licence has been indefinitely cancelled – proved particularly challenging:

> I'm just uncomfortable.... Like, I must look like a hoodlum when I get on the bus because I go straight to the back, sit at the back of the bus. But it's got nothing to do with me wanting to just go to the back of the bus and look cool. It's – I feel uncomfortable sitting in the middle with people behind me.... If you're in front of me, no worries. But I feel funny with people sitting behind me.

This is why he asked Tess to accompany him everywhere he went. He just didn't know how to act.

> I couldn't even read a bus timetable when I got out ten weeks ago.... It was confusing. I couldn't read the dole [social security] form. Like, it would ask me something as small as, 'What's your Tax File Number?' I know what that question means, right, but that overwhelms me so much. I've never had a Tax File Number before. Am I supposed to have a Tax File Number?... Just something small like that [can make] you start sweating.

James's issues around social dysfunction clearly echo those of Chris. However, James had someone to help him keep his nerve. And he was, at least, not in prison (although that's not say he didn't feel himself very heavily constrained and overburdened with obligations). He spoke of wanting to work – of getting his 'white card' – a piece of paper that says to prospective employers he's competent to work in a particular industry. He wanted to earn money to 'contribute financially to my kids'. But James knew the chances of him succeeding were slim. He, did, however, believe something in him was changing for the better:

> I: At this stage in your life... how do you think about yourself? Do you think of yourself as an ex-offender?...
> P: Do you know what?... I've always thought of myself [as] unique, different.... If I'm... standing at the [Drug] Court... I feel like an ex-con that's trying to change.... If I'm

> with my missus and kids, ... I feel like a father ... like someone who's contributed something.... I feel better at home with the kids doing the dishes then I do standing at the courthouse.

Five months later our next interview took place behind bars. James had been remanded back into custody for an apparent 'relapse' (two months earlier he was sent back to custody for two days for returning too many dirty urine tests and breaching his curfew too often). The 'cause' of his current setback was twofold. First, he spoke extensively about never really being able to get used to being 'out'. More particularly, the 'success' of his relationship with Tess was in fact putting immense pressure on him – a self-imposed pressure *not* to mess things up:

> Another big difficulty I found was I've never had a real relationship in my life before.... The only relationships I've had is with my mates and in gaol. I've never had a real intimate relationship....I [went] from gaol... [to] a home D situation straight into [my girlfriend's] house.... [But] I'd never experienced a relationship. I'd never experienced that give and take, that trust, [or] the normal things that have got nothing to do with Drug Court but [have to do with] living with your partner.... I've never experienced that before.

But the main issue related to the stress of trying to manage his curfew in the context of trying to juggle various courses, the collection of his medication, and visits to Tess and the children. James told of events in the following way:

> I've been on something called buprenorphine or the Suboxone program and it's something that's really worked for me. It doesn't make me drowsy, ... [and] it doesn't make me think about drugs.... [I]t's something that really helps me.... I was given time on my home D to go do my urine [tests], my courses and time to also pick up my dose from wherever I was picking it up from – chemist, the doctor's, whatever. Well sometimes because of me... not having enough time ... to go down and get my dose, I used to keep an extra bit of my dose in my wallet. So some of my prescription medication, right, I'd get a 'take-away' once a week. Well, I'd only take half of that and put [the other] half... away for that day that I couldn't make it. I had some of this stuff in my wallet [and] I hopped off the train one day in the city.... [A] police officer with a sniffer dog has grabbed me.... [The police] searched me. [They] found no illegal drugs but they found

some of this Suboxone.... [T]hey've rung up my doctor... and [he said], 'No [he's] not supposed to have it on [him]' – because that's my take-away dose and I'm supposed to take the rest. To cut a long story short, the Drug Dependency Unit has removed me off the Suboxone program and put me on the methadone program.

This 'medical-punitive' decision proved to be a pivotal moment:

Now, methadone affects me totally different. It makes me feel high.... It makes me feel as if I've had heroin. I go on the nod. I fall asleep at bus stops and on buses and I felt on the nod like a heroin junkie. And I was very... aware that I looked like it too. So I was very self-conscious about it and very stupidly it played on my mind so much that I thought I would try to go cold turkey off these opiates. And the only way I thought of doing it was locking myself in a room... at Tess's house.... And if it wasn't for [her] I probably would have done something a lot more silly than I did do. But admittedly I should have gone in and spoke to my Drug Court supervisor about this and said, 'I can't handle the methadone; I need to come off it'. Well, I didn't do that. Instead, off my own back, [I went] and locked myself in my room and because of that I'm crook in bed.

From here, things really started to deteriorate:

I haven't gone in for two of my piss tests... and it's got to the point where I was physically sick and in pain... to the point where it was one of the worst experiences of my life.... [I]t felt like my heart was jumping out of my chest. I was constantly crying [for] about 48 hours. Just crying and crying... methadone's so much stronger than the buprenorphine and it's so much stronger than... heroin.... [C]oming off it just nearly half killed me. Well, it's got to the point where I couldn't handle it anymore and I've just snapped and gone to get [some] drugs or something to make me feel better. I've gone and got drugs and because I've got these drugs I've kind of over-reacted.

It was too late to pull back. Things spiralled down even further:

At that time... I should have come in and talked to my Drug Court supervisor and asked for help there but instead I've panicked and gone, 'Oh I'm going to run away'. And so I did. I ran away for

24 hours because I had already missed two piss tests and then didn't return home one night. 'Bang' – a warrant's been put out for my arrest. Well the next day...I suddenly feel better. But then I find myself sitting alone in the middle of [one of the most deprived suburbs in Adelaide] with no one to support me. No one. I'm thinking to myself, 'Oh I'm stuffed now. I've got a home D bracelet on my ankle I can't go home and I've got no support, [Tess is] going to leave me...' And it wasn't until the next day that she rang me up and she said, 'I don't care, just come home', and I said, 'I can't come home. If I come home my Home D bracelet will [get] pick[ed] up and they'll come arrest me'. So I've removed my home D bracelet, gone home, spoken to [my girlfriend] and she's said, 'I don't care, I'll support you no matter what'.

He and Tess tried desperately to salvage the situation:

[W]e decided that we'd go down to my doctor's [and] tell them that I tried to go cold turkey off my methadone – that I shouldn't have done that, and that I need to be put back on methadone but on a lower dose that doesn't make me feel drowsy. And then we'll talk about handing myself in. And that was the plan – go down and see my doctor, get help with my drug issue, and then hand myself in and explain all this to the courts. Well, I've gone down to the doctor's, I'm at the doctor's surgery, I've got help, they've lowered my dose, given me a dose, [and] as I've left [the doctor's], the police are out the front waiting for me to arrest me. And I've been in here ever since.

After the interview had finished, James kept talking. In fact, he moved seamlessly into a longer and deeper explanation as to why he relapsed. With his consent, the tape was switched back on. It turns out things came to a head on a particular night just prior to trying to go cold turkey. His sister had suffered a cardiac arrest. She was pregnant and doctors had missed the fact that her waters had broken and that she had been carrying the baby in a dry womb for a fortnight. She went into cardiac arrest. The baby was born with brain damage and died after just 48 hours on life support. James was distraught. He was also under curfew at his drug house and trying (unbeknown to authorities) to look after his four-year-old son who'd been dropped off there by his ex-girlfriend so she could spend time with his sister (they were close friends). James was at that time being offered methamphetamines by another drug house resident. He resisted. But the whole thing took a massive toll on James.

He felt physically and mentally spent. That's why he tried to make his Suboxone go the extra yard – to stay on track. And that's why the sniffer dogs got him. In a few days he'd find out whether he'd be kicked out of the Drug Court program and sent back to prison:

> If I don't get out this Monday, right, I get sentenced. Now, ... I used to be very institutionalized... and I still am a bit institutionalized. But I don't think... I could survive any more gaol.... This is the crossroads in my life and if I don't get this, everything that's good [that has] happened in the last six months is going to go down the drain.

James believed he had significantly changed in the roughly six months he was out of prison – the longest time he had spent in the community since he was 13. Asked what mattered to him most during that period he commented:

> Feeling loved.... Not just from my girlfriend but from my two stepchildren and my biological son.... In the last six months... just out of nowhere I remember I'm not in gaol any more... I think to myself, 'Oh my God people love me ...' [T]here's things I've felt now that I've never felt before in my life.... I used to have this strong exterior and I would never cry and all that stuff.... [Well], I've cried more in the last six months than I have in the last ten years.... I've cried for happiness, for anger, for being scared.... I believe that I've changed that much... I'm not a different person, I'm still the same person. But I feel as if I'm a different person.

The court gave him another chance. He was out for less than a month. This time, the scale of the offending would mean a much longer stint in prison. Over a three-hour period James and his co-offender were chased by police for nearly 500km. Multiple cars were used and dumped along the way. Drivers were pulled from their vehicles. Police helicopters, road spikes, and all manner of road blocks were set up and evaded. Speeds approached and sometimes exceeded 200km per hour. Public safety was endangered in major fashion. Eventually, nearing the outskirts of the city, they were finally caught. James said he 'copped a pretty good hiding' from the police. He said he was 'pissing and shitting blood for two weeks' and was still 'poohing blood' at the time we interviewed him. Operation Mandrake police officers told him that the Commissioner of Police had made a special call to the prison to see that he was safely locked up. Every prisoner wanted to hear the details of the chase from

James. He wanted none of it, and regretted his actions from the get go: 'I nearly died fucking four or five times that day... I was overtaking cars in the emergency lane at 200 [km per hour] for God's sake.' He said he once would have loved the fame, but that now it just made him 'depressed'. The phone call to Tess was the hardest call he ever made:

> Today I got on the phone and just broke down and started crying.... It's the dumbest thing I've done in my life ... and I'm at that point where I'm over gaol and I don't want to be in gaol and I want to change.... But I'm at that point in my life where I'm just about to serve my longest sentence ever.

To her great credit, Tess has stood by him. She knew he had come along way even if others could not see that. James remarked that life was going really well prior to that fateful day:

> I was doing excellent. I never had a thought of doing crime. I was going everywhere and if I ever left the house with Tess or I took one of my boys... [it would all be approved by] my home D passes. [Me and] one of my boys were cruising the buses together [and we'd sometimes have] half an hour left at the end of the pass. [So] we'd go to the park for a little while and... catch a taxi down to McDonalds and play in the playground and have a 30 cent [ice-cream] cone.... Even though I was only out for four weeks and I was doing so well.

In the month leading up to the chase, however, James and Tess were arguing more than usual. It came with the territory of still being under the remit of correctional services, of trying to raise kids, trying to get by on a meagre income. James also learned that Mia (his ex-girlfriend) was going to try and stop him having access to his son. Things, in a sense, were on the edge. Here's what happened in the hours immediately prior to the chase:

> [A mate] turned up... and I hadn't seen him for a while and he was already on the run for something minor. He was driving unlicensed.... He's a person, a bit younger than me, but he's been through the same shit, in and out since he was a kid. And he was on the run for bloody, you know, [driving] unlicensed [and] within a couple of months he would have handed himself in. He was planning to hand himself in the next day and so I told him to bring his missus around and his kid around and spend the night with his kid and he insisted, 'Nah, nah, we're drinking, we'll get in an argument'.

Well, I insisted, 'Nah' you know, trying to get him to do the right thing... 'Spend a bit of time with your kid before you go'. Well, he comes around, his missus comes around, they start arguing. Next minute my missus and I start arguing and me and him are running off down the street, you know, like fucking little kids.

James said there was no plan to do anything major. At most he was going to run away for a few days, 'have a break', 'talk to [Tess] over the phone', come back, hand himself in, and serve two or three months in prison for his trouble. Then he would get out, and try and start again. It didn't happen like that. They stole a car to get as far away as possible. They drove through the night. By sunup, James was very much regretting his actions and was on the phone to Tess asking what he should do. She pleaded with him to return. He said he would. Within minutes, he and his co-offender stole another car in preparation for the journey back to Adelaide. But the police saw the vehicle and the pursuit commenced. As mentioned, it lasted for around three hours. At interview, James was forthright in taking full responsibility for his actions. He blamed neither his co-offender nor Tess. He did, though, acknowledge the convergence of factors. In particular, he noted his long-term inability to deal with conflict – his first tactic had always been to run from a fight rather than to reason things through:

> I blame no one but myself.... But in reality... take one of... four things out [of the situation leading up to the chase] and it wouldn't have happened. Like the four, five things together – the drink, him being there, him arguing with my missus, me arguing with my missus, then me getting to the point, that tiny point just before I turn violent – because that's when I run away every time. I've got five or six sisters and I've never hit a girl in my life. And I never even had thoughts of hitting a girl until I've been with Tess, and then... during an argument I start getting these violent thoughts of back-hitting her across a room.... Now that's the point I run away every time – just before I feel I'm going to hurt her... [So] I think [there were] four or five contributing factors. Take one out, it wouldn't have bloody probably happened.... Take the drink out or take my mate out or... take one thing out, I don't think it would have happened. But them contributing factors together just fucked me up.

It's impossible to know the precise dynamics of the household at the time. But it seemed as if something was going to give. And what gave way was James's resolve. He couldn't keep it together any longer. As he aptly put it, '[Things] built up [and] built up and at the time I thought, "Fuck it, I give up", you know what I mean? "I give up".' In his teens, James was asked what it would take for him not to do crime. His answer was: 'Incentive'. In other words, some tangible reward for good behaviour rather than the prospect of punishment for wrongdoing. For James, the thing he always yearned for was always mobility – something which had been put out of reach by his prolific involvement in auto theft:

> I: If... someone had said to you, [when you were younger], 'Here's a $20,000 [car], it's yours'...
> P: I wouldn't steal a car ever again. Never.
> I: You're quick to say that...
> P: Yeah, I'd never – never steal a car again... I would never steal a car again. I would keep that [car and] I'd count my fortune. I'd be that happy.

Whether James would have been true to his word, we cannot say. The 'hook for change' cannot be reduced to possession of a car any more than it can be equated to getting a job, or a house or suchlike. But compared with the millions of dollars spent trying to police and shut down his behaviour, the conditional 'gifting' of his driver's licence and own car might well have been worth the 'risk'. He'll be in his 30s before he can apply for parole.

Chris

Chris is in his mid-twenties. He has spent well over ten years in custody in juvenile and adult institutions. His longest period in the community can be measured in just a matter of months. Indeed, he has lived less than five per cent of his adult life out of lock-up. As a very young boy, he was diagnosed with ADHD and treated for such. But Chris's mother stopped the medication after a few years because she thought it was inflaming his problems. From that point on, his behaviour became unmanageable. His father contends that Chris's mother was in fact diverting his medication in order to supplement her own long and difficult battle with drugs. Things came to a head when he returned home from work to find her 'teaching' Chris's brother (aged under ten at the time) how to inject heroin. Chris's father walked out on the whole family that very day (it's something he regrets deeply and yet simultaneously holds was his only option). At age eight, Chris's uncle (who 'did time for murder') took him along on one of his many criminal jaunts. His usual accomplice was 'off-line' so he used Chris to help him steal goods from a sports store. He told Chris there's no need to buy something 'when you can just take it'.

Chris received his first detention order at age 11. He was then placed in a series of foster homes – always running away to try and connect with his birth family – a family that had literally fallen apart through drugs, alcohol, violence and an inability to comprehend what conventional parenthood could or should look like. At 12 Chris did several months for burglary break and enter and motor vehicle theft. Around this age, he witnessed his 'girlfriend' get hit and killed by a truck. She was running away from Chris after an argument they had. He dropped permanently out of school around Year 8 or 9 (he'd seen his older brother 'wagging'[2] and thought it was 'cool'). Chris also describes how he was expelled for stealing. Either way, educationally, he didn't go much past primary school. At 13 Chris witnessed his uncle sexually abuse his sister. His efforts to convince his parents of the truth of this fell on deaf ears. Chris was also sexually abused by his uncle – something that he has told only a handful of people and which took him seven years to volunteer to us during interview. Around the time of the abuse, his mother moved interstate and left him to the care of his auntie who died shortly thereafter. Chris set out to track one or both of his parents down. He found them but was promptly rejected by them (again).

In his mid-teens Chris made his way to South Australia. He was by this time raising himself – surviving through whatever means he could. Along with his brother, he stole cars and committed robberies to eat but also to fund their methamphetamine habits. The drugs made Chris's offending worse: '[W]hen I'm on speed I have the guts to do anything and I do it,' he remarked. In 'broad daylight' it became routine for him to 'point[ ] a gun [at someone's] throat' to get money. Guns were 'easy to get... because [his] brother already had one'. They also stole guns and ammunition from business premises to ensure they were sufficiently armed. Chris said he was doing all this 'because Mum and Dad didn't give a stuff about me'. The hankering to reassemble the family unit was a theme that would recur throughout most of his interviews: 'I want to go back to when I was about... eight or nine years old... I want to start from back there,' he would say. By the time he was about 16 he was serving time for a home invasion and associated offences. The judge reduced his sentence as the victim testified that Chris had been the one to help nurse her stab wounds until paramedics arrived – wounds inflicted on her by Chris's co-offender. At that time, Chris 'started realizing that crime isn't the way to go'. Still, he would end up offending the day he was released. He had $700 to his name and gave half to his mother (who he had, to an extent, patched things up with). He spent the remainder on alcohol and drugs. His addiction to ice led him to steal a car in order to travel to his dealer. After stealing petrol and running over the attendant, Chris was caught when his car careered out of control during a high-speed pursuit. He was sentenced to a further period of detention.

Around this time Chris learned that his mother was admitted to hospital as a result of injuries inflicted by his father and brother and that they had both been incarcerated for this. Chris was released from detention without conditions ('end of order'). He lasted one week before being locked up again. By then his brother was out of prison and again they started stealing cars and doing drugs. Like so many times previously, Chris was drinking to block out 'bad memories'. And like the times before, he was stealing cars because it was the only 'fun' he knew. On one occasion, to add to the sense of fun, Chris and his brother decided to torch (set fire to) the vehicles – except things went horribly wrong. Over the noise of flames and explosions, Chris's brother could not hear that he was trapped. He failed to realize that the heat had melted the clasp of Chris' seatbelt, rendering it unworkable. The belt itself was also starting to sear into his torso. After being rescued, Chris spent six days in a coma on life support and two weeks in hospital. His mum came to visit him and told Chris that his 'heart had stopped four times'. Chris tells how he woke up with '150 staples in my chest and 150 on my back and [another] 50 on my arms'. Apparently, even the arresting officers had tears in their eyes when they saw him.

Chris went from hospital directly to detention. This time, he got out with $150 in his pocket and was on morphine and speed within two days of release. 'As soon as I had drugs, I was fucked,' he said. He stole a car two days after that and was doing ram-raids and related offences to satisfy his desire for drugs and alcohol. He would swap alcohol and other stolen good for clothes. And he would offend to numb the pain of past events. Over a three-day period Chris estimates he was involved in 17 high-speed pursuits. He was caught and given further time in detention. By this point, lock-up was becoming his home. Chris said as much. '[W]hen I'm out I've got no one...So really in here is like a family to me....All the staff is like my family to me....Essentially, I'm coming back to my friends.'

Around 18 years of age, Chris was transferred to prison for assaulting training centre staff. He was eventually released, returned to custody and bailed all in the space of a few days. Around this time he got together with a new girlfriend (Marie) and she fell pregnant. They lived for a short time with her mother until she kicked them out over an undisclosed argument. She called Chris and Marie 'dogs' – about the worse insult she could throw at Chris. He tried to stab her but the weapon missed its mark. Marie's mother retaliated – not by attacking Chris – but by kicking her own pregnant daughter in the stomach. A neighbour tried to intervene but Chris told him in no uncertain terms to mind his own business (to 'fuck off'). Eventually Chris and Marie stole a car with the aim of heading far away from the sorrow and trauma defining their lives. But Chris lost control of the car on the outskirts of town and crashed, according to him, while doing about 190km per hour. The car was a twisted wreck. Chris says the front bumper was bent to the point of resting against the boot/trunk. With the engine resting on his legs, and the steering wheel pinned against his chest, both he and Marie were cut out by the jaws-of-life.[3] Marie lost the baby. Chris, in a most extraordinary act of desperation and denial, suggested that the baby's death must have been caused through the paramedics strapping Marie too tightly to the stretcher. He again spent time in intensive care. Chris and a visiting friend took this as an opportunity to self-administer (syphon off) the morphine meant to keep Chris's physical pain to a manageable level.

Chris transitioned from hospital to prison and said that the time inside would give him the chance to 'change my life'. He was yet to turn 19. He spoke at that stage of 'want[ing] to stick with my girl [so] she can be my wife and have [my] kids]'. Not long after committing to this, Chris punched Marie in the face for having the temerity to bring another male friend with her to visit him. 'I'm not your fucking mate,' Chris told the 'intruder'. He continued to berate him saying: 'Don't talk to me. Sit there like a dumb cunt'. Marie tried to make the peace saying that Chris shouldn't get so angry. She lost two of her teeth for her troubles – right there in the prison visits room. That evening Marie received a phone call from Chris asking if she was 'still thinking about [him]'. She maintained her rage for a while but eventually started up again as Chris's girl.

After several years he was paroled. This time, Chris lasted a month. And in that month he would perpetrate a wide range of serious offences. This would lead to him being remanded in custody for a period that far exceeded the average time served for most other prisoners (just over four years). Chris spoke of being strung out on ice and of having only 'two hours sleep' for the entire month of his release. During this time, Marie again fell pregnant. Upon learning that Chris was the father-to-be, Marie's father 'cut sick' on her. He 'punched her, choked her, [and] chucked her through [a] window[ ]' causing her to lose her unborn baby (the second such occurrence). Immediately following this, her father 'went and... hanged himself'. Marie, still in her teens, found his lifeless body. The sheer magnitude of the trauma she'd been through reignited her own history of self-harming behavior. Chris, feeling powerless to do anything, did the only thing he could do to illustrate his empathy for Marie's plight. He told her that whatever she did he would also do. '[I]f she kills herself,' Chris declared, 'I'll kill myself... If she cuts herself, I'll hurt myself... Because the way I look at it, if I lose her, I've lost everything.'[4] At that point, Chris felt 'disgusted' with himself saying, 'I hate myself for what I've done'.

Since that time, he has continued to plumb the depths of despair. This has been punctuated with the occasional silver lining – such as the commencement of a new relationship with a woman who, according to Chris, 'understands' who he is and whose children view Chris as a father figure. Chris also briefly re-established ties with his own father. However, just a few days after this *rapprochement*, his older brother – fresh out of prison – attempted to strangle their father to death. Apparently Chris's brother was heavily intoxicated – he'd drunk a slab of beer within hours of being released from a lengthy prison term – and took extreme umbrage at being told by his father to put his seatbelt on for the long trip home. Chris has sworn to take revenge against his brother. This kind of anger, mixed with all the other physical and psychic pain that infuses his life, defines most of his days in custody. His strategy for coping with his plight has been to slowly but surely cut loose from the few people who care about his welfare. It has become almost impossible for Chris to conceive of a future involving anything 'good'. Life, for him, has been a protracted waiting game with prison starting to play hard on his mind: 'I would rather be dead before I come back to gaol,' he said in his last interview. He told himself that any sentence with an expected time to serve of less than ten years would be 'a bonus'. On this count, he was right on the money. He'll be eligible for parole in 2019 – ten years nearly to the day since he was last admitted to custody. How, precisely, did things get to this point?

It would be easy to suggest that Chris's situation is the product of bad choices. If that is so, those choices have been heavily structured by places and contexts beyond his control. No one, for example, gets to choose their family. Chris is an archetypal example of someone who was 'parentified' from a very young age:

I: ... [L]ooking back, ... what was missing in [your] childhood? ...
P: Love. The family upbringing, you know. I didn't want to be brought up by myself.... I wanted to be brought up by my parents.

Chris, in short, raised himself. He was child *non grata*: 'Dad didn't recognize me... as his son. He treated me like a fucking idiot.' This meant Chris had to fend for himself in all situations. He was *made* to grow up well before his time. And he had to assume these responsibilities without effective or positive modelling. Chris's degree of social dysfunction is well illustrated by a comment made by an ex-girlfriend: 'I don't even think [Chris] understands the concept of having a baby. He didn't even know how babies were made. I had to tell him. That's how much he doesn't know anything...' Chris's parents also had very poor beginnings to their lives. Chris touched on the problem of intergenerational dysfunction, saying that 'Mum and Dad didn't have a family upbringing themselves. So they didn't know how to bring us kids up that good'. Years later, Chris's father confirmed this during an interview:

I: ... [Y]ou said you were in foster homes... for a while.
P: Yeah, since the age of two... until the age of 16 ... I was in and out of... kids' homes and foster parents' [homes]...
I: ... So by the time you became a parent yourself...
P: ... I didn't have parents to turn to, to find out, '[I]s this the right way or is that the right, the wrong way'... I had to wing it... I was 22 when I first met my mother.... And three days later she died... of cancer... My Dad, when I first got out [of] the [boys] home, my Dad hit me, knocked me out. When I came to, I said, 'What was that for?' He said, 'That's for coming home.'... I was 16.... And he turned around and said to me, 'I raised you better than that'.... And I said to him, I said – because he grabbed my chin and I knocked his hand away – and I said, 'You didn't bring me up'. I said, 'Welfare, child welfare brought me up'.
I: Can I ask, ... why, ... at two [years of age] were you put into a foster home? What was going on with your parents?
P: My Dad, he was an alcoholic.... [I've been told] by my sisters... that Dad used to come home and bash Mum. He used to bash her until every day she couldn't walk out of the house without a pair of sunglasses on. She always had black eyes.

Chris's mother – who works part-time in an abattoir – has battled her own demons all her life. When she separated from Chris's Dad, she took up with a man who dominated her physically and emotionally:

> [My former boyfriend] controlled me and I needed help. And I'm spewing now because I ended up walking out on him because he was bashing me and everything. Why couldn't I have done it to stick up for my own child?... As a mother [I've] let [my] son down, haven't [I]? Not being supportive of him. That's why I try to get my ass down to [the city to court or prison] to go and visit him.

Lacking the love and support of his parents, Chris found solace in drugs and in crime to fund his appetite for such. Everything he did was about trying to forget the past – to literally blot it out through a self-induced chemical haze. His drug of choice was, catastrophically, ice. But the cornerstone of his offending – its fundamental driving force – was unresolved shame and self-blame associated with the sexual abuse of his sister, and, more pertinently, the sexual violence done to him many years earlier. In interview, the pain of this situation was unmistakable. Chris understood, though, the consequences of this unresolved trauma. Specifically, it meant his pain would be repeatedly transferred to others through his prolific offending:

> My problem is... that I don't go for help because I'm ashamed of what happened... and I don't want to talk to people about it... Even to people I trust... I feel ashamed that it happened.... And that's why I do [crime]. And that's why I take drugs. Like when I drink and take drugs I lose the plot.... [F]or the first couple of hours I might feel good, you know. I'm real happy and then I just lose it.... [A]s much as I want to talk about it to Mum, she doesn't want to know about it... [because it] brings back [bad] memories.... And that's why I try not to talk about it.... Because it all starts bringing back memories about my sister.... I should have done something, but I didn't. I was young back then and I couldn't do nothing...

Chris had to reach back nearly 20 years to recall a time when there seemed to be a modicum of hope that his family might stay together. Here, he spoke of the way one youth worker managed to connect meaningfully with their problems:

I: ... Did [any government agency or person] ever offer any help?...
P: Yeah, [Tony Smith]... He was the best one we ever had ... He would help me out, he would help Mum and Dad, everybody out, the whole family... [He knew about the sexual abuse and] he was real focused on me and [my sister]. He would take me and [her] out. We'd go to the beach, go somewhere, you know.... [H]e'd do that for a week and then the next week he'd do the whole family. And then another week he'd [work with] me and [my brother] and then me and [my other brother] and then me and Mum and me and Dad.... Because back then we were just a family torn apart.... But for them first five years that he was with us, it was like back to normal again, like a happy family... And [then] ever since he wasn't around...

When Tony was transferred to another region, things fell apart. The family literally disintegrated. This set in train a yearning that Chris carries to this day. He wanted to be normal – to do what other people (children) do. He didn't *choose* to do crime. He wanted, in his words, to 'blend' into the community, not stand out for all the wrong reasons:

I: [I]f you could change any two things about your life so far, what would that be, and why?
P: Have a family.... Be like... other people out there.... Like, blend in [with] other people out there, you know, like that bloody go to school, doesn't smoke, doesn't drink, you know, doesn't do crime or nothing.

Chris's life was not going to be 'normal'. With well over four years spent in juvenile facilities between the ages of 10 and 18, he was fast becoming good at living in lock-up and very poor at living in the community. In his late teens his offending made the local news. By his early twenties, his crimes were on the front page of the newspaper and grainy images of him appeared on TV news and police websites. The effects of spending so much time in custody had indelibly left its mark on Chris. He was institutionalized. And he knew it. He said as much in interviews given at 21 and 22 years of age:

I hate to say it. I'm institutionalized. To be honest... I feel more safe in gaol than when... I get outside.

I want to be out. I don't want to keep coming back. I don't want to be here now.... But when the outside gets too hard for me, that's another reason... why I do crime – so I can get locked back up again. Because I feel like gaol is my home ... I've been locked up for so long, in and out, you know. It's just like another different world out there every time and I don't feel comfortable in that... I feel more comfortable being in here because this is where I live.

With these pronounced effects of institutionalization taking hold, the importance of ensuring appropriately calibrated support on release became paramount. But in Chris's case, there seemed always to be a serious mismatch between what he so urgently needed and what appeared to be provided (or not provided). He described the situation pertaining to his last release episode in the following way:

I: And you're saying... that very early on, before you were released, the Parole Board said to you, 'You're going to need to do certain types of programs.'...
P: Right. Well, I picked school.... And that was TAFE [Technical and Further Education].... Nothing...
I: So... within two weeks [of being released]... nothing had started. Is that right, [Chris]?
P: ... [T]hat's right. And I said to my parole officer before I got out, right,... I said to him,... 'Listen here. You'll need to get me in a program straight away, because... I'm the type of bloke that... has to be activated'.
I: You have to be active in doing things, yes?
P: Active. Like, I've got to be doing things every day... I warned them.... They didn't listen to me... I've always got to be up and out... It doesn't matter what time of day or time of night... I've got to be always... doing something.

His girlfriend at the time (Marie) remarked that she could see things were going bad: 'I went to... OARS once, just to see if they could help him in any way. I rang up there to see... what options there [were] for Chris... to try and sort out housing for when he got out.... And, yeah... I got nothing out of it.' Each time Chris was released his emotional and trauma-oriented issues remained unaddressed: 'I got out with a lot of anger.... What happened to my girl, what's happened to me, what's happened in the past,' he would say. More than this, Chris never received ongoing help with the things that went to the heart of his self-esteem – the capacity to read and write, to hold a 'proper' conversation, of how to find a place to live, how to respond to a job advertisement (how to *find* a job advertisement) – how, in short, to function around 'regular' people. As Marie put it:

> He doesn't know how to budget or what to spend his money on, and it all comes back to getting a job.... It's hard for him to get a job when he doesn't know how to write a résumé ... He doesn't know how to go for an interview or even apply for a job.... And I can't do them things for him ... I could apply for him, but when it comes to the interview, God knows what he'll say.... Or how he'll say it.... He wants a job, and he would work good, but he needs help, and I don't think I'm the right person to help him with that.

At interview, we pressed Marie further about Chris's claims that, in terms of meaningful help, 'nothing happened' upon his release:

> I: Chris said in those first couple of weeks, he wasn't actually sure what he was meant to be doing...
> P: Yeah, there was supposed to be school.... But this is where I think they should look more into it ... Chris is not a good speller or reader, and he gets very angry and emotional over it. Like [if I say to him], 'Oh, it was a bit hard to read your letter', he would [get really] defensive.... He's gotten a lot better, ... but ... I would say [he has] a 12-year-old's spelling [level].... And if Chris didn't get something [in class], he is not going to put his hand up and say, 'Can you help me with this? I can't do it'. He'll just get frustrated.... So I said to them, like, 'Don't put him in that kind of stuff' ... I reckon Chris needs one-on-one kind of help.... [Instead] they [keep] put[ting] him in a group of people [where] he'll just go there and not like it, and he won't go back.

It's difficult to understand how both the juvenile and adult systems could fail Chris so badly. There is convincing evidence showing links between behaviour and 'oral language competence' and there are ways to teach children in custodial settings and ways less likely to hit their mark (Snow and Powell 2008). Chris seems to have fallen into a system geared to meeting the needs of residents/prisoners *en masse* rather than as individuals with their own unique circumstances and learning styles. So Chris – as part of some serialized production-line attempt at rehabilitation – was made to do all manner of programs. Anger Management. Challenging Offending. Rock and Water. Victim Awareness. Drugs and Alcohol. He did them all many times over – most often as a hurdle requirement for (early) release rather than out of any genuine commitment to any of them. But at least the system could report it was doing something (even if that something had no positive effect whatever on young men like Chris). In fact, at interview, Chris's needs, as complex as they were at one level, proved quite straightforward at another. He needed basic life skills. He did not need more cognitive behavioural therapy or 'Thinking Straight' courses. What he needed was a means for learning, internalizing and practising the basic building blocks for managing in the community. The following extended excerpt explains the incredible social deficits in Chris's life which, in retrospect, contributed to his extreme sense of feeling like an 'outsider' when he so very much wanted to be 'normal':

P: What I need is a job. [But] I won't get that [situation in here of] having a job where I work six, seven hours a day, go home, [and] you're that stuffed you don't feel like doing any [crime] cos you got to go to work again.

I: ...Let me drill down on that [in terms of life beyond prison]. Do you know how to cook yourself a meal?...Like a healthy, good meal?...

P: No.

I: ...There's no shame in that. I'm not judging you....Do you know how to shop, for instance?...

P: No.

I: ...Do you know how to get the phone connected, or pay a phone bill, or do you know how to get the gas connected?

P: No.

I: Do you know how to buy a bus ticket?...

P: Yeah.

I: ...You can do that, OK. Do you know how to go about organizing housing...getting somewhere to stay?

P: No....I never learnt how to do Centrelink [that is, how to claim housing assistance or social security payments while unemployed, etc.]...I don't even know the way to talk to them...

I: Have you ever had, or would you like it, for instance, if someone [like your parole officer or a mentor] said, 'Chris, the first day you're out ... we're going to drive to Centrelink and I will stand with you in line. I will do a lot of the talking. I will help you fill out the form'...

P: Yeah. If someone was there with me, talking for me [it would help] because I get frustrated when I feel that that person [behind the counter] might not understand what I'm saying.... But [with] someone standing there with me in line... then I'd be able to do it....

I: Do you know how to use a washing machine?...

P: No... I don't know how – and I'm going to be honest with you – how to pay for petrol.... I don't even know how to use a mobile phone...

I: You see, that's the reason I started this conversation.... It's important, really important, that you said what you said. Yeah, doing a lot of gaol and then coming out and trying to somehow live normally is almost impossible [for you].

P: It's impossible.

There is so much to take from this excerpt. But the main point is that Chris never got schooled in how to be a citizen. He missed that train in its entirety. He couldn't cook, pay a bill (he never even received a bill to pay), connect the phone, buy clothes, or a host of other essential things for surviving in modern life. But he could get hold of a sawed-off shotgun at a moment's notice, he could outwit police at high speed while driving the most ramshackle vehicle, he could get as much ice as he needed, he could play the prison system to ensure he was housed away from the madding crowd, he could intimidate enemies in the community from behind prison walls. Chris, in short, had many 'skills'. It's just that they were overwhelmingly centred on criminal and anti-social endeavours. Through it all, Chris knew everything came back to the (lack of) modelling of desired behaviour:

I: [I]f your parents had shown you more attention, or you'd done better at school...

P: ...I wouldn't take drugs. I wouldn't be doing crime. I wouldn't be in here right now. I'd be living with my parents, loving them....

After Tony left his family's life, it took Chris a long time to trust in an 'outsider' again. However, he eventually found another youth worker who came to know him as a person – to know all his obfuscations, justifications as well as his well-founded rationales for why his life took its stated path. Things seemed to look better for a while. He was opening up about his guilt over not 'doing more' to protect his sister, about his social deficits, even about his hopes for the future. But just as progress on these fronts was being made, Chris turned 18. This meant he was an adult and as such was no longer permitted to keep working with his youth worker. As an adult, he would have to cope in the big house (prison) more or less on his own. There would be no continuity of care. His youth worker was permitted to write to him but she could not see him or 'work' with him. Chris never really opened up to another professional again. It was too hard and too painful. He felt as if the process had been sabotaged through no particular fault of his own (other than crossing the line into official adulthood). Chris explicitly acknowledged the importance of having support within and beyond prison. He knew it was his only hope.

> I: So...let's get [this] on the record [Chris]. How ... does someone get their life back together when they've been locked up, if [as you've said], there's no assistance, if there's no help?
> P: If there was someone on the outside that they love, that they know that they're going to stick by them 24/7 all the way, you know, for the rest of their life.

Parole officers and the like rarely fall into this category. Even with the greatest goodwill, their job is primarily to monitor and fill out forms. Parole is geared toward policing and capturing the breach, not rewarding and affirming progress. Chris needed and needs a mentor. In his world, these are in short supply. After nearly five years in prison – with the majority of this spent on remand (and therefore being ineligible for 'programs') – Chris oscillates between the poles of hope and despair. For much of this time he was supported by a long-time friend of his mother. They even struck up a romantic relationship – as romantic as such could be in the context of prison. They talked about getting married, about moving away interstate, about starting a life away from all the hurt. For a time Chris spoke of the way he was becoming something of a father-figure to Penny's children. This seemed to buoy his spirits for a while: 'I'm going to bring them boys up the way I should have been brought up, not the way my family...showed me.... Give them...better advice than what my family gave me...' he remarked in his near final interview. But ultimately the stress of trying to keep a relationship going under such circumstances proved too much. Penny wanted out. She couldn't stand the psychological games Chris was playing. And Chris couldn't get out of his mind that she might be seeing other men 'on the side'. This last is something that incites maximum anger and distress among those doing time. Chris found himself becoming more and more worked up. He never knew if he was shadow-boxing or whether his anger was well founded. In any case, the whole thing was causing him endless 'grief'. They broke up.

Over the past four years, Chris has shown glimmers of generativity. More than anything, he wants a family. If he could, he would want his own broken family to miraculously repair itself.

> I: If you could do anything, anything in the world...when you get out...what is it that you would really like to do?
> P: Have a family....I'm an adult now....It's time for me to grow up....If I did have a family,...[if] I did have a kid, it can make you grow up [so] much.

He's also spoken of looking after his father who has battled mental illness and other more serious ailments in recent times: 'I think [Dad is in his sixties now]...and we're getting to that age when it's our turn now to look after him....Even though he hasn't been there always for me...that's out the window. I don't care about that....I want to have that close relationship I've always wanted before he goes.' Remarkably Chris has shown the capacity to let certain things past be assigned to the past. He wants and needs his father in his life. In the year leading up to his sentencing, Chris chose to cut all ties with him as he found it too painful to talk with him about his predicament. He did not want to lie to his father about what was coming down the line, so he chose silence instead. Now that he knows his fate, he is resuming a relationship with his father and stepmother. At his request, we recently placed a call to inform them both of the sentence and to say that Chris very much wants contact with them. The emotion in Chris's father's voice was palpable. It projected a mix of relief and joy. 'Please give him my love and pass on our address to him,' he said. We did. As with so many young men in his position, the trope of 'next time' came to define Chris' narrative:

> I know for a fact that this is the last time. I know that for a fact. Doesn't matter what time I get I'm going to use that time to better myself, to find who I really am and what I need to do to stay out.

Chris has to believe that.

In sum

At first glance, the three stories told above seem to reflect the worst of human behaviour. Ongoing disregard for themselves and the safety of others appear to be the order of the day. But on closer inspection, these stories show in intricate fashion how situational and structural factors overwhelm some young men's capacities to attain a competent level of citizenship. Sam, James and Chris have become heavily attuned to living in custody and poorly equipped for surviving in the community. They have, though, experienced moments where girlfriends or a parent have tried to assist them to make a go of it. But these people are themselves heavily depleted of the energy and resources needed for making a real difference in such circumstances. It's almost as if the train carrying the three young men had no break/brake – with no way of pulling up let alone turning around and heading in another direction. Prison, of course, is the 'break/brake' society enforces on such people. But prison is not, predominantly speaking, a good means for turning the train around (but see Soyer 2014). In fact, for Sam, James and Chris, it is the means to ensure a further boarding pass. What strikes us most about these stories, then, is the lack of purposeful and productive interface between prison and processes of prisoner (re)integration. These three young men swung hopelessly back and forth between, it would seem, hyper-supervision and under-supervision. Rarely, if ever, did they receive or were they enjoined to participate in appropriate kinds of assistance – assistance, that is, which carefully combined such things as life skills, grief and loss counselling, job training, experiential learning, harm minimization approaches to drug and alcohol abuse, and meaningful opportunities to contribute to rather than take from their communities. Perhaps, on this last count, it is well to admit that each of the young men had, in fact, no legitimate community to return to on release from custody. They were so very heavily stigmatized and atomized – each trying to survive as best they could on their own or with like individuals. This, it should be said, is the way to ensure desistance never gets off the ground. It is, however, a good means for ensuring a return to prison and, ironically, to some kind of community.

7
Points of Unrest

One of the fundamental research tasks is to answer the 'so what?' question. To wit, why do the stories told above matter and what 'larger' meaning or lessons might be taken from them? It is difficult, in this context, to avoid grappling with Moffitt's (1993) claim that all anti-social (criminal) behaviour falls into one of two categories: 'adolescence-limited' *or* 'life-course persistent'. With over 6000 citations, her paper developing that taxonomy must rate as one of the most frequently read articles in criminology and related fields over the past two decades. Prior to discussing some of the key themes emerging from the young men's stories, we feel compelled to understand whether and where they fit into this 'developmental dyad'. With the possible exception of Sean, who we lost touch with some time ago, none could rightly be described as adolescence-limited offenders. All continued to offend (in relatively serious fashion) *beyond* their teenage years. Moffitt posits that adolescence-limited offenders cease offending in or about their teenage years, tend to commence offending later than life-course-persistent offenders, are free from any 'personality disorders and cognitive deficits', and have by their mid-teens (generally the onset of their offending) internalized a sufficient quantum of 'good' behavioural scripts to which they can return/inhabit when the stakes get too high. As she (1993: 690) writes:

> [W]ithout a lifelong history of antisocial behaviour, the forces of cumulative continuity have had fewer years in which to gather the momentum of a downhill snowball. Before taking up delinquency, adolescence-limited offenders had ample years to develop an accomplished repertoire of prosocial behaviours and basic academic skills. These social skills and academic achievements make then eligible for postsecondary education, good marriages, and desirable jobs.

Such a depiction does not adequately reflect the lives of the young men in this book. With the exceptions of Billy (age 14), Lee (age 14), Joel (age 14) and Greg (age 15), they all started 'officially' offending at or below age 13 and self-reported engaging in criminal behaviour from as young as eight years of age (Chris). Sam, it can be noted, was first admitted into custody at age 11 and Charlie at age 12. Further, with the exceptions of Lee and, possibly, Joel and Billy, all came from home environments where modelling of pro-social behaviour was in short supply. They also evinced problems with ADHD (Joel, Matt, Sam, Chris), possible acquired brain injury (Charlie), suspected psychosis (Ben), had completed little beyond seven years of schooling, and between them were committing offences ranging from prostitution, arson, armed robbery and home invasions by, in most cases, age 16. They came from families where crime and incarceration were, to a real degree, considered part and parcel of the life course. Eight of the 14 had a parent who had been incarcerated and in at least three cases (Matt, Reggie, Charlie) the total length of parental incarceration exceeded well over ten years. In two families, fathers and sons had been locked up at the same time – on one occasion, in the same facility. Moffitt (1993: 690) reminds us that 'Adolescence-limited delinquents have something to lose by persisting in the antisocial behaviour beyond the teen years'. While a few of our study cohort were, as teenagers, starting to talk in these terms, in fact there was little for them to reach out to – little on which to hang any desire to desist.

On such a basis, it seems – with the exceptions of Billy, Charlie and David – the young men are best conceived as life-course-persisters. They appear to use Moffit's (1993: 683) terms, to be those 'persons [who] miss out on opportunities to acquire and practice pro-social alternatives at each stage of development'. All but Billy, Joel and Lee were dealt a notably bad hand in life from the get-go. Childhood became a series of reactions to fairly desperate and sometimes violent situations rather than something to be, on the whole, enjoyed. Again, Moffitt (1993: 682) contends that, 'If the child who "steps off on the wrong foot" remains on an ill-starred path, subsequent stepping-stone experiences may culminate in life-course-persistent antisocial behaviour'. The 'home' and the 'school' become pivotal locales in terms of possible mitigation or exacerbation of problems (Moffitt 1993: 682). In our cohort, when one of these sites seemed to be offering some 'protection', some hope, the other would present as a battle zone. For all the young men featured in Chapters 4, 5 and 6 (excepting Lee and Joel), both locales seemed equally hostile on most occasions.

Moffitt further remarks that one of the defining characteristics of life-course-persistent offenders is the 'number and type of ensnaring life events' throughout the teenage years (1993: 691). This is akin to Sampson and Laub's (1997: 153) concept of cumulative life-course disadvantage. As they write:

> If nothing else, incumbency in pro-social middle-class roles provides advantages in maintaining the status quo and counteracting negative life events... Among the disadvantaged, things seem to work differently. Deficits and disadvantages pile up faster, and this has continuing negative consequences for later development in the form of 'environmental traps'.

With regard to our cohort, it is not just that they were committing a greater proportion of serious offences from a younger age than adolescence-limited kids. What also mattered was that the means to break away from the various environmental traps created by such behaviour was, for them, severely limited. Each seemed divested of the social and economic capital that could provide a more immediate path out from crime. 'Teenage parenthood, addiction to drugs or alcohol, school dropout,... patchy work histories, and time spent incarcerated are *snares* that diminish the probabilities of later success by eliminating opportunities for breaking the chain of cumulative continuity' (Moffitt 1993: 684 emphasis in original). None of these events are 'fatal', of course, in themselves. They needn't equate to a life condemned or lived on the run, on the margins, as permanently unemployed or in prison. But when they occur repeatedly and in close proximity, and when they occur in contexts where young people's significant others (parents, girlfriends, aunts, uncles, friends) are themselves struggling to stay one step ahead of the law, to get their next fix, to pull off the next scam, to meet the demands of their own court order or parole conditions, to raise other children, then these things *do* start to take on a determining dimension. They start to become, in short, day-to-day reality. And this reality does not come with instructions for avoiding more snares let alone how to escape those that have already been 'set off'. Here, the 'options for conventional behaviour' become whittled to zero (Moffitt 1993: 684).

This, in effect, describes the situation by age 18 or so for the majority of the young men in our study. Billy, David and Charlie – those who appear in their mid to late twenties to be desisting – were in fact still 'ramping up' in their late teenage years. It is also clear, though, that all the young men viewed the prospect of entering adulthood (turning

18) as something of a milestone. Most measured the significance of the event by whether they were incarcerated or not. Some (for example, Chris, Sam, Ben, Matt and Joel) reflected they hadn't had a birthday in the community for several years. Most made statements about ending offending by age 18. There was a kind of 'taking stock' in evidence: 'Gaols won't see me again' (Charlie); '[N]ow that I'm 18... I'm coming to the big house next.... [I]t's time to stop. I got... one last chance to fuckin' stop this' (Ben). All, it can be noted, failed this test – some in more serious and lengthy fashion than others:

> At the crossroads of young adulthood, adolescence-limited and life-course-persistent delinquents go different ways. This happens because the developmental histories and personal traits of adolescence-limiteds allow them the option of exploring new life pathways. The histories and traits of life-course-persistents have foreclosed their options, entrenching them in the antisocial path (Moffitt 1993: 691).

Moffitt's work seems to encapsulate, in large degree, the various trajectories of those in our study. We note, though, that the binary distinction between adolescence-limited and life-course-persistent does not cover all bases and that, in reality, people's lives are much more complex than either of these concepts permit. For us, *the really challenging work arises in the context of trying to make sense of what happens to the young men as they age out their teens through their twenties* (see Soyer 2014). Is it fair (accurate) to label Chris a life-course offender? He won't, due to his sentence, have the opportunity to offend in the community until his mid-thirties. Is it right to presume he will take up where he left off – that persistence, not desistance, will again define his days out of prison? Is it fair or wise to leave no room for change? Can the same be said of James? Equally, what should be said of Billy? Technically, under Moffitt's typology, he was a life-course-persistent offender since his offending stemmed into his mid-twenties and was becoming increasingly serious. The same can be said of Charlie. And, to a lesser extent, of David. These young men don't fit neatly into the life-course-persistent category. In fact they have managed to slowly break free from the series of environmental traps that ensnared them – but not until they were well *beyond* their teenage years. Perhaps, though, these traps have not altogether disappeared. Instead, with the help of others, we'd argue that they (now) manage such traps better if and when they arise.

And what of Ben, Reggie, Joel and Paul? Aged in their mid to late twenties, they all show varying degrees of progress in terms of the seriousness and frequency of their offending. Certainly, they have not 'desisted' (if by that term we mean 'ceased *all* offending'). But again they don't seem to warrant the label life-course-persistent – especially if severity is in the mix as a dependent variable. Matt and Lee, on the other hand, appear more correctly to 'belong' in that category. But even there, it is impossible to say with certainty what their futures hold. We are, in short, wary about condemning anyone to wear the mantle of life-course-persistent offender without actually knowing how each life course turns out. Here, it is only studies which 'track' people into older age (such as that conducted by Laub and Sampson 2006) that can, in retrospect, comment informatively on Moffitt's taxonomy. In part, this comes down to the intractable problem of wanting to know now (whether someone *will* desist) what can only be known with reasonable certainty tomorrow (whether someone *has* desisted). Finally, as a cautionary note, we point to the vastly different outcomes associated with the life histories of Sam and Charlie. Both were first admitted to juvenile detention at, respectively, ages 11 and 12, both lacked a father-figure in their life, both had 'behavioural problems' in their very early years, both were semi-illiterate and innumerate, both had witnessed or suffered violence in their childhood years, both struggled with long-term drug abuse, and both had roughly the same number of admissions, excluding transfers between such, to juvenile facilities (roughly 20 each). By 'rights', both should be offending well into their 20s and on their way to becoming a life-course-persister. But in fact, they took very different paths even though, to borrow from Laub and Sampson (2006), they very much had 'shared beginnings'.

Turning bad into worse

Although each of the stories relayed in in this book have their own unique antecedents and unfold in ways peculiar to each young man, there are nonetheless several key themes that recur in relation to most, if not all of, their stories. In the remainder of this chapter we discuss each of these themes and note that their defining dimension is, in essence, to make bad situations worse. We do not suggest these are universal issues affecting all young men in similar situations (whether in the UK, US or elsewhere). But we do find they have had a major defining influence on the lives of those in our research.

Parentification

It would be wrong to say there is a generation of kids who have been forced to bring themselves up. Clearly, the majority of children in the western world reside in homes where good behaviour is modelled, food is on the table, clothes are washed, transport is provided to and from school, medical care is available, leisure time with siblings, parents and/or grandparents is in the mix, a roof over one's head is guaranteed, and where, generally speaking, love and affection are the norm. But most of the young men in this book helped 'raise' younger, or were 'raised' by older, siblings at one time or another. Chris, Charlie and David fall squarely into such a situation, as do Sam, Ben, Reggie and Paul. Often, their siblings (particularly, older brothers) were already into crime, setting in train the longer-term 'mimicry' of such behaviour (Moffitt 1993). As Paul commented, 'He [my brother] was just like an idol. He was just someone I looked up to'. None of the families (including Lee's, Joel's and Billy's) from which our cohort is drawn were living anything remotely approximating the Australian or American 'dream'. They survived through a mix of welfare, part-time or seasonal work, and the underground economy (mostly, drug manufacture and dealing). Lee's parents were the stand-out exception to this. They'd worked hard all their lives in the food industry and, conversely, probably dealt least well with the criminal exploits of their child.

The gap between rich and poor in countries often perceived as 'wealthy' is substantial and growing. In Australia one in eight people live at or below the poverty line (Australian Council of Social Services 2012). In the US, the rate is around one in six (see Stanford Center on Policy and Equality 2014), while in the UK, the figure is one in five (see Oxfam 2014). Millions of families, therefore, in these 'lucky countries' are under inordinate economic stress. Many are afflicted by drug and alcohol abuse, intergenerational unemployment, high levels of illiteracy and innumeracy, and by other markers of extreme dysfunction. In these situations it is little wonder that some parents never really 'learn' or have time to be parents and that children never get to be children. At best, some become 'carers' to siblings while their mother and father or both try, around the clock, to make ends meet. At worse – on account of deep-seated behavioural issues, or the incapacity of parents to cope – children end up in some kind of out-of-home care. In fact, nearly 40,000 children in Australia reside in such circumstances with the majority being on some type of supervised order. And the problem is growing. From 2003 to 2012 the number of children in out-of-home care almost doubled (Australian Institute of Family Studies 2013). Roughly five per cent of this group are 'cared' for in secure residential facilities (that is, a young person's prison) or community based residential care settings for children at risk. Of those in remaining types of care, around 25 per cent will experience ten or more placements during their childhood (Australian Institute of Family Studies 2013, drawing on Delfabbro et al. 2001). In such scenarios, children are made to grow up 'before their time' – well in advance of the cultural ideal concerning what childhood should involve.

Beyond this scenario, children are made to grow up fast in other ways. On any day in Australia, more than 100,000 people are homeless. Roughly 17 per cent are aged under 12 while about one in four are aged under 18. Most of these children will, thankfully, be with a parent – typically a mother who is fleeing domestic violence or some other trauma (Homelessness Australia 2014). Again, these children endure hardships to which no child should have to bear witness. But the trouble doesn't end there. Again, on any day in Australia, around 1000 children are incarcerated. In the UK that number is just below 2000 (BBC News, 12 June 2012). Ever the exception, in the US, including those on remand, the number of kids in custody on any day exceeds 80,000 (Mendel 2011: 2). Moreover, significant numbers of children are forced adrift as a result of one or both parents being incarcerated. In the UK, roughly 17,000 children per year are separated from their incarcerated mothers (Travis 2011). In Australia, five per cent of all children and 20 per cent of Indigenous children aged 15 years or under (n=38,000) are believed to experience the incarceration of one or both parents annually (Quilty et al. 2004; Quilty 2005). In the US, a staggering one in 28 children (or 2.7 million kids) under the age of 18 have a parent who is incarcerated (Reilly 2013).

We do not relay such statistics in order to suggest that all children will necessarily do badly under any or all these circumstances. Families in poverty are not *ipso facto* 'bad', violent or dysfunctional. Dedication to children and the struggle to climb out of the cycle of economic hardship in many ways defines such families. Even where this isn't the case, many will find good homes with committed foster carers. Some children will make positive life-changing connections with youth workers and various social service personnel within and beyond custody. Many others, of course, will be reunited with one or both parents at some point. Equally, just because some children have a parent in prison doesn't automatically mean that their own lives will take an exponential turn for the worst. Extended family members frequently come to the fore and battle in earnest to shield children from the otherwise likely fall-out of parental incarceration. But the unadorned reality is that some children *will* fall through the cracks. For those ending up in custodial facilities, the process of parentification – of having to grow up before one's time – is more pronounced. Interviews with 54 young men in secure care settings in South Australia (mentioned above under 'Approach to the field/data') indicated many of these participants did not receive visits from a family member or significant other (Halsey unpublished data). Children under the Guardianship of the Minister for Communities and Social Inclusion (so-called 'GOM kids' or wards of the state) fared particularly badly in this regard. Whether due to familial ties being irrevocably broken prior to admission into custody or to the tyranny of distance (where travel time by family to and from the facility is too great), many kids in such settings are left to do their own emotional labour. This occurs in spite of being surrounded by a host of supportive professionals.

Chris, of course, is the exemplary case of what happens when children are abandoned by their parents. The social costs are immense as is the psychological damage to the child. Greg, whose story was omitted from previous chapters, probably had the worst start to life. His father walked out on him when just a baby and his mother literally couldn't stand to look at him. She beat him until one day eventually welfare stepped in and removed him from her 'care'. The depth of estrangement is illustrated by Greg telling us at interview that his mother was, in his eyes, 'dead' (when in fact she was/is alive and well). He was raised, ultimately, by his grandparents. But in spite of their best efforts, this amounted to trying to control him during the brief periods between custodial events.

Ben's start to life was not much better. He had to battle his mother's life-long drug habit and incapacity to care for herself, let alone her son. His father, as mentioned in Chapter 4, also walked out on them, and Ben has not see him since (that is, for nearly 30 years):

I: What needed to change for you not to do [crime]?...
P: Probably another...chance from my mother....I felt unwanted....She gave up on me heaps...and...went into a lifestyle of drugs....I [also] had an abusive stepfather....[One day] my Mum sold all my electrical goods to support her habit....I just was on my own since I was [age] 12.
I: So that means that...the people that you were doing crime with were almost like a substitute family in a way....
P: Yeah, they were my family, for sure.

At age 25, Ben, it might be recalled, briefly reflected on the costs of never having had a father figure:

It feels like I've never had my Dad in my life at all, ever, ... [s]ince I was one.... [I]t's left me confused and wondering if I had [had] a Dad would I have gone to [the] Boys' Home [juvenile prison]? Would I have gone to gaol if I had that guidance? And so I don't want my kids to have those questions.... [I want to] [g]uide them through their troubles...

Instead of having stability – some kind of moral compass – Ben was forced to flee from 'stepdads that bashed me, racist stepdads, stuff like that.... I always ran away or I always got belted'. In his words, he 'chose the road' and resorted, as previously relayed, to stealing cars to sleep in. He essentially raised himself, all the while yearning for family: 'Sometimes I get envious when I see a happy family with the Mum and Dad,' he commented in a recent interview. The issue of parenting arose quite often in the context of interviews with correctional staff. One prison manager said the solution to crime and incarceration needed to reside upstream: 'People need to be trained to be parents.... I think intervention for the families, right from the beginning, needs to be where all the focus has to be. [It] has to be at the front of the train, not at the end.... It's too late when they get here.' Evidence would seem to bear this out. When kids like Ben, Sam and Chris end up in juvenile detention, they most commonly view such places as a 'respite' from the streets: '[W]hen you go in and you get locked up for the first time, everyone sees that as fun. They don't see it as getting locked up. You know, there's a swimming pool, gym, oval, everything in the detention centres. It takes a while, three or four times to come back into custody [for it] to sink in that it's not fun. But by that time you've already got in the zone of crime and it's heaps hard to get out of' (Ben). In his adult years, Greg also spoke of becoming acclimatized to being locked up. It even became preferable to the hardships of life outside prison walls: '[Y]ou just get accustomed to [gaol]. I mean you get three meals a day, you get a free room, you don't have to pay rent, you get a shower, pretty good food'. In a subsequent interview, he remarked, 'I don't think I'm that far away from wanting to... go back to gaol.... I know I've done so well and that, but fuck, ... out here you've just got to fucking struggle for everything'.

The relationship between being in custody and lost childhood is a complex one (Harvey 2007; Lyon et al. 2000). Generally speaking we find that the experience of incarceration for teenagers is an adverse event that continues to 'rob' them of their childhood years. Incarceration compounds the problem of parentification by asking kids to fend for themselves in what can often present as stark and alienating environments. But there are, to be fair, occasional exceptions to this. For some, custody becomes a place for *recovering* childhood. The following excerpt, taken from an interview with a young man who served time in juvenile facilities with those featured in this book, aptly illustrates this:

> P: In these places you can just act like a kid here.... Like, I still act childish and stuff 'cos at the moment I hate growing up.... I still like to be a kid ... [I] still like to do the childish things and set people up and get people into trouble and stuff and then play around with toys and shit.... It's fun.
> I: ... Right, sure. And do you feel as though you've had a lot of time in your life to be like a child or not?...
> P: Not really.... In here it's really the only time I can express it 'cos you're with other people and they're doing the exact same thing. So you don't feel like an idiot for doing it.... You just fit in. It's easy, you can just be your childish self...
> I: So [do] you think there are a number of other people in here in a similar situation to you?...
> P: Well, ... we're all sort of the same in one way or another.... [W]e're all ... in the same shit.

There is a sense in which all the young men in our study are seeking, at one level or another, to recover lost childhoods. The iconic moments of going to the beach with friends and family, going on long family drives, going to school each and every day, playing until sunset in the back yard without fear of being randomly yelled at or beaten or otherwise humiliated, of making the important transitions from kindergarten to primary school to high school, are all conspicuously absent in their life histories. Some have managed to make up ground while serving time – a bit of cognitive behavioural therapy here, a bit of education and job training there, a bit of anger management, and maybe even some participation in grief and loss sessions. But the cold hard truth is that this has rarely been sufficient to the task of assembling the well-adjusted person forsaken in those early years. Reggie recounted the perils of parentification in stark terms:

> One of the boys in here [in the juvenile facility] sees staff as his parents... because he's never had parents and he's fucking down and out.... He comes back just so he's got that secure feeling that someone's watching, and he knows they're there every day for him.... Me, I'd probably just fucking well kick his ass in. Yeah, tell him how to fucking live.... He's come here and he's found a little bit of love

and affection where he'll never have it again unless he goes to the adult system, and then they're really going to love him there...in the worst way.

It is difficult to imagine how a child emerges from such a scenario as anything other than psychologically and socially damaged. And on that count it is of little surprise that so many do, in fact, progress to adult custodial facilities.

Personal need versus systemic offerings

Another prominent theme to emerge from interviews concerns the gap between what is required to desist from crime as against what is available to support this process. The role of *people* rather than 'things' was paramount here. The young men spoke consistently of needing someone – akin to a mentor – to help them handle issues large and small. This could involve getting to appointments on time or it could mean, for instance, assistance with obtaining better, more permanent, accommodation. In his first interview – over a decade ago – Lee observed, 'The criminal needs a [different] footstep to follow instead of...the footstep of [the] criminal life or gangster life.... He needs someone to show him a straight path, not the crooked path'. Paul also noted the lack of systemic support for the 'individual' and highlighted, in particular, the pressure for staff within and beyond prison to treat people as if they were components on an assembly line:

> [T]here's not much support.... [Y]ou've probably got ...two social workers that are running around the whole gaol trying to see...so many prisoners a day that they're not actually getting the time to sit down [properly] with [each] prisoner. They've just got to rush through everything.... Even while they're out,...like [when they're on] parole,...I can probably vouch for every prisoner [that they'd] be sick of signing in to parole – just how strict parole is.... It's just the way they do it, it's just all crap.... [M]ost criminals [are] not making [enough] money...to get through day-to-day.... [S]ome can't even afford a bus ticket to get to parole half the time [and] if they don't have that money for a bus ticket they...can't sign that piece of paper...for their freedom.

So often the views of (ex)prisoners are interpreted with suspicion or as serving some ulterior motive (Maruna and Mann 2006). Criticism by offenders of the way things run tends to be quickly recast as an attempt to displace one's own role in creating a life of crime and reincarceration. But Paul has some very powerful allies – namely, correctional personnel. As one prison manager remarked:

> [F]or us, it's very frustrating. We will have somebody here, they'll get released, sentence served, or even out on parole, automatic parole, and they've got nowhere to go and we've used up every resource we've got to try and find them some form of accommodation. We've actually released prisoners here with a tent and a sleeping bag.... And that's been the best we can do to address the accommodation needs for them.... [W]e had a chap who ... we did that to and he had mental health issues.... [T]he best we could get for him to move forward ... as a valued member of the community was that he had a tent. He was going to try and find somewhere along the river where he could pitch his tent... and... to try and find work picking grapes or picking oranges.... And [all the while] we're saying ... 'In no time he'll be back in'.... Before long we had him back again and [we asked him] what happened? 'Oh, well, you know, this happened and that, someone stole my sleeping bag and tent, so I had nowhere to go, so I caught up with some friends and ended up staying at their house. They went out to do a [house] break [burglary break and enter]. They told me to come along with them, so I went along with them and I was the one the police found outside the house'.... And, you know, that happens so often. It happens so often.

Numerous studies have noted the way in which people emerging from prison are set up to fail (Petersilia 2003; Travis 2005; Wacquant 2009). This continues, in our view, to be one of the enduring issues surrounding resident and prisoner reentry and reintegration (see Thompkins 2010). If things get off to a bad start for those already at the limits of economic stress and social marginalization, then the chance of these same people getting on track (that is, not having to resort to crime) is slim at best. As James commented during one of his many attempts to hold things together, 'At the moment [I'm] living [way up north of the city but] everything I feel comfortable with – the only Centrelink I feel comfortable with – is [way down south of the city].... So here I am [risking my curfew by] going all the way out of my way from [the north] to [the south] just to feel comfortable... because I feel like I'm just going to get up and walk out [of any other social service agency]'. We found time and again that the correctional system provokes risky behaviour in those under its remit. And it does this not out of any ill-will or malice toward young offenders – or offenders generally – but because it is in fact a system within a system. It is beholden to all manner of political forces and is always one step away from being judged in the court of public opinion about how it manages the 'dangerous' among us (Pratt 2007). Corrections itself is under strain and this strain is passed on in all kinds of ways to prisoners and their families (where such exist) (Halsey and Deegan 2014; Comfort 2003, 2007). The system is also a highly irrational one. It does things that could only be described as senseless – high-risk, even. James, again, gives the following example:

> P: [T]hey released me [at] 2.30 in the afternoon with no paperwork ... [Instead], they've given me a cab fare to go to the local Centrelink and I've rocked up ... and I said that I've just been released from prison and they said, 'Prove it'.... [So] I said, 'Ring the prison'. And they said, 'Oh, we could be ringing anyone and anyone could answer the phone and tell us you've just got released'. So I had to go from [mentions location] Centrelink back to [the] prison ... to the ... admin guy and say, 'You didn't give me no papers saying that I was released. [And those papers would have helped me get my Emergency Bank Transaction]'.... I [then had] to go from Centrelink, back to [the prison and from the prison] back to Centrelink....
> I: What if it was closed?
> P: Exactly. That's the thing.... If I had walked to [the prison] and then walked back again, Centrelink would have been closed by the time I got back.... It's only luck that I ran into people that I've known for a long time ... and they understood my situation and said, 'Yeah, no worries,' and took me back to [the prison] and brought me back down [to Centrelink].... If it wasn't for that ... there was a good chance that I would have stolen a car or ... did a runner or something.

Lee also tells of a major mistake in terms of his progression through custody into the community:

> I didn't get any resocialisation. I didn't get [to go to the pre-release centre]. I didn't get a job. I didn't save up no money. I was back and forth from medium to high security because someone that had the same name as me ... had 14 house break charges ... and that stuffed up my chance [to go to the low-security prison].... [T]hey had the wrong person. I [had to go] down to the ... magistrates court just for

them to have both of us there and say, 'Yeah, we have the wrong person'. [But] by then... I'd already thrown... my hopes and dreams out the [window]. Like, 'Stuff it. I've been doing the right thing... [but] I'm not going anywhere. I'm not progressing [toward a lower security rating and my release]'.

In a system (at the State level) that manages more than 2000 prisoners (and roughly 3000 probationers/parolees) on any day, mistakes are bound to happen. But in the end we are talking here of people and their futures (however precarious those futures might appear). What happens to people within prison very likely structures, as we have earlier remarked, the attitudes carried beyond the gate (Contreras 2013: 85–6). The blend of bad decision-making mixed with overtly harsh treatment can leave a lasting impression. Ben describes a recent 'short stay' in G Division – the most secure and sparsest place for prisoners in South Australia.

P: I forgot to sign in on my bail... [so] I handed myself into the police station. They gave me bail again through the courts.... At first it was with a guarantor and I had to get that sorted because my phone was flat and I didn't have any of my numbers.... [T]hey put me in Yatala [Labor Prison] for six days even though I had bail. It was just because I couldn't get hold of a guarantor and then I went back to court. While I was in Yatala I tried to kill myself.... [W]ith everything going on, getting screwed over by [my ex-girlfriend], my bail [problems], and my mate dying [from a criminal gunshot wound to the head], ... I [was] burning inside, and, yeah, [I] slashed up. [So they put me in] G Division [because I] was going a bit loopy...

I: Right.... [D]id that make things worse?

P: It did.... I told them before they put me in there too, they've gone, 'You're going to G Division'. I was like, 'That's a punishment place. Like, I need help. I don't need to be punished'. No one was listening to me when I was asking for help. No one was listening to me about the way I felt inside... I just lost it. They just stripped me down and put me in a canvas skirt and put me in a room with the light on 24 hours a day, a prison officer sitting at the full glass door.... So you've got a prison guard watching you all day plus a camera, the light's on 24 hours a day, and you're in a skirt. It was pretty [terrible].

I: ...What's in that G Division cell?...
P: Nothing. You don't even have a mattress or a pillow or anything. Just a wooden board to lay on and then there's a hole in the floor and when you go to the toilet you've got to squat over the hole.... It's disgusting...
I: And the bed scenario?...
P: Wood slats, yeah.
I: No pillow?
P: No.... I was that cold and uncomfortable. I had a sore back for weeks after that. They treated me like I was the worst person in the world when all I really needed was some help.... [O]ut of all the... years I've done, that six days was probably the lowest point.... Very inhumane in there. Yatala's the worst prison out of them all.

For someone, who, as it turns out, was in the midst of a psychotic breakdown, this is the best 'care' the prison could show Ben. The day after he was released he called us in a highly distressed state saying he felt himself slipping into mental disarray – he said, specifically, that he felt like his mind was 'caving in on itself'. We asked if there was any mental health plan in place for him. There wasn't. Had the prison put him in touch with a service, with anyone who could help? Apparently, they hadn't. We made some calls and did what we could. But it shouldn't have to work like that. There are thousands of people who don't have our numbers at their disposal and the potential connection to our networks of expertise and support. Ben had even tried to call us from prison but he was reputedly denied the right to phone calls. Again, we needn't take Ben's word regarding his situation. As one intervention manager commented, 'the provision of psych[ological and psychiatric] services... is a huge issue for us. We have many people incarcerated... that need access to psychs. We only get a psych two and a half days a month'. Another intervention manager, from a different facility, remarked that 'bed space takes all priority over rehabilitation and rehabilitation programs'. One prison manager commented specifically on the officer culture at Yatala: 'when you have staff sitting on one side of the barrier, it's like being at the zoo.... It's a dreadful... way to run any facility.'

The problem of systemic offering versus personal need does not just affect the young men themselves. As with many (ex)prisoners, their support network often includes those struggling with their own battles to keep abreast of correctional rules and court-related matters. One of Reggie's NSOs (Jane) suffered major (and unnecessary) hardship due to the overzealous 'risk-crazed' (Carlen 2008) approach to managing parolees – even those who, in this case, had not put a foot wrong for many years:

> P: [I was on parole and] I had a breakdown.... I was nervous about flying on big planes... to Sydney ... I was just so nervous... and I wanted to see my granddaughter [and] be there for her first birthday.... [A]nd I just had a bit of a breakdown and [was] accused [by my parole officer] of not taking my medication.... And apparently the Parole Board approved my two weeks in Sydney... [but] I wasn't told until the last minute.... And when I did find out, I booked all my plane fares and I was getting phone calls [from corrections] to say, 'Well, you'd better not get connecting flights so you're not hanging around in Melbourne 'cos we don't know who you're associating with'.... And it was just stress, stress, stress, stress.... The warrant was out for two days before I was picked up at my house [and] transferred to... prison.
>
> I: [H]ow long were you in... prison before you [were permitted] to appear before the Parole Board?
>
> P: ...Three and half months.... [And] [t]he breach was never proven.... It was just, 'You are now free to go'.... [Not even] a simple, 'Sorry... We fucked up your life'. [But] it's not [just] my life. It's my granddaughter's, it's my parents', it's my daughter's [life as well], you know?

Jane called us just prior to being taken away by the police. Again, we thought long and hard about 'intervening'. We had a fair idea of what was at stake (the house, her mental health, her relationship with her daughter and granddaughter, her hitherto impeccable contribution to building 'community' – in short, her continued desistance). On balance, we decided that this kind of injustice needed at least some redress. We sorted a lawyer and, with Jane's full knowledge and permission, we put a call into Corrections suggesting her current parole officer was causing more problems than it was worth. To the Department's credit, they organized a more experienced officer. The relief in Jane's voice and the change in her demeanour upon seeing her some months later was palpable. Her whole family were so incredibly thankful – they knew they could have struggled, literally, for years, to get the same result. Again, getting good support shouldn't have to be this hard. It shouldn't depend on some kind of social lottery – whether you happen to be involved in a research project or not.

One of Lee's NSOs (Tim) – someone universally admired within the prison system by officers and prisoners alike – also fell foul of the overly conservative approach to managing prisoners. A lifer, Tim thought his application for parole had been languishing for months with the Executive Council of the State Government (post the recommendation of the Parole Board). In fact, there had been a mix-up and no such recommendation had been made nor forwarded to the Executive. Another hearing was arranged. We were permitted to attend and also submitted a letter of support on his behalf. The Board gave Tim their strongest endorsement but mentioned they could only *recommend* him for parole. The final decision as to when and whether he would be released would be up to the Executive Council (essentially, all Cabinet Ministers who meet to decide such things). He was rejected. And to add insult to injury, no reason was offered or, under the relevant Act, was required to be offered by the government for its decision. With the exception of having tried to escape from custody when first admitted, Tim had an impeccable custodial history. He was, understandably, gutted. In anticipation that the Parole Board's recommendation would be upheld, the correctional system had, as it turned out, already transferred him to the pre-release cottages. There, he was doing many 'normal' things – cooking, working, cleaning and sharing a 'living space' (not a cell). Indeed, he'd done all this at the much larger low-security facility within which he was incarcerated prior to his transfer. We'd never seen him so happy and so motivated to do well. Then word came that his application had been denied. With that news, he was placed straight into G Division. He was now a lifer who'd been refused parole and as such was deemed a flight risk. Watching him 24/7 became 'necessary' to avert any danger he posed. Tim, like many other lifers, was something of a 'political prisoner'. News from interstate at that time reported a succession of parolees who, shortly after release, had gone on to commit serious crimes (including murder). This, it is fair to say, reverberated through the political corridors of South Australia. Whatever the case, it was an incredibly efficient way to destroy Tim's hope – his sense that he may have a future beyond bars.

It is not, we note, the Parole Board nor Correctional Services that is the problem. For its part, the Board is incredibly overburdened and, on the whole, does an admirable job of assessing applications. Instead, it's the whole conception of what parole is or should be about that's the key issue. Just as there are, no doubt, problematic parolees who snub their nose at the various chances given them, there are also problematic parole officers. Such officers are driven by checklists and rarely spend time getting to know 'clients' (people). Evidence has emerged suggesting that good parole officers *can* make meaningful differences in people's capacity and motivation to desist. This might not be explicitly acknowledged by parolees at the time of their supervision, but in time there is a tendency to look back and view the parole officer as, at least, partly important to reducing or stopping offending (Farrall and Calverley 2006). Still, in our cohort, even 'success stories' like David, Billy and Charlie had to engage in a difficult if not risky dance with the parole system. It was a system, which, in their eyes, failed to understand that compliance is not the same thing as reintegration:

> They expect you to report [to corrections every week].... It was impossible.... I was working five days a week or more, six [days], sometimes seven.... Please, I can't [report] there every week. [But] [i]f they were open until 6 [pm], I would be there every week... (David)

Ben had a similar experience of being prohibited from doing things he knew would strengthen his involvement in positive networks:

> I got in contact with my DJ again and there's some gigs coming up that I can't do because of the parole. There was a couple [of gigs] in Sydney... which would be good.... [E]veryone's been waiting for me to get out and continue on again.... But I'm not allowed in licensed premises.

At the other end of the spectrum, we found some young men surrendering the possibility of early release in favour of getting out 'end of order'. There were, apparently, too many rules to follow and so it was better to stay in prison than to be brought back for a minor breach. The exchange with Joel illustrates this:

> I: So did you have to go before the Parole Board?
> P: No, I just wrote them a letter saying, 'Look I, don't want my parole back, fucking don't let me let out early, don't'.... I put in there, like, 'Parole's just a pathetic excuse for fucking following me around and telling me how to do my business and run my life and... tell[ing] me I have to be at this course and do that course and then pick up rubbish on this main road'. Nah.

Lee, admittedly a more serious offender, also found parole to be a strange and unhelpful experience:

> You see, I'm not even meant to be here... [in a café].... [Corrections say] to us, 'Tell us two to [or] three days ahead if we [want to] go to a licensed premises'. [But] [e]verywhere's a licensed premises. I haven't even gone clubbing since I got out. I haven't even gone partying since I've been out. I haven't gone anywhere.... I've been eating at home... the majority of the time.... And they say, 'If you feel like going somewhere, just ring us two days before'. [But] [w]hen you go out [and] you want to eat something, you don't [think] two days [in] advance, 'I want to eat that'.... It's weird...

The kind of subject required by parole is not the kind of person who inhabits society writ large. Parole – especially for those deemed 'high risk' requires a heavily managed subject – someone who is consistently reminded of their 'offenderhood' through the management of their whereabouts (place), the things they consume (drugs, alcohol) and the people they converse with or meet (co-offenders and other parolees are deemed particularly problematic). Across all our interviews (including the larger sample of 54 young men), it is hard to find a parolee who tells of the right kind of support – someone who has found a point where the system appropriately balances personal need and systemic offerings. Our sense is that community corrections evince an all-or-nothing approach to supervision. There is either hyper-vigilance or next to nothing in terms of monitoring offenders (we note, again, that 'monitoring' is *not* the same as helping). Interviews with intervention managers bear this out:

> [W]e kick them out the front door and say, 'See you later'. And there's absolutely very minimal follow-up.... If a prisoner is on parole, community corrections, in my opinion, are just overwhelmed. There are an unrealistic number of supervisions... per case officer.... And so they quickly move them from a high-intensity level of reporting and monitoring to a much lower level. They do that as quickly as possible, with just the sheer numbers that they have, and so you get people falling through the cracks at that point.

Here, the pressure involved in managing large caseloads exacerbates the very problem one is trying to solve – people coming repeatedly back to custody. This is the derailment of desistance by design. There are few better illustrations of this than putting people back into *known* criminogenic circumstances – the precise contexts that all the prison-based and community programs tell offenders, at all costs, to *avoid*. James and Paul capture, respectively, this circumstance:

> [W]hen I was at [the] Drug Court house at [mentions suburb], I really did feel that it was no better than gaol. I was surrounded by people – next door, in my house, other side of me – that were in and out of prison, that had drugs around [them], that were using.... [There was] no difference between that Drug Court house and the gaol cell that I'm in now.

> [The suburb I was in was] not a bad area. [But] the block of units [I was living in] was bought by [OARS to house people] released ...from gaol.... [So] you're usually surrounded by dickheads... [engaging in] drunk and disorderly behaviour.... I was...bringing...my kids ...there [and] just wanted to do my family thing. But it's hard being surrounded by that. And across the road from th[e] units was another set of townhouse units and they're all for mental patients.... So I was surrounded by a lot of criminals and dickheads. And I was surrounded by loopy criminal dickheads.

These situations would be laughable were the stakes not so high. Housing – stable living arrangements in good streets and suburbs – ranks as probably the most important material thing a prisoner needs post-release (see Baldry et al. 2006; Halsey 2007b). Through a decade of interviewing, housing came up time and again as central to getting desistance going. Of course, employment, education and learning to adjust to life in the 'free world' also featured prominently. But having a place of one's own was central to sustaining these other events. It is no coincidence that Billy, Charlie and David have all had somewhere stable and safe to reside – somewhere relatively 'protected' from old networks – and that they are the only young men who could rightly be said to be progressing (even in light of Billy's most recent relapse) along the desistance path.

There are also real questions surrounding what prison is being used for. Many are coming back to prison for *breaches* as opposed to new offences. Indeed, in 2012, after 'sexual assault and related offences', the category 'offences against justice procedures, government security and operations' accounted for the most frequent major charge for which people were admitted to prison in South Australia (15 per cent of all prisoners) (ABS 2013a). The bulk of this offence category reduces to breaches of parole or probation conditions. Consistent with situations evidenced by the stories in Chapter 4, about 40 per cent of those coming back to prison for such 'offences' are aged 19 to 29 and around 70 per cent had served at least one prior period of imprisonment. This creates an inordinate churn at the front end of the prison such that 10 per cent of all prisoners now serve less than 12 months, with the average time on remand being just over two months. At the 'back end', there is evidence of greater numbers of longer-term prisoners with the proportion of those serving more than ten years having risen by 50 per cent in South Australia in the last decade (ABS 2013a).

But the real story here is the economic and social costs attached to reincarcerating people for less serious, non-violent matters. Reggie describes one such situation:

> P: I went in to get a pack of cigarettes from the shop in the car.... And got caught driving disqualified.
> I: And how far... would you have driven from the house to get the cigarettes?
> P: ...It would have been quicker to walk there ... than take the car.... It wasn't as if the cigarettes were even for me. I had cigarettes. I was getting them for my brother's girlfriend because she's got no ID.

Given that bed space is acknowledged to get in the way of doing rehabilitation, the use of prison in such circumstances has to be seriously queried. One intervention manager concurred, saying 'finding people being remanded in custody for minor offences – you've just got to question, "Is that what a place like this should be for?"' Many of the stories in this book tell of the damage done when people are brought back to prison for minor infractions. Relationships, accommodation, jobs – the motivation to stay out – are all adversely impacted. And this occurs at substantively great cost to the taxpayer. Locking someone up is roughly 20 to 30 times more expensive per day than supervising someone in the community. Again, prison managers – not just prisoners – can see the game for what it is:

> We had... [a] fellow that came... into prison for something relatively minor. [Well], his wife [subsequently] left him because she was sick of him always being arrested. [She] took his kids away [and] didn't tell him where they'd gone to. [Before being locked up], he was in a

> Housing Trust house [which was then taken] ...away from him. His employer said, 'Look, I can't hold your job for you', so he lost his job. Eight weeks he was [in prison for].... So this guy, he went out and he [had] nowhere to live, nothing. [His] family has fallen apart. [He] got into the drugs again, finished up doing...a massive amount of break and enters [burglaries] and [has] just come back to us for three years. Now, this was a mature...30-[year]-old chap who basically [had] just got his head together, but because we brought him back in for eight weeks, we cost him everything.

This harks back to the irrationality of the correctional enterprise. In truth, it doesn't always correct so much as induce new problems and aggravate old ones. Those on parole so often get caught up in a bizarre world of checks and balances that the main goal of reintegration recedes from view. Lee related this type of scenario:

> [One time] I had a urine [test] at DASSA [Drug and Alcohol Services South Australia] and [while I was there my parole officer] rang [me] up...I said [to him], 'Yeah, I'm at DASSA giving a urine'. And then the [parole officer told the DASSA worker that I needed to give another urine in an hour's time to the Parole Board at 9.30am].... [I was worried] because [I thought I] might not be able to [urinate] because [I've] just [urinated] here [at DASSA].... Then I go [to the Parole Board] and...they make me sit there for an hour.... [And then when I gave them the urine], they said to me, 'This is a bit clear'. I said, 'What do you mean? I drank a lot of water. I knew I was going to get urined...and I've just done a urine, right?' I said, 'How else was I going to [urinate]?' And [the Parole Board] goes, 'If [your urine] keeps coming [back] like this we can [write up] your dilute[d] [urine] as a dirty [urine]'. I said, 'What? If I can't give it, it's a breach. [But] if I give [it] too clean, it's a breach. Come on, make up your mind'.

Trying to read 'progress' from a urine sample is like trying to assess artistic greatness from a child's drawing. It's possible, but mostly fraught with inaccuracy and conceit. Technology – whether electronic bracelets, urinalysis, mouth swabs, random phone calls – does not really substitute for consistent, respectful and individualized support (McNeill and Maruna 2008). 'You've got to treat each kid differently' (James). As Wacquant (2010: 614) writes, 'If the authorities were serious about "reentry", they would ...start by reestablishing the previously existing web of programs that build a bridge back to civilian life – furloughs, educational release, work release, and half-way houses – which has atrophied over the past two decades and avoid locating "reentry services" in decrepit facilities located in dangerous and dilapidated inner-city districts rife with crime and vice'. Beyond the US, this remedy has direct relevance in Australia and other locales as well. Importantly, Wacquant goes on to mention additional steps which could promote the reintegration process, such as prison college programs, dismantling the culture of the 'rap sheet' (which tends toward entrenched discrimination against those looking for work), expansion of drug and alcohol programs, and decoupling the prison from administrative breaches of parole. Without such efforts, many (ex)prisoners – young men like those in this book – will continue to be stuck in what Rose (2000: 324) calls the 'circuits of exclusion'. Here, '[e]xclusion itself is effectively criminalized, as crime control agencies home in on those very violations that enable survival in the circuits of exclusion: petty theft, drinking alcohol in public, loitering, drugs and so forth. These new circuits cycle individuals from probation to prison because of probation violations, from prison to parole, and back to prison because of parole violations' (Rose 2000: 336). That, to a very large degree, fittingly sums up our take on things.

Beckoning help

Another theme which resonated across all the young men's stories concerns the reluctance to ask for help when things turn bad – or, better still, prior to things going seriously off-track. We surmise that this is in part to do with many years' exposure to the 'responsibilized self' (Bosworth 2007) which custodial programs try to incite. A good prisoner takes control of her/his life within prison and beyond. S/he doesn't use others as a 'crutch'. They don't make excuses for wrongdoing or setbacks. They *own* each and every 'failure' (see Reich 2010: 126). Such beliefs – such a correctional hegemony – have major implications when it comes to young men's perceptions of their *actual* ability to 'make it' on release:

> Anytime something gets tough, something gets hard...I run away...It doesn't matter what it is, I avoid conflict. I avoid anything that stresses me out: 'I don't have to put up with this. Let's go'. Well, when you're on home detention, yes, you do have to put up with it or you're going to go to gaol....[But] I don't think like that at the time. (James)

This response echoes Chris's situation ('My problem is that I don't go for help'). Indeed, Chris tried calling us while in the midst of the major crime spree which eventually led to his current term of imprisonment. He even reputedly drove a stolen vehicle to the boom gate of the facility he was locked up in as a juvenile – trying desperately to speak with someone through the intercom – to find someone who could 'talk him down', to stop the carnage. But that was to no avail. He was apparently told it wasn't their business. He was, after all, an adult now and so beyond their 'jurisdiction'. Paul also reported being at a loss to know where to turn for help: 'I've never really known who [to see] or where to go to see anyone.... [I] try and deal with my emotions.... [But I'm] really struggling to deal with life now... [and I'm] out there doing what I used to do when I was seventeen.' Ben, in one of his many low points, sent the following text as a plea for help:

> Hey Mark. It's [Ben]...I'm coming off the rails pretty bad at the moment. I'm not with [my girlfriend]. I'm not seeing my kids at the moment. I've lost my clothes and car coz police took one and [my girlfriend] burnt the other. Things are falling down around me and I don't know what to do any more. Ran out of ideas and patience.

We managed to organize a food hamper and made sure he had temporary shelter. It's all we could do. Marie, speaking in the context of trying to get Chris some help, aptly articulated the key problem with service delivery:

> There's no support there for him.... [Y]ou could only ring ... to speak to someone between... normal work hours.... [Y]ou can't get help outside of those hours.... [I]t hasn't even been like a month and he's back inside. And, yeah, it just really spun us out, like, the lack of support... on the outside.... [And I even] said to [Chris] before [he got locked up], I said, 'Well, why don't you just go down to the police station if you want to talk to someone? Isn't that what an officer is there for, to be able to talk to you if you've got a problem or you feel you've got to do something?' He goes, 'The fucking cunts will lock me up.' I said, 'Not if you just want to go down and talk to them.' He goes, 'I'm [Chris]. They'd lock me up.'

It's as if there should be, on exit from custodial facilities, a warning sign above the gate reading: 'Personal crises only addressed between normal business hours.' In a state like South Australia, the only real hope outside these times is to place a call to the Crisis Care number. But even with that someone can be on hold for inordinately long periods. When we called, a 45-minute wait was not uncommon before a 'live' person picked up the call. A lot can happen in that time. People can snap. They can go further off the rails. In any case, such an agency can only really help if there are beds available or if the queues for other services are not haemorrhaging with demand. Here, the inability to get the right help in timely fashion can lead to the 'fuck it' mentality flagged repeatedly in earlier chapters. It's the point where young men give up hope that they can pull through – with their 'freedom' intact – whatever crisis might be besetting them. As Matt commented: 'The gaol's a revolving door for most people. It's a fucking trap. You get out on bail and you stay on bail for the rest of your life because you're breaching over stupid shit.... I just got fed up and thought, "Fuck it, I'm not going to just breach my bail, I'm going to do something else". And then you get another charge.' That 'other' charge, as it turned out, for Matt, was endangering life and a host of other offences.

In *Delinquency and Drift*, Matza (1990) [1964] insightfully draws attention to the 'mood of fatalism' that envelopes many young offenders. Where fatalism predominates, 'the delinquent...experiences himself [sic] as effect' rather than 'as cause' (Matza 1990: 88–89). Here, immediately prior to (re)offending, there is 'the feeling that one's self exercises no control over the circumstances surrounding it and the destiny awaiting it' (Matza 1990: 188). Fatalism in turn induces a state of personal desperation – a kind of paralysis of self. This paralysis is certainly apparent in many of the stories told above. In such circumstances, it is crime – what Matza famously refers to as the *infraction* – that helps 'to restore the mood of humanism in which the self is experienced as cause' (Matza 1990: 189). The key point here is that the infraction (committing more crime, going 'off the rails', throwing all caution to the wind, 'fucking it') is not necessarily about doing deliberate damage to oneself or to others. Instead, it is a means for ending the existential turmoil of young people who feel their emotional and psycho-social well-being to be under imminent threat with no legitimate way of addressing such insight. As Matza (1990: 190) writes, 'An infraction is among the few acts that immediately and demonstrably make things happen'. Under this scenario, young men don't commit crime to leave or get beyond the 'moral order' but to rejoin it through the institutional (enforcement, juridical, correctional) attention subsequently given them (Matza 1990: 189).

There are, it seems, few circuit breakers for warding off the mood of fatalism and/or the sense that further offending is the solution to such.

The 'skills' taught through programs tend not to resonate on the street. David said as much in his first interview:

> Nobody takes any notice of [the programs]. Nobody takes in anything.... [L]ike [the program dealing with] conflict management... they just ask you stupid questions, like, give you scenarios like, 'What would you do if somebody spat in your face?' Like, what would you do if I spat in yours? I mean, it's pretty fucking obvious. You're not going to stand there and take ten deep breaths and say 'Look, mate, just leave me alone'. We tell them [the program coordinators] what they want to hear. We can't say, 'Yeah, I'd fuckin'... stomp on his head'. We have to say, 'Yeah, I'd walk away', you know. Tell them what they want to hear.

For us, it comes down to trust and timing. Young men who've spent long periods in custody need to know someone has their back (and is not constantly *on* their back). And they need to know that asking for help does not conflict with their sense of masculinity (one which likely considers 'reaching out' to be a sign of weakness or incompetence). In Reich's (2010) terms, assistance needs to be attuned to the 'outsider masculinity' that envelopes so many young men involved in crime and reincarceration (toughness, brashness, belief in absolute self-efficacy and the like). Help also needs to be timely and relevant. It needs to get results in order to counter the belief that turning a small breach into a major offence is the best form of conflict resolution. This requires persistence from several quarters. And the heavy lifting can't all be done by young men's partners or families. Coleman (1990: 590–7) reminds us that the family (in whatever form) is a key institution through which social capital (access to legitimate opportunity structures) is transmitted. But we know that parents 'deeply engulfed by the stresses that accompany living in poverty or who use, sell, or are dependent on drugs are less likely, less inclined, and have less capital to forward to their youth' (Wright 2001: 7). Someone has to stick through good times and bad and resources need to be there to see to it that the good outweighs the bad. Sean's NSO commented insightfully on this aspect:

> He hasn't had an example.... [A]ll his influences have been negative influences.... [I]t's people yelling at him, telling him off.... [H]e's not had a positive influence in his life which is sort of what I am.... As much as it pains me to say it he needs a lot of guidance,

he needs a lot of help and he's just not getting it. Like, I mean he'll come out of [a custodial facility] and they'll be like, 'OK, well that problem's out of the way. See you later. Let's move on to the next one'. The workers he's had have come and gone.... He's bounced around through every organization... and no one's stuck through.

One of the (many) damaging things that happens to young men in and out of custody is that they cannot continue working with their youth worker beyond the age of 18 years (that is, into adulthood). This can prove disastrous for some young men who have taken years to let down their guard and to start to connect with someone in a position of authority. Chris, it will be recalled, spoke passionately about the time things seemed to be getting on track. But that assistance took years – not months, weeks or days – to get right. And it took courage. Telling traumatic stories can itself be another form of trauma for young men (for anybody, in fact) (Day et al. 2008). Here, we would note that the degree and number of traumatic events in the lives of the young men featuring above are extensive – far exceeding, we would suggest, those in the general population. Death (drug overdoses, fatal shootings, car accidents), sexual abuse, beatings, foster care, dealing with solitary confinement and intergenerational incarceration all leave their mark. These are things we sense never properly get resolved within and beyond custody. Recall Chris's words: 'I got out with a lot of anger.... What happened to my girl, what's happened to me, what's happened in the past'. Agnew (1992, 2006) argues that coping with loss compels vulnerable adolescents into crime as they attempt to correct perceived injustices or make use of illegitimate channels for achieving particular goals. Crucially, angry or frustrated individuals are 'less likely to consider the long-term consequences of their behavior' (Agnew 2006: 33). Again, the correctional system – trying to deal with its own strains – has managed to make the process of recovering from grief and loss more difficult. As one intervention manager explained:

> [O]ften the young men with the death by dangerous driving [offences arrive here] and they've seen nobody [even after years of being locked up in other facilities].... And, you know, that's really difficult in the victim awareness group, dealing with that kind of stuff. But, you see, we're not even supposed to deliver them [victim awareness courses] one-on-one. So...as you'd understand, there's a huge potential to re-traumatize people in a group situation.... Historically, I have

delivered those on [a] one-on-one [basis].... We're not supposed to do that anymore, so I'm not sure how that's going to [go].

In the absence of carefully calibrated assistance from the system, the chief form of help (if any should exist) comes from family members. But, as we've demonstrated, they can only do so much to assist the likes of Chris, Sam or James, but also Ben, Lee, Paul or Matt. This is because the families in such situations are so heavily fragmented and poorly resourced. They lack the requisite skills and time (not to mention emotional energy) to pull their kin through (see Halsey and Deegan 2014). Too often, the only thing standing between the young men and more crime are pleas from their family to think again. Recall here the words of Matt's father: 'I'm trying to feel for my son and tell him that it's all a waste of fucking time. Time you can't get back.' This is a stark and forceful appeal. Indeed, with Matt subsequently taking to waving shotguns in people's faces, his father's fears were right on point. But what we take from this is a profound sense of being alone in the battle for desistance. It can't just come down to one or a few significant others wishing things were different. There needs to be a collective effort – a concerted 'partnership' between juvenile justice, corrections, service agencies, and the people and contexts to which (ex)prisoners return. Of course, in a perfect world there would be no juvenile justice or correctional system. But given these systems are in place and only getting larger, it is important to ensure they and the social service agencies they interface with are properly funded. Crucially, that funding needs to be geared not just toward the management of prisoners and parolees but to the equally if not more important task of 'turning prisoners back into citizens' (Maruna 2011: 4).

Managing the scorned self

For us, so much of the crime and suffering endured and/or inflicted by the young men in this book reduces to the deep and abiding sense of being *jilted* or disrespected from a young age (see Moran 2014). Each commenced offending – at least in more serious fashion – on account of feeling humiliated, shamed and/or marginalized in ways that were not immediately recoverable by the young men themselves nor by those in their milieu. Katz (1988: 24) describes humiliation as akin to situations where people 'become morally impotent [and] unable to govern the evolution of [their] identity'. Most, if not all, of us know what it is to be humiliated – the situation where 'we have made fools of ourselves or have been made fools by others [such that] we may wish or feel we are sinking into the earth' (Katz 1988: 28). But most of us manage to deal with humiliation in ways that don't involve harming others (or ourselves). Typically this is through being able to laugh at what could otherwise linger as 'threatening' psycho-social events. From boardrooms to the streets, humour, in particular, has been noted as an immensely important social device that enables potentially serious situations to be immediately recast as trivial and for the recasting to be done in ways that ultimately keep people's reputations intact.

We mentioned earlier that most of the young men in our cohort are trying to make up for lost childhoods – trying to recover from events that more or less put them on a path to crime and incarceration. One variable that seems firmly in the mix here is the experience of having being repeatedly humiliated, or, in more colloquial parlance 'dissed', from a young age. They have all variously been labelled by parents and/or professionals as 'misfits', 'delinquents', 'incorrigibles', 'menaces', 'hyperactive', 'deficient', 'slow to learn' and the like. They have all at different times acquiesced in these labels or acted out against them. Crime, for them, was a form of rage – a kind of early to mid-life course protest. And rage, as Katz (1988: 27) reminds us, is the chief means for 'turn[ing] the structure of... humiliation on its head'. Each young man in our cohort (including Lee) felt seriously betrayed by someone or something early in their lives and, for most, this feeling never really got resolved as they aged through their teenage and early adult years. As Katz (1988: 27) puts it, 'Humiliation drives you down; in humiliation, you feel suddenly made small, so small that everyone seems to look down on you'. Crime became the way for young men like Chris and Sam – indeed all – to feel 'big' again. They weren't just 'frustrated' with their lot – it wasn't a matter of being unable to get this bit of clothing, do this bit of maths, learn that bit of spelling, or attend to this or that rule set by a teacher, parent, sporting club or the like. Things ran much deeper than that and struck in far more personal and lasting ways.

For Chris it was having his claims of sexual abuse fall on deaf ears and watching his family, literally, disintegrate, before him. It was being forced to bring himself up and to surrender any hope of a normal childhood. For Matt it was being beaten and scorned by successive 'stepfathers' while his own father was doing time. It was never being able to rely on his mother due to her chronic alcoholism and battles with depression. For Ben, it was being abandoned in infancy by his father, only then, some years later, to lose his baby brother in a fatal accident. Instead of being able to turn to his mother, she became a drug addict, selling anything and everything to fund her habit and bringing countless men to the house who were violent to her and threatened violence to Ben. Cars became his home and crime became his means of survival. For James it was being bullied persistently at school, to the point where no school would accept him due to the nature of the schoolyard violence he attracted ('That's...when I started getting into trouble really,...people picking on me'). With his father having long fled the family scene, and his mother addicted to ice, James took to the streets and was made a ward of the state. For Lee, it was never being able to 'integrate' into his community and to abide his parents' relentless demands that he refrain from taking his own path. He didn't want to be dirt poor. He wanted to have what other kids had, and he wanted it sooner not later. Dealing heroin by age nine gave him a taste of the good life.

For Reggie, although he rarely spoke of it, the abandonment by his parents, and the violence done to him by successive foster carers, were defining events. The streets were a safer option, as was custody. For Billy, it was the sense that he'd been lied to for so long about who his real father was, and, by default, who he thought himself then to 'really' be. For Joel, like James, it was being bullied mercilessly at school because he was 'slower' to learn than other kids. Violence, for him, became the way to build some kind of reputation. For Charlie, it was the feeling that he was destined to do crime because that's what everyone in his family had done and were doing. Dealings with police, courts and custodial facilities were the norm – like the sun rising and setting. For David, it was the toxic household – his parents' verbal abuse of each other and of drugs and alcohol – that led to his childhood being cut short. Even after his father left, dealing with his mother's alcoholism was too much. Crime became a type of solace.

Sam never really knew his father. His mother was deeply ensconced in the drug world both prior to and after his birth. All kinds of 'clients' came to and went from the house. From age three Sam's behavior was, by all accounts, 'uncontrollable'. He never had a chance. Paul's learning difficulties caused him endless problems. His own father judged him to be a bitter disappointment and abandoned him at age seven. Paul's problems with anxiety and depression only worsened as he bounced for years from the street, to his grandparents' houses, to custodial facilities, to emergency accommodation. He knew little of stability and his self-esteem took a severe hit – something that has only started to improve in recent times. Sean also had psychiatric issues. He never knew his father and, following a broken arm given him by his despairing mother, was made a ward of the state. The experience of going from one foster care scenario to another left him seriously traumatized. At age four, Greg was also surrendered by his mother to the State. And when his father re-entered the scene over a decade later, the damage had already been well and truly done.

We do not suggest each of these lives can be reduced to a single event or point in time. There are, after all, countless children who face similar adversities and come through things relatively unscathed. We do argue, though, that *no two lives share exactly the same circumstances* and that this fact is fundamental to understanding why, as mentioned at the outset, the correctional and wider social support systems appear broken. Gadd and Farrall (2004: 148 emphasis added) rightly argue that 'criminal careers researchers need to think through what the risk and protective factors they routinely cite – (un)employment, (in)adequate parenting, marriage and divorce, social exclusion and inclusion, drug use and abstinence – *mean* to their research subjects, as well as how these correlate with rates of offending at aggregate levels'. Moralizing and didactic statements such as, 'If I was in James' position ...', or, 'If I was faced with Chris' dilemma...', or, 'If I had Sam's start to life...', become, here, null and void. They literally don't make sense since none of us was there, struggling each and every step to walk in their shoes. Life, as Deleuze (1994) says, is characterized by *alterity* – a kind of radical difference that refuses any attempt to serialize the diversity of experience.

In the context of thinking about young people and their involvement in crime, this means acknowledging that the capacity to fend off various crises will be different in small but critically important ways for *each and every child*, and for each and every 'family'. Again, drawing on Gadd and Farrall (2004: 148), 'answers to the question "why do people stop offending?" are unlikely to be evident in the surface-data we gather about criminal careers. The latent or unconscious meanings embedded in offenders' narratives are as important as the actual words, narratives and discourses used. These unconscious meanings can only be "got at" through in-depth interpretive work'. In other words, the nuanced view from the inside looking out will always be fundamentally distinct and more complex to the chiefly homogenizing view from the outside looking in (especially those which try to glimpse 'crime causation', 'criminogenic need', or even 'basic need' from profiles, tables, actuarial data and the like). The prime purpose of this book has been to explicate the consequences of this tendency – to show something of the complexity and 'underlying' troubles investing each young man's story and to demonstrate that the stories are *not* reducible to one or the other. Yes, all the young men 'graduated' from juvenile to adult custodial facilities and, yes, most lacked a stable father figure, were kicked out of school for bad behaviour, had slept rough on occasion, battled their own and others' problems with drugs and alcohol, and commenced offending to 'escape' the turmoil of their lives. To an extent they *are* cut from same cloth. But in so many ways their circumstances are different and this difference requires carefully calibrated responses that, to be blunt, no standardized 'program' or court order seems capable of delivering. Again, as Deleuze (2007: 216) writes, 'There is no beginning, there is no end. We always begin in the middle of something'.

Arguably, it is the inability of various agencies – and indeed family members themselves – to understand precisely what this 'something' is that results in so much heartache. Chris, for instance, wasn't just 'in the middle' of a pattern of sexual abuse. He was also in the middle of trying to understand his parents' refusal to believe in him. He was in the middle of trying to protect his sister. He was in the middle of trying to muddle through school with all this on his mind. But he was also in the middle of wanting to be a child. Even as a man, Chris has always been in the middle of that struggle. At each point where agencies 'intervened' in the lives of the young men in this book, they singularly failed to grasp the nature of the 'middle' – of the personal and social milieus in which each resided and would most likely return subsequent to arrest or release from custody. In the words of one prison manager:

> [W]e send them out quite often in the early stages [of their offending career] without getting intervention. We send them back to the same environment that we took them out of, usually into the same house with the same peers.... [I]f anything they develop additional... networks within gaol that support the need for ongoing criminal activities.... And we don't address the unemployment issue, we don't address the family issue.

Perhaps most tellingly, so much of what happened to the young men within and beyond custody only heightened their sense of disempowerment and personal humiliation. When incarcerated as juveniles they swung between the poles of *infantalization* ('You cannot know what is best since you are still a child') and *responsibilization* ('As a young man, you need to take control over your life'). How could a capable well-adjusted young person ever emerge from this 'Alice in Wonderland' scenario (Maruna et al. 2004b)? It's like Reich (2010) says, being locked up as a juvenile is the time when young men temporarily play the Game of Law (obey staff, dutifully attend programs, start 'thinking right') only in order that they can get out and resume, with even greater vigour, the Game of Outlaw (get high, offend, consolidate or expand their hold in the underground economy). Keeping kids 'safe' in custody is of paramount importance. But it's typically not going to put them on the path to primary, less, secondary desistance. This is because most young men leave such environments not knowing how to cope in legitimate ways beyond the perimeter of the facility. Incarceration, in short, is a humiliating and disenabling experience writ large – the excerpts throughout this book, in spite of the occasional positive moment – overwhelmingly testify to this.

In this context, Margalit (1998: 128–9 emphasis added) makes the important distinction between 'humiliating agents' and 'humiliating situations', observing that the distinction 'is important because institutional humiliation is *independent* of the peculiarities of the humiliating agent, depending only on the *nature* of the humiliation'. This is why one can find genuinely good staff (agents) in both juvenile and adult custodial environments (situations) and yet also find that their efforts don't, in most cases, help to fashion competent citizens within and beyond the gate (but see Burnett and McNeill 2005). Ultimately, prisoners bear the brunt of an institutionalized disrespect – one that carries on and entrenches the feeling of already having been 'passed over' well before being admitted to custody. Recall here Ben's experience in solitary confinement, James's release without his parole papers, Sam's proximity to his mother's alleged assailant, Jane's near loss of her house and kids, the process surrounding Tim's parole rejection, Chris's incapacity to keep up a professional relationship with his youth worker, the refusal to permit Reggie to attend a funeral, and more. Katz (1988: 30) writes, 'Humiliation is a painful awareness of the mundane future, a vivid appreciation that once I get out of the current situation I still will not be able to get away from its degradation. I become humiliated just as I discover that despite my struggles to do so, I cannot really believe that the meaning of the moment is temporary'. This so very neatly captures the situation for most of the young men in our study. So how might such situations be ameliorated or, better, averted? Are there any points of light concerning the plights of young male repeat offenders? To our minds, there are, and several of these are discussed in the next chapter.

8
Points of Light

In their UK study of 113 persistent male offenders interviewed repeatedly from ages 19 to 26, Shapland and Bottoms (2011) found overwhelmingly that the cohort felt shame at being labelled 'offenders' and aspired to lead conventional lives centred around respect for the law, good jobs and stable home environments. In Farrall's (2004: 99 emphasis in original) UK-based study of 199 probationers, around 95 per cent of that cohort 'said that they *wanted* to stop offending'. The most common factors, beyond the 'right mind-set', associated with probable cessation from crime involved 'family support' (including accommodation) and 'employment' (Farrall 2004: 158). In Burnett's (2004: 157) exploration of persistence and desistance among 130 property offenders – mostly aged in their 20s – more than 80 per cent 'said they wanted to go straight'. This required, in the main, sufficient income in order not to have to resort to crime. In her ethnography of 15 young men transitioning from a reform school to the community in Philadelphia, Fader (2013) similarly showed that, far from embracing or permanently desiring the criminal life, each young man wanted ultimately to become a good employee, father, student or the like. They wanted, simply, to become better people. Even Contreras' (2013: 233) participants – the 'stickup kids' – wanted out of the extreme violence that characterized their world. Gus – the central protagonist in that work – 'spoke', finally, 'of pursuing a quiet, humble life'. And this from a man who once only knew how to trade drugs and guns, and kill, maim or torture drug rivals. Reich's (2010: 240) work examining the masculinity games of young men in and out of a Rhode Island training school (young men's prison) told how, as adults – especially as *incarcerated* adults – all wanted to live life beyond the traps set by the 'Game of Outlaw'. They wanted, instead, the means to build a life around children, a job and, importantly, in relation to social inquiry into the world around them.

So often – too often – in researching and thinking about offenders, there is a tendency to overlook the fact that the majority of such people would choose a different life if only they knew how and if, in transitioning to a different circumstance, they could somehow maintain or enhance their dignity and standing. This is one of the defining lessons from Philippe Bourgois' classic work *In Search of Respect*. Through a meticulous ethnographic immersion in the milieu, he laid bare all the mayhem associated with dealing crack cocaine in East Harlem. While he recorded a particular kind of 'pleasure' and 'prestige' for those involved in that life, Bourgois demonstrates these benefits to be short-lived and only 'desired' because there is precious little else offering a means for survival. Beyond providing an income, though, drug dealing is shown to be motivated by more than 'simple economic exigency' (Bourgois 1996: 324). Instead, '[l]ike most humans on earth ... [the crack dealers were] also searching for dignity and fulfillment'. The catch for Primo and Caeser – the book's central participants – was that in 'scrambling to obtain their piece of the [economic] pie', their stocks of respect, in the eyes of the general community, plummeted (Bourgois 1996: 326). Only in relation to other drug dealers, users and suppliers did their prestige remain steady. These other players understood the game – its rules, its risks, its potentials and its costs.

So with the young men in our study. As their criminal capital grew, their stocks of social legitimacy plummeted. Perhaps, as juveniles, they could expect to be cut some slack. After all, everyone mucks up some time, especially as a kid. But when one's offending starts to span well beyond teenage years – or becomes extremely serious in those years – it becomes increasingly hard to rebuild the reservoir of goodwill and respect that most 'normal' citizens enjoy. This in part accounts for why the secondary stage of desistance has proved so difficult to attain for the majority of young men in our research. That stage is not just about the development of internal scripts – the story built and rehearsed from within about past, present and future. Rather, it's equally about how others with standing interpret such stories and about the stories these others invest in and put into wider circulation on behalf of would-be desisters. Young men struggling to desist from crime undeniably do so in relation to the hardships and possibilities of the street. But they also must confront the obstacles and possible turning points in particular types of *discourse* (pre-sentence reports, sentence management plans, parole plans, review board decisions, job application forms, rental agreements and so on) and *chatter* (of friends, family, police, court staff, youth workers, correctional officers and the like). Overcoming such obstacles is an immensely difficult task. But there are practical ways to ensure that 'hooks for change' as well people's openness to such stand a higher likelihood of engagement.

Remedy

We don't profess to offer an instruction manual for desistance early in the life course – let alone desistance more generally. Even after several hundred interviews over many years it's clear there is no set path or combination of factors that guarantee success. So often we've thought that one or another of the young men were on their way to better things when, seemingly out of nowhere, things took a turn for the worse (recall the precarious circumstance of Billy, our 'leading desister'). Sometimes the turn was, in retrospect, reasonably fathomable, but other times it remained unclear why the young men veered off the rails. But given this caveat, we start from the basic premise that any society interested in effective crime prevention will invest as heavily as possible in the services and infrastructure known to enhance social inclusion and personal opportunity. This, at minimum, includes:

- functional, well-located, and readily available stocks of low-rent housing;
- meaningful and market-relevant opportunities for job training within prison and beyond as well as integration of ex-prisoners into workplaces fit to manage the stigma and assortment of issues accompanying the hiring of such persons;
- strong investment in primary and tertiary education within custodial facilities but also, and especially, in suburbs/communities known disproportionately to 'feed' the work of police, courts and prisons;
- responsive and supportive psychological and psychiatric counselling and/or mental health wards capable of dealing with the complex needs of various court users including those currently sent to prison for, essentially, lack of such services;
- well-resourced 24-hour state-of-the-art crisis response lines capable of dealing immediately with ex-prisoners and/or their support persons who may feel themselves overwhelmed by circumstances and on the brink of collapse/reoffending; and
- a universally accepted commitment to work with the family and/or social context to which prisoners and/or residents of juvenile custodial facilities return on release in order to more appropriately distribute the heavy 'load' of re-entry and reintegration

(for a discussion of obstacles to desistance, see also Maguire and Raynor 2006).

We turn now to highlighting some of the more effective measures which, either locally or internationally, seem to make a notable difference in terms of life within and beyond custody, and which enhance the motivation and capacity of people to desist from crime. Importantly, all of the examples mentioned below tap into the generative dimensions of prisoners' and ex-prisoners' lives. That is to say, they are fundamentally concerned with opportunities for positive legacy-making and 'giving back' to the community (McNeill and Maruna 2008). In that sense, each initiative is based on a fluid notion of the custodial and post-custodial subject. Here, people are not 'nailed down as one' – they are no longer relentlessly defined in relation to their past (criminality). Instead, they are valorized for who they are becoming. After all, the struggle for desistance, in the end, is in many ways akin to the struggle for a new emergent self, or, as Stevens (2012) puts it, 'the person...I was always meant to be'.

Respite care

One of the most important things that can be done to reduce the number of young people ending up (permanently) in out-of-home care and/or the juvenile justice system (and subsequently the prison system) is to assist families at crisis point to get back on track, or perhaps on track for the first time. It is manifestly clear from the stories in this book that so many of the young men could have benefited from a circuit breaker in 'managing' dynamics on the home front. Children need a place to retreat to which doesn't subsequently carry the threat or possibility of them becoming a ward of the state or fostered out with successive families. It is not unusual for young men in custody to report being moved from upwards of 20 foster families in their teen years – most of which exacerbates the instability and turmoil in their lives. In South Australia, one of the most effective organizations assisting children in this regard is Time for Kids. Founded in 1960, it has placed in excess of 5000 children (aged from birth to 17 years) with hundreds of volunteer carers who provide respite for children – children who tend to be on the cusp of falling into crime and other types of anti-social behaviour. This type of arrangement seeks to reduce and preferably remove the stigma attached to helping families under excessive strain. In any year around 200 carer families open their homes to children at weekends, school holidays and other mutually agreed times. As a Time for Kids Ambassador, the lead author knows something of the importance of the organization's work. The fundamental aim of Time for Kids is to ensure that families stay together and that children from highly marginalized households or communities get to experience things which most kids take for granted – holidays, movies and, perhaps most importantly, the chance to just be 'children'.

In 2006, a report based on interviews with past 'clients' of Time for Kids highlighted their understanding of the role respite foster care played in shaping (or not) their life course (Halsey 2006b). It is significant that many – although aged in their mid-twenties – had stayed in touch with their carer family. A selection of comments from those 'children' tell of the positive impact:

> Every summer we'd go down to [a little place on the coast] and we'd stay in the caravan and we'd camp out.... I don't remember a family holiday that our mum had. So I was so lucky in that respect. (A)

> You kind of learn a lot of new skills seeing people that you haven't before.... Like more communications skills, and things like that. And just being positive and being able to... go and talk to people that you haven't met before.... It makes you feel really good about yourself as well. So instead of feeling really crappy about yourself, it just makes you feel a lot better as a person. (C)

> I just had this kind of huge family existence, that's what resonates for me the most. Just being completely acknowledged by people that don't owe me one single thing but treat me like their own. (E)

> They treated me like their family, like I was their daughter.... It sort of felt like a dream childhood. (F)

> [B]efore I went there [to my Time for Kids family] I was in foster care a lot and I hated the way they treated me [there], whereas this family was different. Like, they weren't getting paid to look after me... whereas in foster care they do.... So going there, they were genuine people, they weren't doing it for the money or anything else. They just wanted to help out a random kid.... [I]n foster care... they make you feel like shit... and they treat you pretty bad. (H)

What strikes here is the way ordinary things are perceived as extraordinary. More than this, it was the sense of finding somewhere safe that mattered most – somewhere where children can get their faith in adults (and the world generally) restored. Somewhere they can laugh and just be happy. Part of feeling safe was the knowledge that each child was not required to 'choose' between respite care and their own family (whatever that might have looked like). Time for Kids works because they put considerable effort into ensuring strong and open connections between a child's parent(s) and their carer family. It is, in effect, one of the best means for building social and emotional capital among families who find, for whatever reason, that they are low in these. Overwhelmingly, children assisted by Time for Kids come from sole-parent families where the challenge of bringing up children has proved too burdensome. Typically first placed at around eight or nine years of age, the relationship with a carer family can continue over many years. When asked to look back, as adults, on their experience, and to frame it in terms of a possible turning point, the following responses were given:

> It definitely shaped who I am. It's given me such a compassion for other people, to see the best for people.... Recognizing what was done for me really makes me want to go, 'Hey, I want to help others', and in the same respect that I wasn't aware that I was being 'helped', I want to do that for other people. (A)

> I: Can you draw any link between [who] you [are] today and these experiences?
> P: Definitely.... You kind of learn a lot of new skills seeing people that you haven't before.... Like... more communications skills, and things like that... It makes you feel really good about yourself as well ... (C)

> I wouldn't be the person that I am right now if it wasn't for [my carer family].... Like, [at] 13, you know, when you go through that whole teenage stage, I used to always feel like whenever I went there I could just be myself, and I could find myself again. (D)

> It was great.... I got to see what the dynamic [of a family] was, what they were like as parents. They were role models to me, and [I saw] how [a] family should be run.... [T]hey gave me understanding, yeah, I have no regrets about staying with them. (G)

It is impossible to say precisely the impact Time for Kids has had and is having in terms of keeping kids out of the juvenile justice system. But as a guide, the 14 young men in this book spent close to 12,000 days (around 33 years) in juvenile custodial facilities from ages 10 to 18. The costs of incarceration amount, as mentioned in Chapter 1, to approximately $12 million for this small cohort. Even if, over the years, just one in every 100 children assisted by Time for Kids had prevented them from spending a year in custody, the economic saving would be in the vicinity of $16 million. It is difficult to imagine what Paul, Matt, Ben, Chris or James would have made of the opportunity to engage in respite care. Perhaps they would have rejected it outright. But the gamble, in retrospect, would have been well worth the risk.

Sport

Recent work in the UK has shown promising results linking carefully crafted sporting opportunities for young men in prison and subsequent likelihood of desistance from crime. Meek (2012) undertook a major evaluation of the 2nd Chance Project run out of Portland Young Offender Institution. The Project involved three to four months of intensive training in football (soccer) or rugby but also, importantly, linked physical skills training to a host of other supportive interventions for those enrolled. This included a '2nd Chance transition worker' responsible for engaging agencies and services needed for each young man to stand the best possible chance of reintegration following release (Meek 2012: 6). Participants were aged, on average, 20 years and had been sentenced for violent and/or property crime as well as drug offences. Most participants, though, had some history of violent offending. Meek (2012: 16) determined that 'Of the [50] academy participants who have been released from prison in the past 18 months, 41 (82%) have successfully desisted from re-offending'. On available data, at such time nine had 'been in the community for a year or more', '15...in the community for between [six] months and [one] year, and a further 15 ...for under six months' (Meek 2012: 16). The reoffending rate of 18 per cent is substantively less than the national figure of 48 per cent (measured up to one year following release). Clearly, there is something about this initiative that seems to have garnered success where so many other 'interventions' have failed or made only marginal gains. Key here is the fact that 2nd Chance is premised on the understanding that good work built behind prison walls requires equally hard work following release. There must be continuity of support – support which functions as if the barrier dividing custodial and post-custodial assistance is invisible. Reflecting on the success of 2nd Chance, Parker and Meek (2013: 80) observe:

> [T]oo often, on release from prison, young people find themselves without the personal or social skills to engage with the agencies

which are designed to support them. For these young people the easiest way to survive is to return to the life that they know best and around which they feel most secure: a life of crime. The 2nd Chance Project aims to act as some form of corrective in this respect, by creating a climate in which marginalized and vulnerable young people can develop a sense of confidence and belief in themselves, trust in others and hope for the future. At a practical level this means empowering young people to think positively about life, to develop coherent self-advocacy, to interact with multi-agency support and, where appropriate, to re-establish familial connections and relationships.

So much of what presently passes for 'rehabilitation' falls well short of making inroads into (ex)prisoners' lives. 2nd Chance, though, seems to permit cognitive, emotional and situational transformations to powerfully converge.

Mentoring

Another project – again South Australian-based – which has showed promising results for young people in detention is the Step Out: Youth At Risk of Re-offending Mentoring Initiative (SOMI) coordinated by the Red Cross. Over a 15-month period spanning 2011 and 2012, six paid mentors and a number of support volunteer mentors connected with 19 young people in detention in South Australia. The average length of each mentor-mentee relationship was 11 months and the maximum 14 months. Visiting each of their mentees for a period of three to six months prior to release, mentors and mentees slowly established trust and worked together to plan the final stages of their time in custody and, importantly, what they hoped to achieve upon release. Each constructed a Personal Development Guide outlining short and long-term goals. These were reviewed at set intervals by mentors and each of their mentees. Short-term goals included finishing school, ceasing drug use, making new friends, dealing better with painful emotions, saving money and the like.

Of the 15 mentees who reported their progress at the first point of review, 12 (80 per cent) had succeeded or were well on the way to meeting their short-term goals. Long-term goals were rightly more lofty and 'included such things as: "Attend university and work toward becoming a manager of a family business", "Work in a helping profession with animals or people", "Become a truck driver", "Work as a chemist and liv[e] with my family", "Have a stable life with a family and own a home",

"Have a car licence, go back home with Mum, have a job", "Work as a youth worker", and "Be in high school".' Of the 13 mentees who reported their progress at the second review, two were 'well on the way to realizing their long term plans' and 'a further six...had taken steps in the right direction' (Halsey 2012: 14). Overall, and even with several cycles of release and return to custody, 'The clear majority of mentees believed their journey toward integration into mainstream society had been made easier, better, or more likely, on account of their participation in the SOMI' (Halsey 2012: 2). But the really telling result to emerge from this initiative was that young people who had previously viewed all 'help' with suspicion considered mentoring a means for bringing 'someone in their life they could rely upon and trust'. For them, this was the 'single most important stated benefit' of the SOMI (Halsey 2012: 2). The importance of the connection with a trusted capable other – someone who does not condemn or judge – is a vastly undervalued resource in juvenile and criminal justice:

> I: ...So what do you know now about having a mentor that you didn't know before you commenced with Step Out?
>
> P: Just that there's people out there in the community in general that are gonna help you no matter what. And even if you, you know, you fuck up, or you do something wrong, and you think, 'Well, I'm fucked. I'm going back...to gaol', you know, 'I'm going back to [a juvenile or adult custodial facility] or wherever. And, ah, I'm fucked. I don't know what I'm gonna do'. And then all of a sudden you get this phone call and, you know, you look at your screen and 'Step Out program', you know [my mentor is calling]. And you [answer the phone] and it just feels like all your worries have just gone. You know, they sit there and they talk and they say, 'It's not the end of the world. Here's a taxi I'm gonna call. Then come into the office [and] we'll sit down [and] we'll talk about it'. And you...just feel like a big weight's been lifted off your shoulders straight away. Like, you feel like you've...mess[ed] you up, so you might as well go hard with all the crime and things.... Then all of a sudden you get this phone call and everything's alright and it's just magically fixed like, you know, it helps so much coz you think, 'Well,...I'm going back anyway, I might as well just commit more crime', and then you get this phone call and then afterwards you think, 'Fuck, that would have been a stupid decision because it wasn't even nothing to worry over...I've

> been [in] lot[s] of situations... where it's happened... [E]ven drug withdrawals. I tried stopping drugs and... [the people from Step Out]... they sort of said, 'Well, hey, look. If you're gonna stop, you might as well fucking, you know, you might as well do it properly'. And they sort of helped me with that as well. And even when I was on drugs they said, 'Hey that's your business, you know. Just don't do it round the office and don't come in off your head of course'.

This is one the very few ways to effectively address the 'fuck it' mentality (spoken of elsewhere) that arises in the minds of so many young people when trying to desist. Trusted relationships – not overzealous policing, insensitive case management, admonishment or threat of further punishment – is the key to getting people in desperate situations to reconsider their trajectory. These kinds of results, it should be noted, were achieved with minimal financial cost and with an average mentor-mentee contact time of just two hours per week. One mentor summed up the basics of helping young offenders:

> I: What was the most important thing you were able to offer or do for each of your mentees?
> P: Just be there for them. If they got something to say, listen. If they got somewhere to go, take them. If they're hungry, feed them. You know, whatever they need, within reason.... [J]ust be there for them.

Education

Education can form a fundamentally important part of the desistance process. Yet, all of the young men in our study arrived at adulthood without any meaningful educational qualifications to their name. Although education is mandated in juvenile custodial settings, it is far from an ideal learning environment. Too often classes devoted to academic learning devolve into classes where management of difficult behaviour becomes the norm. On release, all the young men in this book found it virtually impossible to settle into a school without feeling an acute sense of paranoia and stigma. Most, at 17, had only passed eight or nine years of schooling and so, in the broader community, could expect to sit in class alongside students several years younger than them. Such a scenario proved wholly unworkable. Young men who've done a lot of custodial time need to catch up on their lost years of learning in ways that protect their dignity (that is, in ways which ensure they aren't humiliated). While most custodial facilities offer classes in basic literacy and numeracy, many prisoners (young and old) need more than that. Klein et al. (2004: 1 quoted in Travis 2011) reminds us that '[T]he most educationally disadvantaged population in the United States resides in our nation's prisons'. The same, without any doubt, could be said of Australia, the UK, New Zealand and Canada. Perhaps only one per cent or so of the prison population in these countries held a tertiary (university/college) degree immediately prior to being admitted into custody. Most will not have completed more than ten years of schooling. And yet it is also known that education is a major means for reducing recidivism. Coley and Barton (2006) highlight several studies showing around a 30 per cent reduction in repeat incarceration where post-secondary education is attained prior to release. A recent meta-analysis of correctional education by the RAND Corporation demonstrated 'that participation in correctional education programs is associated with a 13 percentage-point reduction in the risk of reincarceration three years following release'. The economic savings of such reductions are substantial. Brazzell et al. (2009: 19) cite evidence showing that for roughly every one dollar spent on correctional education of the *academic* 'non-programmatic' kind, five dollars will be saved downstream in criminal justice costs. The fact that so few people with university degrees go to prison is testimony enough to the protective dimensions associated with such an award. Education opens up new horizons and new pro-social networks.

Two well-known initiatives in the US that have – since the demise of the Pell grant scheme in the early 1990s – sought to restore college education to a central position within select prisons include the Bard Prison Initiative (BPI) and the Prison University Project (PUP). BPI commenced in 1999 under the stewardship of former Bard student Max Kenner. Since that time, Bard has built steadily to the point of offering college classes in six prisons in New York State. It has 'granted nearly 275 degrees to BPI participants and enrolled more than 500 students' (BPI 2014a). In terms of enhancing public safety and rebuilding lives, BPI has made significant inroads: 'Among formally incarcerated Bard students, less than 4 per cent have returned to prison. The estimated cost per person, per year of the BPI program is a small fraction of the price of continuing incarceration' (BPI 2014b).

The PUP is based in California, and is run entirely through philanthropic support. Starting from small beginnings in 1996, it became an 'incorporated' not-for-profit entity a decade later. It now enrols, on any day, around 300 of the 4500 prisoners at San Quentin State Prison.

Prisoners from all around California make it their business to get transferred to the facility just to have the opportunity to enrol in college education. Since its inception, in excess of 100 students have graduated with an Associate Arts degree – all taught, voluntarily, by faculty from surrounding Universities (UC Berkeley, Stanford, UC Davis, to name a few). Many of the graduating students are serving long sentences and so, while awaiting possible parole, take up the opportunity to assist other prisoners with their education. This process of 'giving back' and helping others strengthens the 'value' of the educational experience even where release might not be imminent. Jody Lewen, Director of the PUP, has noted that studying subjects such as history, philosophy, biology, politics and the like can complement other 'offence based' programs within the prison (such as those dealing with drug and alcohol issues, anger management or sexual abuse). This is no doubt because gaining a degree equips prisoners with hope for their futures. And with hope comes the capacity and motivation to tackle problems one might otherwise traditionally have shied away from addressing. After all, if someone perceives they have no real future, why sign up for involvement in programs aimed at addressing one's problems? (Voice of America 2011).

Commenting on his involvement in the PUP, one student remarked: 'College helps give me a sense of direction, of purpose, and accomplishment. It seems to have broadened my perceptions of others, of the humanities, and even of myself: [I'm immersed in] a functioning part of society, *even in my remoteness*' (PUP 2014a emphasis added). This is what the PUP and like initiatives do – they remind prisoners they are *part* of society – more than this, such projects affirm them as people capable of engaging in critical thought about the world and their place in it. In Reich's (2010: 50) terms it provides prisoners with the means to directly challenge the 'outsider masculinity that [otherwise] secures their ongoing marginalization' in the world. Again, the pay-offs associated with investing in people typically cast off as 'unworthy' is immense. Prisoners graduating through the PUP and released into the community reputedly return to prison at far lower rates than those who have no such qualification. Perhaps only around 10 per cent are reincarcerated – a rate about six times less than the state's overall rate of reincarceration within three years of release (California Department of Corrections and Rehabilitation 2011).

The lead author has been privileged to witness the work of BPI and the PUP first hand. The initiatives stand as concrete reminders that good and generative things happen in environments geared more fundamentally toward stagnation and deprivation. It seems beyond doubt that education impacts in vitally positive ways on prisoners' sense of self and prison climates more generally. Other correctional systems could do worse than replicate such approaches. As one student of the PUP reflected:

> I sometimes ask myself if there is a price for peace? Or whether there is a price for hope? I do not think that there is. In addition, there is no price that can be affixed to the education I am receiving free of charge. I do know that there is a social and monetary price for crime and recidivism. I can only wonder if me, and the other men here, had had this opportunity years ago if any of us would be here. I do not pretend to know the answer to this question, but I do know that many of us will not return to prison because of the possibilities opened to us through education (PUP 2014b).

Drawing inspiration from these 'models', the Department of Correctional Services (DCS) in South Australia recently collaborated with Flinders University to deliver the first face-to-face 'in-prison' course aimed at qualifying prisoners for university entry. In late 2013, ten prisoners completed the Flinders Foundation Studies Program with six receiving graduation certificates in a ceremony held at Mobilong prison about an hour's drive east of Adelaide (Flinders Marketing and Communications 2013). This is a small but important step to opening up new horizons for such persons – most of whom will be the first in their family to ever have contemplated study at tertiary level. At the time of writing, DCS is in the midst of a system-wide review of educational delivery but there are signs of a commitment to support another iteration of the Foundation course.

Employment

Another promising initiative – again South Australian-based – has been the Prisoner Reintegration Employment Opportunity Program (PREOP). Conceived by the General Manager of Port Augusta Prison (three hours' drive north of Adelaide), the program commenced in 2009 and aims to provide on-the-job training in the mining industry for select prisoners (particularly Indigenous prisoners). In three two-week blocks, prisoners work under the supervision of staff of mining giant BHP Billiton in remote northern South Australia. Some work in the kitchens providing food for the sizeable workforce, others receive training in use of machinery and the like. Several prisoners, in recognition of this rare opportunity, have been known to ask for their parole date to be 'put off' in order to maximize their chances of acquiring work and sorting out housing options through involvement in the PREOP (see ABC News Radio 2012). To date, around half of participants completing the program have managed to find employment. And of those, only five per cent have returned to prison. Conversely, of those who did *not* complete the program or find employment, 95 per cent have been reincarcerated. This points starkly and directly to the importance of employment in the desistance process.

> Work is not simply a way to make a living and support one's family. It also constitutes a framework for daily behaviour and patterns of interaction because it imposes disciplines and regularities. Thus, in the absence of regular employment, a person lacks not only a place in which to work and the receipt of regular income but also a coherent organization of the present – that is, a system of concrete expectations and goals. Regular employment provides the anchor for the spatial and temporal aspects of daily life. It determines where you are going to be and when you are going to be there. In the absence of regular employment, life, including family life, becomes less coherent (Wilson 1996: 73 quoted in Wright and Decker 1997: 132).

Given that around half of all prisoners (in Australia) and approaching two-thirds of Indigenous prisoners report being unemployed in the 30 days leading up to their incarceration (Australian Institute of Health and Welfare 2013: x), the provision of job training and connection to meaningful work *immediately* on release is a critically important feature for putting desistance on track. This is not to say that those who are fortunate to find work will stay out of trouble. But it stacks the odds in their favour. The case of 'Alan' – a participant of the first PREOP intake – gives some clue as to the potentially transformative effect of employment. 'Prior to [his involvement in the] PREOP he had been incarcerated 20 times over a period of 16 years...[with]...[t]he longest time...spent out of prison [being] six months'. Since completing the PREOP, Alan 'was awarded a job on one of the pastoral leases with BHP Billiton'. He 'is still employed today and has not come back to prison in the four years since' his initial participation (Unpublished data, supplied by Brenton Williams, General Manager, Port Augusta Prison).

Art
Art by Offenders in the UK is another outstanding example of a not-for-profit initiative making an important difference to the quality of life for juvenile and adult prisoners, mental health patients, asylum

detainees and those serving sentences in the community (probationers and the like). Stemming from the efforts of former prisoner and author Arthur Koestler, Art by Offenders commenced in 1962 and now receives around 8000 submissions annually from across the UK. Poems, paintings, drawings, ceramics and numerous other artistic forms are sorted, judged and curated in the old governor's house of HMP Wormwood Scrubs. The curating of the art is a deliberately shared task with victims of crime, established artists, musicians and many other groups having been involved over the decades. The 'flagship event' of Art by Offenders is a major exhibition that, in recent years, has been held at the South Bank Centre, London. More than 20,000 people visit the exhibition each year and gain some understanding of life behind bars and, more importantly, of the humanity and potentially positive forces existing there. Around 75 per cent of works are available for purchase with the income generated going to victim support (25 per cent), the artist her/himself (50 per cent) and the Koestler Trust (25 per cent).

Recent work has posited art as assisting primary and secondary stages of desistance. 'It has been found, for example, that art therapy can support "primary desistance" by inciting introspection, confrontation with one's offending, and communication of hitherto suppressed cognitive and emotional states'. Further, 'Arts-based programmes may be said to promote "secondary desistance" insofar as they enhance prisoners' commitment to learning in contravention of previously internalised identities ...' (Cheliotis and Jordanoska forthcoming). Stemming from the work of the Koestler Trust, DCS in South Australia has supported a similarly run initiative for the last three years (Flinders Marketing and Communications 2014). One of the lead author's PhD students coordinates the initiative and his dissertation examines the role of art in challenging public perceptions of prisoners and imprisonment as well as the links between artistic expression and prisoner well-being. One viewer commented: 'Again this exhibition makes me think about prisoners, their lives, and their families in a different way. It re-frames them... Thought provoking, perspective changing, and visually interesting.' Another remarked: 'I had never really thought about prisons as sites of creativity, but this exhibition has helped me to imagine it.' While another observed: 'This exhibition provides inmates with a purpose for vital creative output. It also challenges the viewers' pre-conceived ideas about what makes a criminal.' Equally important, though, are prisoners' own perceptions of their involvement. A selection of comments follows:

> I see art as a very important part of my life. I am now 44 years old and as I have another 10 years before I can go for [parole] it gives me a reason to keep going.
>
> Getting a certificate is in itself a sense of achievement and it shows my family that I'm actually doing something positive with my time in prison.
>
> It showed another side to us and highlighted that we are not just a number on a door.
>
> I found it liberating to be able to express myself via a painting, as in prison, expressing yourself, and your opinions, is somewhat limited... [L]ooking forward to the next one (Unpublished data, supplied by Jeremy Ryder).

Many of the key aspects of desistance and generativity are in evidence here – self-fulfilment, critical reflection, giving to and communicating with others, reconceptualizing identities, challenging stereotypes and permitting the physical and psychic space for change, to name several. Art, of course, is not a panacea for correcting all the ills of incarceration let alone one's entire life history. But it would seem, for some, to be an inexpensive but important part of the desistance journey.

In sum

Ultimately, none (or even all) of the initiatives mentioned above will transform the juvenile justice, correctional and social landscapes. In many ways such initiatives are very small pebbles in a very large river that seems to flow ineluctably against a wider, grounded commitment to prisoner well-being and effective pathways toward prisoner reintegration. The problem here, of course, is not a just a juvenile justice or correctional one. It is in addition a political and social challenge. While it is essential to remain positive about the various innovative things happening locally and internationally to support prisoners and processes of (re)integration, it is also essential to be realistic about overarching trends. Misplaced optimism really only leads to further damage because it misreads (or frames out) the fundamental issues and practices in need of serious and sustained critique. We are doubtful whether Chris's, Sam's, James's or Matt's involvement in art or mentoring or employment or sport or education would have changed their life histories in meaningful ways. It would be naïve to suggest otherwise. But what we can say is that where such options are entirely lacking, the outcome for such young men will be particularly bleak. Yes, young men need to develop a new redemptive-oriented script (Maruna 2001), and they need to become generative rather than stagnative in their routines and outlooks. But for this to occur, they also need – desperately so – things to hang their hopes on (Giordano et al. 2002). They need, in short, the widest possible array of opportunities whereby the struggle to desist can begin, let alone be consolidated.

Concluding Remarks

In her fourth interview, Shirley (grandmother of Reggie), relayed the following life-changing moment that happened in the early 1950s in central Australia:

> I: [Y]ou mentioned that [it] was a real eye-opener when you went to Alice Springs [and worked as a nurse].... [And you said that's where] you saw Aboriginal people for the first time.
>
> P: That was where I decided to adopt... because there was a little boy in there, a two-year-old he was... in Alice Springs [Hospital].... [H]is mother had died of tuberculosis... [and] his father was in the bush somewhere, they didn't know where.... So he had to stay [in the hospital]. He had been there from a baby. When I... went down to the ward, he was in a cot.... [T]hey had... a whole lot of kids in cots... but he was in this cot and nobody went near Anthony. And he used to sit in his cot [and defecate], and then he'd make patterns all over [the walls with it].... [T]hat little kid never smiled and I thought, 'This is terrible that this little baby's here and nobody cares for him'. So I did. And in the three weeks I was in there... I took him and I cleaned him up... because nobody wanted to clean him up because of the mess and everything. I cleaned him up, I took him out to play with the other kids and all that sort of thing. And in a couple of weeks that kid was smiling and trying to talk. And [when] I came home, I wanted to adopt him.... [But] I couldn't...
>
> I: Did you ever find out what happened to that little two-year-old or not?
>
> P: No.... No I never [did].

228 *Young Offenders*

Reflecting on a more recent event, a prison officer told of the following scenario:

> There's one... prisoner here that wouldn't go outside... and I just got talking to him and... [eventually] got him outside walking around for a bit.... [H]e'd spent a long time in [isolation] and he wouldn't socialize with anyone.... [News]papers get delivered [to the prison] so... I'd take them straight to him and, as soon as he finished reading them, he'd slip them under the door, and then other prisoners would read them. You know, he'd ask for a shave [so]... straight away [I'd] go and get a razor, where other officers might not have.... [And over a period of months] we ended up... walking around the prison yard.

At first glance, the events relayed in these excerpts appear poles apart. One speaks of the impetus to devote one's life to helping disadvantaged children. The other speaks of a 'one-off' attempt to engage with a prisoner. But in fact they both speak to the transformative power of caring for others – no matter what their colour, creed, religion or what they have been convicted or accused of. Along with her husband, Shirley went on to dedicate her life to raising orphaned Aboriginal kids. She hung in through thick and thin – watching most of them and *their* children go into and out of custody. But always – always – being there at visiting time and awaiting them at home upon release. Hers, arguably, has been the very definition of a selfless generative life. The prisoner in the above excerpt, is, in fact, one of South Australia's most high-profile and despised offenders. In prison he became in many ways like Anthony – rejected, ostracized, withdrawn. It took months before someone decided to offer up a human gesture toward him. When it came, that gesture came from an unexpected quarter – a prison officer (a screw, the enemy, 'them'). It took many more months for those gestures to translate into the prisoner possessing the courage to leave his cell. But eventually the prisoner did just that. Slowly he began to feel a little bit of his dignity return – just enough to become, within the confines of prison, a functional human being. It wasn't some set of programs, or persistent yelling and harassing by other prisoners or prison staff, or a boot camp, or being made to talk endlessly about one's 'criminogenic needs', that made the difference. It was the fact that someone cared enough to engage in a very simple but instantly recognizable way. And to do this where others had seen fit to allow stagnation to set in. For us, whether it is someone like Anthony (an innocent baby) or a notorious offender serving many years, people's futures are inextricably bound to the actions and omissions of others. That is what the struggle for desistance is about – the actions and omissions of others intermingling with the actions and omissions of oneself. If the stories of the young men in this book reduce to anything, it is to that.

We recognize that the age crime curve for persistent serious offending works against the majority of participants whose lives unfold in this book. It is all too easy, though, on that count, to surrender the quest to ensure opportunities to lead non-violent and dignified lives are distributed throughout communities rather than to certain sections thereof. Far from being utopian, this really is the only way to make serious inroads into juvenile crime and, subsequently, adult offending trajectories. People do, of course, desist from serious repeat offending in their mid to late 20s. David, Charlie and, on balance, Billy, stand as evidence of that. But they are the exception. Many more will keep turning to crime because they don't have the means to turn to anything else. It seems clear that progression from persistent offending to desistance from crime is the outcome of a complex interaction between subjective factors and environmental factors (LeBel et al. 2008). But as Laub and Sampson (2001) argue, there is 'currently no way to disentangle the role of subjective vs. objective change as the cause of desistance' (2001: 41). McNeill (2006: 47) also captures this sentiment by remarking that 'desistance resides somewhere in the interfaces between developing personal maturity, changing social bonds associated with certain life transitions and the individual constructions which offenders build around these key events and changes'. We fully concur with this.

However, we favour the idea that sociogenic factors are of penultimate importance – especially in sparking desistance and in turning 'lulls' into, eventually, a more or less extended state of affairs. Charlie, for example, couldn't have made something out of nothing. He needed the connection to an intimate. He needed the prison environment to help crystallize his desire to be with Michele. He needed somewhere to reside away from 'bad influences'. And he also needed the means to pay for that accommodation. Certainly, Charlie also had to *want* these things and be motivated to stick at them. For him that motivation stemmed, uniquely, from three sources: the belief in his moral goodness; weariness over being repeatedly incarcerated; and love of Michele. What caused these factors to hold weight at one time and not another is the really big question. It's also impossible to answer. '[T]he 'chicken and egg' of subjective and social factors in desistance from crime is not, we contend, a resolvable riddle (LeBel et al. 2008). But in our opinion the riddle doesn't need to be solved. Instead, it's enough to know that one *or* the other (subjective *or* social factors) is insufficient for accomplishing any kind of desistance (primary or secondary). That means any and all efforts to think about prevention of crime cannot rest on flawed notions of the responsibilized self any more than they can rely on the occasional offering of public housing, or job training, or education or drug counselling as magical change agents. All these things and more need to be in the mix. And they need to be available not just when crises set in but well ahead of things turning bad.

In concluding we would therefore make five key points. The first is that desistance from crime is hard. Generally speaking, unless one is personally affected by crime – unless one has walked alongside someone trying to work their way out of years of offending – the difficulties associated with this tend to be poorly understood. As such, public and political debate tends to revolve around one of two poles – either people fail to desist because they *choose* to do more crime (since being out of lock-up means they are, after all, 'free' to make good or bad choices) or, more 'generously', people don't desist because they suffer some psychological malady. Their behaviour is therefore pre-determined and to that degree understandable. The truth, of course, lies between these two poles and is much more complex. There are very few offenders who actively and consciously want to live their lives through the rubric of crime. Crime is hard work and the gains to be had from offending are few. Kudos, wealth – even happiness – can all be derived from offending. But for the vast majority of offenders, these are fleeting rewards. Crime is also tiring, dangerous and ultimately unsatisfying. The people who don't desist from serious repeat offending generally 'fail' not because they are malicious or 'stupid' or uncaring or selfish or the like. Instead, they fail because they can't find the right set of personal and social hooks onto which they might hang the idea of a future really distinct from their past. The trend, in such instances, is for people to become overwhelmed by 'life on the outside' and to fall back into the 'skin' which feels most comfortable.

Second, the mythologies about crime (what causes it) and desistance (how it occurs) typically lead to underinvestment in the things which actually support major transformations of 'self'. What Deirdre Healy (2010) and others have called the 'crucible of change' needs to be surrounded by structured pathways whereby *primary* desistance can get off the ground (pathways to school, job training, stable accommodation and so on). These structures need, most crucially, to employ at least some 'professional ex's' (Brown 1991) – people whose own desistance project is strengthened by 'giving back' to others and who are just starting out, perhaps for the third or fourth time or more, on the desistance journey. This kind of help is called 'retroflexive reformation' (LeBel 2007) and it is a powerful but hugely underutilized resource in the area of rehabilitation and reintegration. In short, we need to do better at getting desistance started (in, literally, the days and weeks following release) in order to have something to build on as those days and weeks turn, very quickly, into months and years.

Third, there is a desperate need for development of processes of social certification/validation for people released from custody. The most critical part of doing or supporting desistance is ensuring that would-be desisters have real and ongoing opportunities to receive social affirmation of their change process. Think about how seriously we take the process of trying to convert primary school children into high school graduates. Or the amount of time and energy invested to turn an amateur athlete into an Olympic gold medallist. Or the resources it takes to turn a cadet into a soldier. All of these things involve monumental commitments of time from various quarters. They involve extensive avenues for entry/recruitment and training as well as strategies for assisting those who might go temporarily 'off-track'. In addition, and perhaps most crucially, they involve rituals of certification that signify the completion of what Maruna (2001) calls a 'rite of passage'. It's important to ask what quantum of time and resources are allocated to the really complex task of 'turning prisoners back into citizens'. What formal social recognition (beyond the lapsing of the requirement to report to a community corrections officer or give a urine sample) is awarded to those who have desisted from crime? What types of 'de-labelling' processes are built into people's desistance journeys? Many ex-offenders will say it is vital for them to have some kind of formal process whereby their process of change is acknowledged – and many think that this should be done by the institution which sentenced/denounced them.

Fourth – and harking back to an earlier point made about compliance and reintegration – there is an important distinction to be made between control and support. We have shown – as have others – that the pathway from serious repeat offending to desistance is 'curved', not straight. People get to desistance very often through scaling back the severity and frequency of offending rather than stopping all offending at a particular point. This means that parole officers, and those working in community corrections more generally, need to think especially hard about the longer-term social impact of being control-oriented as opposed to supportive of 'clients'. Most studies of probationers and parolees talk about the fixation on offenders' past lives rather than the one they actually want to build going forward. Deficit understandings of 'personhood' and personal change don't actually leave much room for change to occur – for the spark of desistance to turn into something more durable (like a predominantly law-abiding life). For support rather than control to be the order of the day, youth workers, community correctional officers and the like need, we would argue, regular professional training in 'what works' in terms of desistance (what doesn't work is more cognitive behavioural therapy or the instruction to do this or that course for the umpteenth time). People working in custodial and post-release environments also probably need to be better remunerated and recast in the public mind as playing a socially valued role. Of course, to move even marginally away from a control-oriented model of offender supervision requires real political strength and leadership. We're certainly not saying that this is an easy task.

Fifth, and finally, we think a very high premium needs to be placed on opportunities for would-be desisters to stumble. Swift reaction to serious 'failure' or real threats to public safety is warranted, but (over)reaction to small setbacks or breaches is not. The desistance process is, for most people, a fragile thing (witness Billy and David). This is why, for instance, the role of the community corrections officer and juvenile release worker needs to be re-examined. Only dedicated and active support people can hope to gain any sense about where someone is at in the elusive thing called 'the desistance process'. And that's because there is no such thing as *the* desistance process. But desistance has a kind of logic and a key aspect of this should be the provision of the space for setbacks to occur. Not turning a setback into a disposition to do additional and far more serious crime is probably the most important but least well understood part of the desistance conundrum. The stories in this book reflect that.

Custodial-Grams

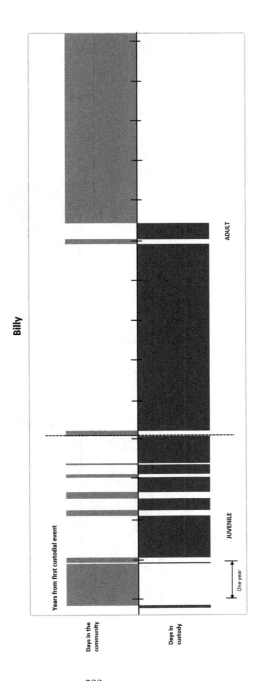

233

234

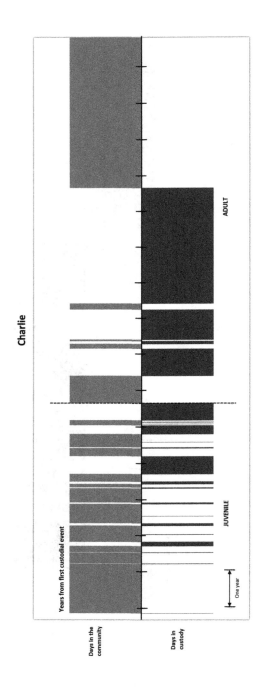

235

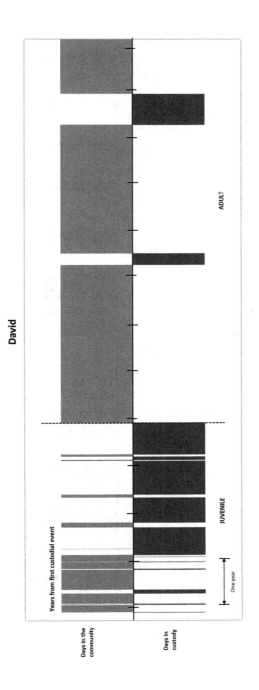

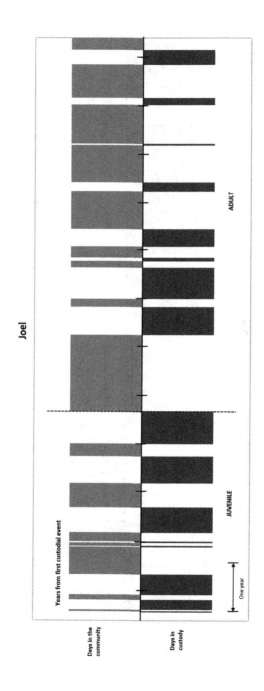

237

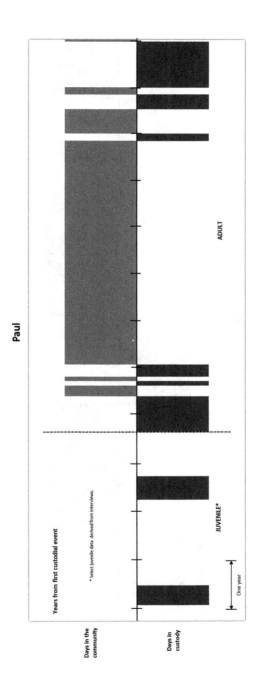

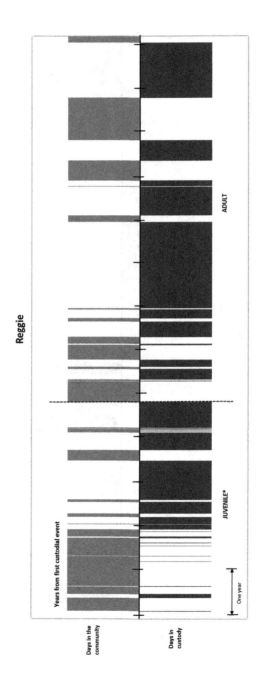

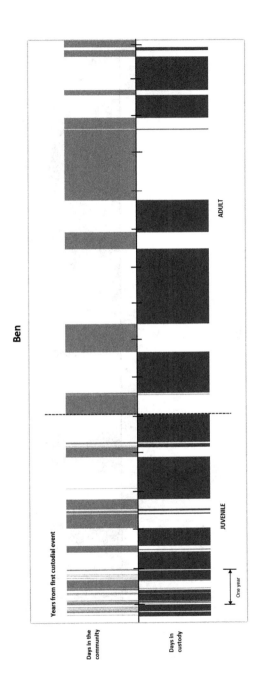

240

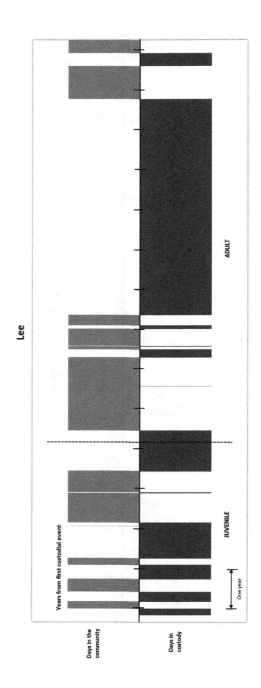

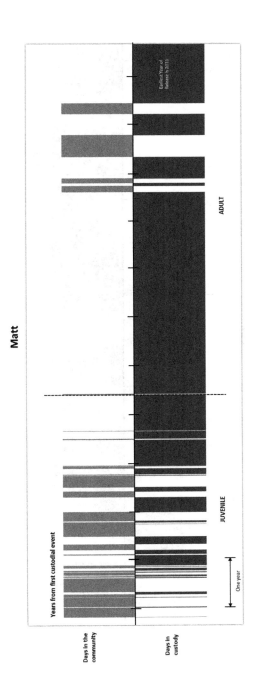

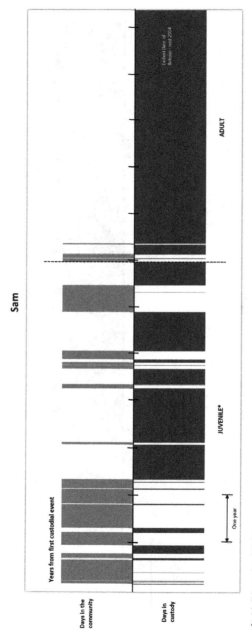

* includes 66 days spent in an adult facility;

243

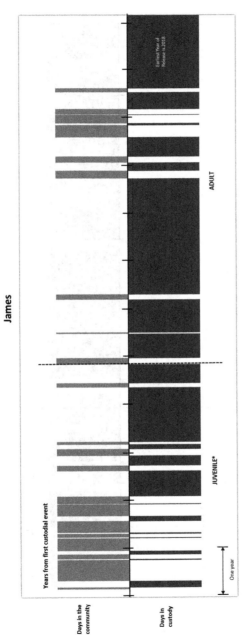

244

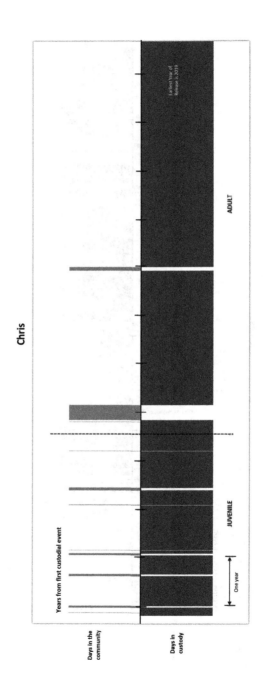

Notes

1 Setting the Scene

1. There is no published aggregated national data on the number of *sentenced* persons discharged annually from prisons around Australia (but see Baldry et al. 2006 for an estimation of total discharges). Inferences can, to an extent, be made from state and territory data. In South Australia, for example, the annual number of sentenced discharges in 2011/12 was 1680, about 80 per cent of the daily average prison population of 2078 (South Australian Department for Correctional Services, South Australia 2012: 104, 106). In New South Wales, the annual number of sentenced discharges for 2010/11 was 7846, again, around 80 per cent of the average daily prisoner population of 10,208 (Corrective Services New South Wales 2013: 6, 18).
2. The age standardized rate of incarceration is 13.6 times higher for the Indigenous population (SCRGSP 2013: 8.7).
3. This was a phrase used by Fergus McNeill but the precise source is unknown. The most likely context was his public lecture 'Five Forms of Rehabilitation: Towards an Integrated Perspective', delivered at Flinders in the City, Victoria Square, Adelaide, 19 September 2012.
4. That rate sits in the order of 8 per cent (19.7 million in 2002 to 22.7 million in 2012).
5. Excludes 'capital costs and payroll tax' (SCRGSP 2013: 8.24).
6. All monetary amounts are expressed in Australian Dollars unless otherwise indicated.
7. The real net operating cost per day per prisoner in 2011–12 was $226 (SCRGSP 2013: 8.24) compared with $23 per day for managing those under a community correctional sanction.
8. New South Wales, for instance, generated just under 145,000 prisoner movements in 2011–12 (61 per cent of which involved prison to court events) (Corrective Services New South Wales 2012: 55).
9. The cost per day to keep a juvenile in detention in South Australia for 2012–13 was $880.33 (SCRGSP 2014: Table 16A.24). This puts the annual recurrent cost per juvenile at $321,540.53.
10. This places to one side the Marxist-functionalist view recognizing the connection between offending and those whose livelihoods rely on a continuous supply of offenders – academics/criminologists included.

3 On Track

1. Home detention.
2. I=Interviewer; P=Participant. We acknowledge, of course, that interviewers are also 'participants' in the research process.

3. 'Lock-up' is the term used by the majority of participants to describe incarceration in juvenile and/or adult custodial facilities.
4. A colloquial term used by all the young men to describe their own and each other's 'out of control' behavior.

4 Recurring Breakdown

1. Ram-raiding is the term used to describe the crime of driving a vehicle through a business premise in order to load it up with stolen goods then speed off.
2. These 'poles' are officially known as 'bollards'. These are installed at regular intervals in front of business premises to prevent cars being driven through shop fronts and loaded up with merchandise.
3. A South Australian Police operation targeting prolific offenders (mostly Indigenous) involved in motor vehicle theft, ram-raiding and, later, armed robbery and torching of stolen vehicles (see Goldsmith and Halsey 2013).

5 Major Derailment

1. Originally built in the mid-19th century using prisoners as labourers, Yatala is a maximum-security prison located about 20 minutes' drive from Adelaide's central business district. It is generally recognized as evincing the worst living conditions of any prison in South Australia (the possible exception to this would be the Adelaide Women's Prison which, at the time of writing, is undergoing building improvements).
2. Social Security Number.
3. A so-called 'enforcer' affiliated with an outlaw motorcycle gang.

6 Catastrophic Turn

1. Police cells used typically for overnight stays.
2. Truanting from school.
3. A mechanical device used to free people from crashed vehicles.
4. This threat of self-harm was reported to the prison manager directly following the interview.

References

ABC News Radio (2012) 'SA Prisoners Delay Release to Stay on Work Program'. Available at: www.abc.net.au/pm/content/2012/s3553572.htm. Last accessed 30 May 2014.

ABC1 Television (2014) *David Bowie: Five Years in the Making of an Icon*. Television program, Adelaide, 29 January.

ABC2 Television (2014) *Hard Time*. Television program, Adelaide, 21 January.

Agnew, R. (1992) 'Foundation for a General Strain Theory of Crime and Delinquency', *Criminology*, 30(1), pp. 47–87.

Agnew, R. (2006) *Pressured into Crime: An Overview of General Strain Theory* (Los Angeles: Roxbury).

Allard, T., Stewart, A., Smith, C., Dennison, S., Chrzanowski, A. and Thompson, C. (2014) 'The Monetary Costs of Offender Trajectories: Findings from Queensland, Australia', *Australian and New Zealand Journal of Criminology*, 47(1), pp. 81–101.

ABS (Australian Bureau of Statistics) (2013a) *4517.0 Prisoners in Australia, 2013*. Available at: www.abs.gov.au/AUSSTATS/abs.nsf/Lookup/4517.0Main+Features100022013?OpenDocument. Last accessed 27 May 2014.

ABS (Australian Bureau of Statistics) (2013b) *4512.0 Corrective Services, Australia, December Quarter, 2013*. Available at: www.abs.gov.au/AUSSTATS/abs@.nsf/Lookup/4517.0Main+Features100022013?OpenDocument. Last accessed 27 May 2014.

Australian Council of Social Service (2012) *Poverty in Australia*. Available at: www.acoss.org.au/uploads/html/ACOSS_PovertyReport2012.html. Last accessed 10 May 2014.

Australian Institute of Family Studies (2013) *Fact Sheet: Children in Care*. Available at: www.aifs.gov.au/cfca/pubs/factsheets/a142092. Last accessed 16 May 2014.

Baldry, E., McDonnell, D., Maplestone, P. and Peeters, M. (2006) 'Ex-prisoners, Homelessness and the State in Australia', *Australian and New Zealand Journal of Criminology*, 39(1), pp. 20–33.

BPI (Bard Prison Initiative) (2014a). Available at: http://bpi.bard.edu/what-we-do/, Last accessed 29 May 2014.

BPI (Bard Prison Initiative) (2014b). Available at: http://bpi.bard.edu/faqs/, Last accessed 29 May 2014.

Barry, M. (2006) *Youth Offending in Transition: The Search for Social Recognition* (New York: Routledge).

Barry, M. (2011) 'Explaining Youth Custody in Scotland: The New Crisis of Containment and Convergence', *Howard Journal of Criminal Justice*, 50(2), pp. 153–70.

Barry, M. (2013) 'Desistance by Design: Offenders' Reflections on Criminal Justice Theory, Policy and Practice', *European Journal of Probation*, 5(2) pp. 47–65.

BBC News (2012) *Tackling Violence in Europe's Largest Youth Prison*, 12 June. Available at: www.bbc.com/news/uk-18166236. Last accessed 16 May 2014.

Bonczar, T. (2003) 'Prevalence of Imprisonment in the US Population, 1974–2001', Bureau of Justice Statistics Special Report (Washington DC: US Department of Justice).

Bonta, J., Rugge, T. and Dauvergne, M. (2003) *The Reconviction Rate of Federal Offenders*, User Report, 2002–03 (Ottawa: Solicitor-General, Canada).

Bosworth, M. (2007) 'Creating the Responsible Prisoner: Federal Admission and Orientation Packs', *Punishment and Society*, 9(1), pp. 67–85.

Bosworth, M., Campbell, D., Demby, B., Ferranti, S. M. and Santos, M. (2005) 'Doing Prison Research: Views from Inside', *Qualitative Inquiry*, 11(2), pp. 249–64.

Bottoms, A., Shapland, J., Costello, A., Holmes, D. and Muir, G. (2004) 'Towards Desistance: Theoretical Underpinnings for an Empirical Study', *Howard Journal of Criminal Justice*, 43, pp. 368–89.

Bourgois, P. (1996) 'In Search of Masculinity: Violence, Respect and Sexuality among Puerto Rican Crack Dealers in East Harlem', *British Journal of Criminology*, 36(3), pp. 412–27.

Bourgois, P. (2012) *In Search of Respect: Selling Crack in the Barrio* (2nd ed) (Cambridge: Cambridge University Press).

Box, S. (1983) *Power, Crime and Mystification* (London: Tavistock).

Brazzell, D., Crayton, A., Mukamal, D. A., Solomon, A. L. and Lindahl, N. (2009) *From the Classroom to the Community: Exploring the Role of Education during Incarceration and Re-entry* (Albany: CUNY Urban Institute).

Brotherhood of St Laurence (2014) 'Youth Unemployment Jumps 67 Per Cent in South Australian Areas'. Media Release. Available at: www.bsl.org.au/Mediacentre/Media-Releases?id=1032. Last accessed 10 May 2014.

Brown, D. (1991) 'The Professional Ex-: An Alternative for Exiting the Deviant Career', *The Sociological Quarterly*, 32(2), pp. 219–30.

Burnett, R. (2004) 'To Reoffend or Not To Reoffend? The Ambivalence of Convicted Property Offenders', in S. Maruna and R. Immarigeon (eds), *After Crime and Punishment: Pathways to Offender Reintegration* (Cullompton: Willan), pp. 152–80.

Burnett, R. and Maruna, S. (2004) 'So "Prison Works", Does it? The Criminal Careers of 130 Men Released from Prison under Home Secretary, Michael Howard', *Howard Journal of Criminal Justice*, 43(4), pp. 390–404.

Burnett, R. and McNeill, F. (2005) 'The Place of the Officer–Offender Relationship in Assisting Offenders to Desist From Crime', *Probation Journal*, 52(3), pp. 221–42.

Bushway, S. D., Piquero, A. R., Broidy, L. M., Cauffman, E. and Mazerolle, P. (2001) 'An Empirical Framework for Studying Desistance as a Process', *Criminology*, 39(2), pp. 491–515.

Bushway, S. D., Thornberry, T. P. and Krohn, M. D. (2003) 'Desistance as a Developmental Process: A Comparison of Staticand Dynamic Approaches', *Journal of Quantitative Criminology*, 19(2), pp. 129–53.

California Department of Corrections and Rehabilitation (2011) *2011 Adult Institutions Outcome Evaluation Report* (Sacramento: Office of Research/Research and Evaluation Branch).

Campbell, R. (2002) *Emotionally Involved* (London: Routledge).

Carlen, P. (2008) 'Imaginary Penalties and Risk Crazed Governance', in P. Carlen (ed.), *Imaginary Penalties* (Cullompton: Willan).

Chatwin, B. (1988) *Songlines* (London: Penguin).
Cheliotis, L. K. and Jordanoska, A. (forthcoming) 'The Arts of Desistance: Assessing the Role of Arts-based Programmes in Reducing Reoffending', *Howard Journal of Criminal Justice*.
Chen, S., Matruglio, T., Weatherburn, D. and Hua, J. (2005) *The Transition from Adult to Juvenile Criminal Careers*, Crime and Justice Bulletin No.86 (Sydney: NSW Bureau of Crime Statistics and Research). Available at: www.bocsar. nsw.gov.au/agdbasev7wr/bocsar/documents/pdf/cjb86.pdf#xml=http://search. lawlink.nsw.gov.au/isysquery/bace3404-3ede-4fd2-a229-cb45fc4d8191/25/ hilite. Last accessed 31 May 2014.
Codd, H. (2008) *In the Shadow of Prison: Families, Imprisonment and Criminal Justice* (Cullompton: Willan).
Cohen, M. A. and Piquero, A. R. (2009) 'New Evidence on the Monetary Value of Saving a High Risk Youth', *Journal of Quantitative Criminology*, 25, pp. 25–49.
Coleman, J. S. (1990) *Foundations of Social Theory* (Cambridge, MA: Harvard University Press).
Coley, R. and Barton, P. (2006) *Locked Up & Locked Out: An Educational Perspective on the US Prison Population* (Princeton: Educational Testing Service), pp. 20–1.
Comfort, M. (2007) 'Punishment beyond the Legal Offender', *Annual Review of Law and Social Science*, 3, pp. 271–96.
Comfort, M. (2003) 'In the Tube at San Quentin: The "Secondary Prisonization" of Women Visiting Inmates', *Journal of Contemporary Ethnography*, 32(1), pp. 77–107.
Contreras, R. (2012) *The Stickup Kids: Race, Drugs, Violence and the American Dream* (Oakland: University of California Press).
Copes, H. (2003) 'Streetlife and the Rewards of Auto Theft', *Deviant Behaviour*, 24(4), pp. 309–32.
Corrective Services New South Wales (2013) *Statistical Profile: Characteristics of NSW Inmate Receptions*. Available at: www.correctiveservices.nsw.gov.au/_ _data/assets/pdf_file/0005/484178/Statistical-Profile-Characteristics-of-NSW-Inmate-Receptions.pdf. Last accessed 31 May 2014.
Cunneen, C., Baldry, M. E., Brown, M. M., Brown, M. D., Schwartz, M. M. and Steel, A. (2013) *Penal Culture and Hyperincarceration: The Revival of the Prison* (London: Ashgate).
Davis, F. (1961) 'Deviance Disavowal: The Management of Strained Interaction by the Visibly Handicapped', *Social Problems*, 9(2), pp. 120–32.
Day, A., Nakata, M. and Howells, K. (eds) (2008) *Anger and Indigenous Men* (Sydney: Federation Press).
Deleuze, G. (1994) *Difference and Repetition* (trans. P. Patton) (New York: Columbia University Press)
Deleuze, G. (2007) *Two Regimes of Madness – Texts and Interviews 1975–1995* (trans. M. Taormina and A. Hodges; edited by D. Lapoujade) (New York: Semiotext(e)).
Deleuze, G. and Guattari, F. (1996) *A Thousand Plateaus* (Minneapolis: University of Minnesota Press).
Delfabbro, P. H., Barber, J. G. and Cooper, L. (2001) 'A Profile of Children Entering Out-of-Home Care In South Australia: Baseline Analysis for a 3 Year Longitudinal Study', *Children and Youth Services Review*, 23, pp. 865–91.
Department for Correctional Services, South Australia (2012) *Annual Report 2011–2012* (Adelaide: Department for Correctional Services).

de Viggiani. N. (2007) 'Unhealthy Prisons: Exploring Structural Determinants of Prison Health', *Sociology of Health & Illness*, 29(1), pp. 115–35.

Erikson, E. H. (1982) *The Life Cycle Completed; A Review* (New York: W.W. Norton & Co).

Fader, J. J. (2013) *Falling Back: Incarceration and Transitions to Adulthood among Urban Youth* (New Brunswick: Rutgers University Press).

Fagan, J. and Wilkinson, D. (1998) 'Guns, Youth Violence, and Social Identity in Inner-Cities', *Crime and Justice*, 24, pp. 105–88.

Farrall, S. (2004) 'Social Capital and Offender Reintegration: Making Probation Desistance Focused', in S. Maruna and R. Immarigeon (eds), *After Crime and Punishment: Pathways to Offender Reintegration* (Cullompton: Willan), pp. 57–84.

Farrall, S. (2002) *Rethinking What Works with Offenders* (Cullompton: Willan).

Farrall, S. and Bowling, B. (1999) 'Structuration, Human Development and Desistance from Crime', *British Journal of Criminology*, 39(2), pp. 253–68.

Farrall, S. and Calverley, A. (2006) *Understanding Desistance from Crime* (London: Open University Press).

Farrington, D. (2007) 'Advancing Knowledge about Desistance', *Journal of Contemporary Criminal Justice*, 23(1), pp. 125–34.

Farrington, D. P. (2003) 'Key Results from the First Forty Years of the Cambridge Study in Delinquent Development', in T. P. Thornberry and M. D. Krohn (eds), *Taking Stock of Delinquency: An Overview of Findings From Contemporary Longitudinal Studies* (New York: Kluwer Academic/Plenum), pp. 137–83.

Flinders Marketing and Communications (2013) 'Flinders Foundation Studies Program'. Available at: http://blogs.flinders.edu.au/verbatim-flinders-law-school-news/2013/12/04/verbatim-e-newsletter-november-2013-prisoners-build-a-new-foundation-for-life. Last accessed 30 May 2014.

Flinders Marketing and Communications (2014) 'Art by Prisoners'. Available at: http://blogs.flinders.edu.au/flinders-news/2014/05/02/arts-insights-on-both-sides-of-the-prison-wall. Last accessed 30 May 2014.

Frauley, J. (2011) 'Critical Realist Criminology', in K. Kramar (ed.), *Criminology: Critical Canadian Perspectives* (Toronto: Prentice-Hall), pp. 145–58.

Freiberg, A. (2001) 'Affective versus Effective Justice: Instrumentalism and Emotionalism in Criminal Justice', *Punishment & Society*, 3(2), pp. 265–78.

Gadd, D. and Farrall, S. (2004) 'Criminal Careers, Desistance and Subjectivity: Interpreting Men's Narratives of Change', *Theoretical Criminology*, 8(2), pp.123–56.

Gavazzi, S., Yarcheck, M., Rhine, E. and Partridge, C. (2003) 'Building Bridges between the Parole Officer and the Families of Serious Juvenile Offenders: A Preliminary Report on a Family Based Parole Program', *International Journal of Offender Therapy and Comparative Criminology*, 47(3), pp. 291–308.

Giordano, P. C., Cernkovich, S. A. and Rudolph, J. L. (2002) 'Gender, Crime and Desistance: Toward a Theory of Cognitive Transformation', *American Journal of Sociology*, 107(4), pp. 990–1064.

Glaser, B. (1992) *Basics of Grounded Theory Analysis: Emergence vs. Forcing* (Mill Valley: Sociology Press).

Glueck, S. and Glueck, E. (1968) *Delinquents and Nondelinquents in Perspective* (Cambridge, MA: Harvard University Press).

Goldsmith, A. and Halsey, M. (2013) 'Cousins in Crime: Mobility, Place and Belonging in Indigenous Youth Co-offending', *British Journal of Criminology*, 53(6), pp. 1157–77.

Gottfredson, M. R. and Hirschi, T. (1990) *A General Theory of Crime* (Stanford: Stanford University Press).

Greenberg, D. (1993) *Crime and Capitalism* (Philadelphia: Temple).

Hagedorn, J. (2008) *A World of Gangs: Armed Young Men and Gangsta Culture* (Minneapolis: University of Minnesota Press).

Hagen, A. and Foster, H. (2012) 'Children of the American Prison Generation: Student and School Spillover Effects of Incarcerating Mothers', *Law and Society*, 46(1), pp. 37–69.

Haigh, Y. (2009) 'Desistance from Crime: Reflections on the Transitional Experiences of Young People with a History of Offending', *Journal of Youth Studies*, 12(3), pp. 307–22.

Halsey, M. (2006a) 'Negotiating Conditional Release: Juvenile Narratives of Repeat Incarceration', *Punishment and Society*, 8(2), pp. 147–81.

Halsey, M. (2006b) 'Preface', in B. Parsons and D. Maguire (eds) (2010), *It's About Time: Giving Kids a Break* (Kent Town: Digital Print Australia), pp. 11–15.

Halsey, M. (2007a) 'On Confinement: Client Perspectives of Secure Care and Imprisonment', *Probation Journal*, 54(4), pp. 339–68.

Halsey, M. (2007b) 'Assembling Recidivism: The Promise and Contingencies of Post-Release Life', *Journal of Criminal Law and Criminology*, 97(4), pp. 1209–60.

Halsey, M. (2008a) 'Pathways into Prison: Biographies, Crimes, Punishment', *Current Issues in Criminal Justice*, 20(1), pp. 95–110.

Halsey, M. (2008b) 'Narrating the Chase: Edgework and Young Peoples' Experience of Crime', in T. Anthony and C. Cunneen (eds), *The Critical Criminology Companion* (Sydney: Federation Press), pp. 105–17.

Halsey, M. (2008c) 'Risking Desistance: Respect and Responsibility in Custodial and Post-Release Contexts', in P. Carlen (ed.), *Imaginary Penalities* (Cullompton: Willan), pp. 218–51.

Halsey, M. (2012) *'Step Out': Youth at Risk of Reoffending Mentoring Initiative*. Final Report. Prepared for Australian Red Cross, Adelaide.

Halsey, M. and Armitage, J. (2009) 'Incarcerating Young People: The Impact of Custodial Care', in F. McNeill and M. Barry (eds), *Young People, Crime and Justice* (London: Jessica Kingsley), pp. 154–75.

Halsey, M. and Deegan, S. (2012) 'Father and Son: Two Generations through Prison', *Punishment & Society*, 14(3), pp. 338–67.

Halsey, M. and Deegan, S. (2014) ' "Picking Up the Pieces": Female Significant Others in the Lives of Young (Ex)Incarcerated Males', *Criminology & Criminal Justice*. Available at: http://crj.sagepub.com/content/early/2014/03/12/1748895814526725.ref.html. Last accessed 13 March 2014.

Halsey, M. and Groves, A. (unpublished) 'Intergenerational Incarceration: Emerging Issues from a Mid-range Australian State', Law School, Flinders University.

Halsey, M. and Harris, V. (2011) 'Prisoner Futures: Sensing the Signs of Generativity', *Australian and New Zealand Journal of Criminology*, 44(1), pp. 74–93.

Harvey, J. (2007) *Young Men in Prison: Surviving and Adapting to Life Inside* (Cullompton: Willan).

Healy, D. (2010) 'Betwixt and Between: The Role of Psychosocial Factors in the Early Stages of Desistance', *Journal of Research in Crime and Delinquency*, 47(4), pp. 419–38.

Healy, D. and O'Donnell, I. (2008) 'Calling Time on Crime: Motivation, Generativity and Agency in Irish Probationers', *The Probation Journal*, 55(1), pp. 25–38.

Huebner, B. M., Varano, S. P. and Bynum, T. S. (2007) 'Gangs, Guns, and Drugs: Recidivism among Serious, Young Offenders', *Criminology & Public Policy*, 6(2), pp. 187–221.

Holland, S., Pointon, K. and Ross, S. (2007) *Who Returns to Prison? Patterns of Recidivism among Prisoners Released from Custody in Victoria in 2002-03*, Department of Justice, Victoria. Available at: https://assets.justice.vic.gov.au/corrections/resources/50606073-3dee-4ded-b214-d8160ce3bc83/who_returns_to_prison.pdf. Last accessed 31 May 2014.

Homelessness Australia (2014) *Fact Sheet: Homelessness and Children*, Available at: www.homelessnessaustralia.org.au/images/publications/Fact_Sheets/Homelessness_and_Children.pdf. Last accessed 16 May 2014.

Jacobs, B. A. and Wright, R. (2006) *Street Justice: Retaliation in the Criminal Underworld* (New York: Cambridge University Press).

Kazemian, L. (2007) 'Desistance from Crime: Theoretical, Empirical, Methodological, and Policy Considerations', *Journal of Contemporary Criminal Justice*, 23(1), pp. 5–27.

Katz, J. (1988) *Seductions of Crime: Moral and Sensual Attractions in Doing Evil* (New York: Basic Books).

King, S. (2013) 'Early Desistance Narratives: A Qualitative Analysis of Probationers' Transitions Towards Desistance', *Punishment & Society*, 15(2), pp. 147–65.

Klein, S., Tolbert, M., Bugarin, R., Cataldi, E. F. and Tauschek, G. (2004) *Correctional Education: Assessing the Status of Prison Programs and Information Needs*, Department of Education, Office of Safe and Drug-Free Schools.

Kupers, T. (2005) 'Toxic Masculinity as a Barrier to Mental Health Treatment in Prison', *Journal of Clinical Psychology*, 61(6), pp. 713–24.

Kyckelhahn, T. (2011) 'Justice Expenditures and Employment, FY 1982–2007 – Statistical Tables', Bureau of Justice Statistics (Washington, DC: US Department of Justice).

Langan, P. A. and Leven, D. J. (2002) *Recidivism of Prisoners Released in 1994*, Bureau of Justice Statistics (Washington, DC: US Department of Justice).

Laub, J. H. and Sampson, R. J. (2001) 'Understanding Desistance from Crime', *Crime and Justice: A Review of Research*, 28, pp. 1–69.

Laub, J. and Sampson, R. (2006) *Shared Beginnings, Divergent Lives: Delinquent Boys to Age 70* (Cambridge, MA: Harvard University Press).

Laub, J. H., Nagin, D. S. and Sampson, R. J. (1998) 'Trajectories of Change in Criminal Offending: Good Marriages and the Desistance Process', *American Sociological Review*, 63(2), pp. 225–38.

LeBel, T. (2007) 'An Examination of the Impact of Formerly Incarcerated Persons Helping Others', *Journal of Offender Rehabilitation*, 46(1/2), pp. 1–24.

LeBel, T., Burnett, R., Maruna, S. and Bushway, S. (2008) 'The "Chicken and Egg" of Subjective and Social Factors in Desistance from Crime', *European Journal of Criminology*, 5(2), pp. 131–59.

Le Blanc, M. and Loeber, R. (1998) 'Developmental Criminology Updated', in M. Tonry (ed.), *Crime and Justice*, 23 (Chicago: University of Chicago Press), pp. 115–198.

Liebling, A. (1999) 'Doing Research in Prison: Breaking the Silence?', *Theoretical Criminology*, 3(2), pp. 147–73.

Liebling, A. (2004) *Prisons and Their Moral Performance* (Oxford: Oxford University Press).

Lynch, M., Buckman, J. and Krenske, L. (2003) 'Youth Justice: Criminal Trajectories', *Trends and Issues in Crime and Criminal Justice*, No. 265, (Canberra: Australian Institute of Criminology).

Lyon, J., Dennison, C. and Wilson, A. (2000) *'Tell Them So They Listen': Messages from Young People in Custody*, Home Office Research Study 201 (London: Home Office).

Maguire, M. and Raynor, P. (2006) 'How the Resettlement of Prisoners Promotes Desistance from Crime: Or Does It?', *Criminology and Criminal Justice*, 6(1), pp. 19–38.

Margalit, A. (1998) *The Decent Society* (Cambridge, MA: Harvard University Press).

Maruna, S. (2001) *Making Good: How Ex-Convicts Reform and Rebuild Their Lives* (Washington, DC: American Psychological Association).

Maruna, S. (2007) 'N=1: Criminology and the Person', *Theoretical Criminology*, 11(4), pp. 427–42.

Maruna, S. (2011) 'Reentry as a Rite of Passage', *Punishment and Society*, 13(1), pp. 3–28.

Maruna, S. and Farrall, S. (2004) 'Desistance from Crime: A Theoretical Reformulation', *Kölner Zeitschrift für Soziologie und Sozialpsychologie*, 43, pp. 171–94.

Maruna, S. and Mann, R. (2006) 'A Fundamental Attribution Error?: Rethinking Cognitive Distortions', *Legal and Criminological Psychology*, 11(2), pp. 155–77.

Maruna, S. and Roy, K. (2007) 'Amputation or Reconstruction? Notes on the Concept of "Knifing-Off" and Desistance from Crime', *Journal of Contemporary Criminal Justice*, 23(1), pp. 104–24.

Maruna, S., LeBel, T. and Lanier, C. (2004a) 'Generativity behind Bars: Some "Redemptive Truth" about Prison Society', in E. de St. Aubin, D. McAdams and T. Kim (eds), *The Generative Society* (Washington, DC: American Psychological Association), pp. 131–51.

Maruna, S., LeBel, T. P., Mitchell, N. and Naples, M. (2004b) 'Pygmalion in the Reintegration Process: Desistance from Crime through the Looking Glass', *Psychology, Crime & the Law*, 10(3), pp. 271–81.

Matthews, R. (2009) 'Beyond "So What?" Criminology: Rediscovering Realism', *Theoretical Criminology*, 13(3), pp. 341–62.

McAdams, D. and de St. Aubin, E. (1998) *Generativity and Adult Development* (Washington, DC: American Psychological Association).

McCarthy, B. and Hagan, J. (1995) 'Getting into Street Crime: The Structure and Process of Criminal Embeddedness', *Social Science Research*, 24(1), pp. 63–95.

McCarthy, B. and Hagan, J. (1992) 'Mean Streets: The Theoretical Significance of Situational Delinquency among Homeless Youth', *American Journal of Sociology*, 98(23), pp. 597–627.

254 References

Maguire, M. and Raynor, P. (2006) 'How the Resettlement of Prisoners Promotes Desistance from Crime', *Criminology and Criminal Justice*, 6(1), pp. 19–38.

Mailer, N. (1979) *The Executioner's Song* (Boston: Little, Brown and Company).

Matza, D. (1990/1964) *Delinquency and Drift*, 2nd revised edition (New York: Transaction Publishers).

McDonald, K. (1999) *Struggles for Subjectivity: Identity, Action and Youth Experience* (Cambridge: Cambridge University Press).

McNeill, F. (2009) 'What Works and What's Just?', *European Journal of Probation*, 1(1), pp. 21–40.

McNeill, F. (2006) 'A Desistance Paradigm for Offender Management', *Criminology and Criminal Justice*, 6(1), pp. 39–62.

McNeill, F. (2004) 'Desistance, Rehabilitation and Correctionalism: Developments in Scotland', *Howard Journal of Criminal Justice*, 43(4), pp. 420–36.

McNeill, F. and Maruna, S. (2008) 'Giving Up and Giving Back: Desistance, Generativity and Social Work with Offenders', in G. McIvor and P. Raynor (eds), *Developments in Social Work with Offenders*. Series: Research Highlights in Social Work (48) (London: Jessica Kingsley), pp. 224–339.

Meek, R. (2012) *The Role of Sport In Promoting Desistance from Crime: An Evaluation of the 2nd Chance Project Rugby and Football Academies at Portland Young Offender Institution* (Southampton: University of Southampton/2nd Chance Project).

Mendel, R. (2011) *No Place for Kids* (Baltimore: Annie E. Casey Foundation).

Ministry of Justice Statistics Bulletin (2013) *Offender Management Statistics Quarterly Bulletin, October to December 2012, England and Wales*. Available at: www.gov.uk/government/uploads/system/uploads/attachment_data/file/192314/omsq-q4-oct-dec-2012__2_.pdf. Last accessed 31 May 2014.

Moffitt, T. (1993) 'Adolescence-Limited and Life-Course-Persistent Antisocial Behaviour: A Developmental Taxonomy', *Psychological Review*, 100(4), pp. 674–701.

Moran, K. (2014) 'Social Structure and Bonhomie: Emotions in the Youth Street Gang', *British Journal Criminology*, first published online November 12, 2014, doi:10.1093/bjc/azu085.

Nadescu, A. (2008) *Reconviction Patterns of Released Prisoners: A 48-months Follow-up Analysis*, Department of Corrections, New Zealand. Available at: www.corrections.govt.nz/resources/reconviction-patterns-of-released-prisoners-a-48-months-follow-up-analysis.html. Last accessed 17 April 2014.

Oxfam Policy and Practice (2014) *Poverty in the UK*. Available at: http://policy-practice.oxfam.org.uk/our-work/poverty-in-the-uk. Last accessed 31 May 2014.

Ozanne, J. L., Hill, R. P. and Wright, N. D. (1998) 'Juvenile Delinquents' Use of Consumption as Cultural Resistance: Implications for Juvenile Reform Programs and Public Policy', *Journal of Policy and Marketing*, 17(2), pp. 185–19.

Parker, T. (1990) *Life after Life: Interviews with Twelve Murderers* (London: Pan Macmillan).

Parker, A. and Meek, R. (2013) 'Sport, Physical Activity and Youth Imprisonment', in A. Parker and D. Vinson (eds), *Youth Sport, Physical Activity and Play* (New York: Routledge), pp. 70–82.

Paternoster, R and Bushway, S. (2009) 'Desistance and the "Feared Self": Toward and Identity Theory of Criminal Desistance', *Journal of Criminal Law and Criminology*, 99(4), pp. 1103–56.

Payne, J. (2007) *Recidivism in Australia: Findings and Future Research*, Research and Public Policy Series No.80, Australian Institute of Criminology. Available at: www.aic.gov.au/documents/0/6/B/%7b06BA8B79-E747-413E-A263-72FA37E42F6F%7drpp80.pdf. Last accessed 31 May 2014.

Pearson, G. and Hobbs, D. (2003) 'King Pin? A Case Study of a Middle Market Drug Broker', *Howard Journal of Criminal Justice*, 42(4), pp. 335–47.

Perry, B. D. (2001) 'Bonding and Attachment in Maltreated Children: Consequences of Emotional Neglect in Childhood', adapted in part from *Maltreated Children: Experience, Brain Development and the Next Generation* (New York: W.W. Norton & Company, in preparation). Available at: www.childtraumaacademy.org. Last accessed 3 June 2014.

Petersilia, J. (2003) *When Prisoners Come Home: Parole and Prisoner Reentry* (Oxford: Oxford University Press).

Pew Center on the States (2011) *State of Recidivism: The Revolving Door of America's Prisons* (Washington, DC: The Pew Charitable Trusts).

Pinkerton, J. and Dolan, P. (2007) 'Family Support, Social Capital, Resilience and Adolescent Coping', *Child and Family Social Work*, 12(3), pp. 219–28.

Piquero, A. (2004) 'Somewhere between Persistence and Desistance: The Intermittency of Criminal Careers', in S. Maruna and R. Immarigeon (eds), *After Crime and Punishment: Pathways to Offender Reintegration* (Cullompton: Willan), pp. 102–25.

Piquero, A., Farrington, D. P. and Blumstein, A. (2003) 'The Criminal Career Paradigm', in M. Tonry (ed.), *Crime and Justice: A Review of Research*, 30 (Chicago: University of Chicago Press), pp. 359–506.

Pocket Macquarie Dictionary (1995).

Pratt, J. (2007) *Penal Populism* (London: Routledge).

Presser, L. (2009) 'The Narratives of Offenders', *Theoretical Criminology*, 13(2), pp. 177–200.

Prison Reform Trust (2013) *Prison: The Facts*. Available at: www.prisonreformtrust.org.uk/Portals/0/Documents/Prisonthefacts.pdf. Last accessed 31 May 2014.

PUP (Prison University Program) (2014a) 'Pete Bommerito'. Available at: www.prisonuniversityproject.org/student/pete-bommerito. Last accessed 29 May 2014.

PUP (Prison University Program) (2014b) 'Aly Tamboura'. Available at: www.prisonuniversityproject.org/student/aly-tamboura, Last accessed 29 May 2014.

Quilty, S. (2005) 'The Magnitude of Experience of Parental Incarceration in Australia', *Psychiatry, Psychology and Law*, 12(1), pp. 256–57

Quilty, S., Levy, M., Howard, K., Barratt, A. and Butler, T. (2004) 'Children of Prisoners: A Growing Public Health Concern', *Australian and New Zealand Journal of Public Health*, 28(4), pp. 339–43.

Reich, A. D. (2010) *Hidden Truths: Young Men Navigating Lives in and out of Juvenile Prison* (Berkeley and Los Angeles; University of California Press).

Reilly, K. (2013) 'Sesame Street Reaches out to 2.7 Million American Children with an Incarcerated Parent', Pew Research Centre, 21 June. Available at: www.pewresearch.org/fact-tank/2013/06/21/sesame-street-reaches-out-to-2-7-million-american-children-with-an-incarcerated-parent. Last accessed 16 May 2014.

Rose, N. (2000) 'Government and Control', *British Journal of Criminology*, 40(2), pp. 321–39.

Ross, S. and Guarnieri, T. (1996) 'Recidivism Rates in a Custodial Population: The Influence of Criminal History, Offence and Gender Factors', *Criminological Research Council*. Available at: www.criminologyresearchcouncil.gov.au/reports/35-89.pdf. Last accessed 31 May 2014.

Rumgay, J. (2004) 'Scripts for Safer Survival: Pathways out of Female Crime', *Howard Journal of Criminal Justice*, 43(4), pp. 405–19.

Sabol, W. J. and West, H. C. (2010) *Prisoners in 2009*, US Department of Justice, Bureau of Justice Statistics. Available at: www.bjs.gov/content/pub/pdf/p09.pdf. Last accessed 31 May 2014.

Sampson, R. J. and Laub, J. H. (1997) 'A Life-Course Theory of Cumulative Disadvantage and the Stability of Delinquency', in T. P. Thornberry (ed.), *Developmental Theories of Crime and Delinquency* (New Brunswick: Transaction).

Shapland, J. and Bottoms, A. E (2011) 'Reflections on Social Values, Offending and Desistance among Young Adult Recidivists', *Punishment and Society*, 13(3), pp. 256–91.

Shover, N. (1996) *Great Pretenders* (Boulder: Westview Press).

Snow, P. and Powell, M. (2008) 'Oral Language Competence, Social Skills and High-risk Boys: What Are Juvenile Offenders Trying To Tell Us', *Children and Society*, 22(1), pp. 16–28.

Snyder, C. R. , Harris, C., Anderson, J. R., Holleran, S. A., Irving, L. M., Sigmon, S. T., Yoshinobu, L., Gibb, J., Langelle, C. and Harney, P. (1991) 'The Will and the Ways: Development and Validation of an Individual-Differences Measure of Hope', *Journal of Personality and Social Psychology*, 60(4), pp. 570–85.

South, N. and Brisman, A. (2013) *Routledge International Handbook of Green Criminology* (London: Taylor & Francis Ltd).

Soyer, M. (2014) 'The Imagination of Desistance: A Juxtaposition of the Construction of Incarceration as a Turning Point and the Reality of Recidivism', *British Journal of* Criminology, 54(1), pp. 91–108.

Stake, R. E. (1995) *The Art of Case Study Research* (Thousand Oaks: Sage).

Stanford Center on Policy and Inequality (2014) *Poverty and Inequality Report*. Available at: http://www.stanford.edu/group/scspi/sotu/SOTU_2014_CPI.pdf. Last accessed 31 May 2014.

SCRGSP (Steering Committee for the Review of Government Service Provision) (2013) *Report on Government Services 2013*. Available at: www.pc.gov.au/gsp/rogs/2013. Last accessed 31 May 2014.

SCRGSP (Steering Committee for the Review of Government Service Provision) (2014) *Report on Government Services 2014*. Available at: www.pc.gov.au/gsp/rogs. Last accessed 16 August 2014.

Stevens, A. (2012) ' "I Am the Person Now I Was Always Meant To Be": Identity Reconstruction and Narrative Reframing in Therapeutic Community Prisons', *Criminology and Criminal Justice*, 12(5), pp. 527–47.

Sykes, G. (1958) *The Society of Captives: A Study of a Maximum Security Prison* (Princeton: Princeton University Press).

Taylor, J. (1997) 'Niches and Practice: Extending the Ecological Perspective' in D. Saleebey (ed.), *The Strength Perspective in Social Work Practice* (2nd ed.) (New York: Longman), pp. 217–27.

Thompkins, D. (guest editor) (2010) Special Issue: The Prison Reentry Industry, *Dialectical Anthropology*, 34(4).

Trammell, R. (2012) *Enforcing the Convict Code* (Colorado: Lynne Rienner Publishers).
Travis, A. (2011) 'Prison Leaves 17,000 Children Separated from Their Mothers', *The Guardian*, 30 September. Available at: www.theguardian.com/society/2011/sep/30/prison-17000-children-separated-mothers. Last accessed 16 May 2014.
Travis, J. (2005) *But They All Come Back: Facing the Problem of Prisoner Reentry* (Washington, DC: The Urban Institute Press).
Travis, J. (2011) 'Rethinking Prison Education in the Era of Mass Incarceration', Keynote Address at the University Faculty Conference on Higher Education in Prison, John Jay College of Criminal Justice, City University of New York, 4 February.
Uggen, C., and Piliavin, I. (1998) 'Asymmetrical Causation and Criminal Desistance', *Journal of Criminal Law and Criminology*, 88(4), pp. 1399–1422.
van Onselen, L. (2014) 'Assessing the Impact of the Car Industry's Closure', *Macrobusiness*, 11 February. Available at: www.macrobusiness.com.au/2014/02/assessing-the-impact-of-the-car-industrys-closure. Last accessed 10 May 2014.
Vaughan, B. (2007) 'The Internal Narrative of Desistance', *British Journal of Criminology*, 47(3), pp. 390–404.
Voice of America (2011) 'Prison University Gives Inmates Hope'. Available at: www.voanews.com/content/prison-university-gives-inmates-hope-117519304/163512.html. Last accessed 29 May 2014.
Wacquant, L. (2009) *Punishing the Poor* (Durham: Duke University Press).
Wacquant, L. (2010) 'Prisoner Reentry as Myth and Ceremony', *Dialectical Anthropology*, 34(4), pp. 605–20.
Walker, L. (2010) 'My Son Gave Birth to Me: Offending Fathers – Generative, Reflexive, Risky?', *British Journal of Social Work*, 40(5), pp. 1402–18.
Ward, T. and Maruna, S. (2007) *Rehabilitation* (London: Routledge).
Warr, M. (2002) *Companions in Crime* (Cambridge: Cambridge University Press).
Weaver, A. (2008) *So You Think You Know Me?* (Hook: Waterside Press).
Whyte, W. F. (1943) *Street Corner Society* (Chicago: University of Chicago Press).
Wilkinson, D. (2001) 'Violent Events and Social Identity: Specifying the Relationship between Respect and Masculinity in Inner-City Youth Violence', *Sociological Studies of Children and Youth*, 8, pp. 231–65.
Wilson, W. J. (1996) *When Work Disappears* (New York: Vintage).
Wright, J., Cullen, F. and Miller, J. (2001) 'Family Social Capital and Delinquent Involvement', *Journal of Criminal Justice*, 29(1), pp. 1–9.
Wright, R. and Decker, S. (1997) *Armed Robbers in Action* (Boston: Northeastern University Press).
Yin, R. K. (2006) *Case Study Research* (Thousand Oaks: Sage).

Index

aboriginal
   heritage, 81, 88, 227, 228
   population, 4, 82–3
adolescence limited offending, 8, 9–10, 108, 144, 177–81
affirmation/encouragement
   lack of, 37, 42, 72–3, 74, 85
   significance of, 57, 132, 136–7, 154, 162, 213, 221
   social affirmation, 231
Agnew, R. (1992, 2006), 202–3
alcohol, 52, 58, 65, 81, 87, 108–9, 123, 176
Allard, T. et al. (2014), 16, 17–18
Art by Offenders, 223–5
art and desistance, 224–5
Asian community, 105, 106, 111
associates *see* criminal peers/associates
Attention Deficit Hyperactivity Disorder (ADHD), 63, 64, 116, 128, 162, 178

background *see* disadvantaged background
bail *see* parole
Bard Prison Initiative (BPI), 220
Barry, M. (2013), 108
basic life skills, 140, 171, 172–3
beckoning help, 10, 199–204
Bourgois, Philippe, In Search of Respect, 210, 211
Brazzell, D. et al. (2009), 220
Burnett, R. (2004), 210
Burnett, R. and Maruna, S. (2004), 123

car crime, 141, 142–3, 164, 165
   see also driving
care
   as generative moment, 7–8, 23
   for parent, 100, 120–1, 133, 135, 175
   for siblings, 44, 46, 53, 54–5, 133, 158
   transformative power of, 227–9
change
   desire for, 53, 67–8, 103, 118–20, 148
   love as agent of, 159
   offenders' perception of, 155–6, 159
childhood
   abuse, 116, 117, 123
   and juvenile custody, 185–7
   lost, 185–7, 204
cognitive dissonance, 124–5, 136–7
Cohen, M. A. and Piquero, A. R. (2009), 18
Coleman, J. S. (1990), 202
Coley, R. and Barton, P. (2006), 220
communities of interest, 2
community service, 76, 79, 80
conflict, inability to deal with, 161
Contreras, Randol, *Stickup Kids* (2012), 27, 210
corporate crime, 24–5
corporate generativity and the public good, 24
correctional staff *see* prison officers/correctional staff
correctional system *see* societal and systemic failure
crime, 230
   as career choice, 126
   as habit, 53, 129
   prevention, remedy, 212–13
   seductive elements, 104
criminal, 'training', 105–6, 117, 128–9, 142, 163
criminal/negative environment, 80, 84, 105–6, 127, 129, 178, 196, 205
criminal peers/associates, 47–8, 52–3, 55–6, 64, 84, 105–6, 109, 110, 120, 128–9
   community of, 176

distance from, 47–8, 55–6, 140, 196
temptations of, 147–50, 158, 160–1
Crisis Care, 200–1
crisis response, 212
cumulative life-course disadvantage, 179
custodial experiences, 29, 67, 69, 70, 96–7
custodial-grams, 34, 233–44

Davis, E. (1961), 136
Deleuze, G.
  (1994), 207
  (2007), 208
Deleuze, G. and Guattari, F. (1996), 2
desire for desistance, 84, 137–8, 164, 175, 178, 210–11
  acceptance by the system, 138
  continuity of support, 216–17
  determination, 55–6
  genuine sentiments, 138
  motivation, 111–12, 130–1
  need for change, 53, 67–8, 103, 118–20, 148
desistance
  antecedents of, 21–3, 134, 148
  concept of, 19–20
  difficulties of, 104, 126, 230
  economics of, 15–18
  and generativity, 6–8
  law enforcement, 50–1
  multiple obstacles to, 103, 211–12
  political value of, 16
  potential desisters, 12–15, 103
  significance of, 11–12
  social contract, 50–1
  sociogenic factors, 229–30
  strategies for, 48–9, 53–4, 55–9, 109, 140–1
desistance process, 20–1, 60–1
  case histories, 35–44, 44–51, 51–9, 111–15
  fragility of, 43–4, 59–61, 150, 232
  individual approach, 18–19, 126, 207
  primary, 20, 230
  push and pull factors, 37–9, 54
  secondary, 20–1, 211
  victim awareness, 137–8, 144–5

detention *see* incarceration
'deviance disavowal', 136
de Viggiani, N. (2007), 113
disadvantaged background, 4–5
  case histories, 36–7, 45, 51–2, 75–6, 81–2, 89–91, 92, 115–16, 117
  poverty and need, 141–2, 182
  see also criminal/negative environment; dysfunctional families
driving
  and freedom, 150–1, 162
  importance to offenders, 36, 50, 54, 85–6, 88, 89, 102–3, 109
  joy-riding, 93, 94, 116–17, 118, 142, 164
  licence, 44, 48, 114
  stolen cars, 45, 53, 82, 84, 100–1
  while disqualified, 53–4, 58, 85–6, 88, 98, 102–3
  see also car crime
Drug Court
  housing, 154, 196
  program, 153–4, 157–8, 159
drugs
  and alcohol programs, 108–9, 176
  and crime, 163, 164, 165–6, 168
  dealing, 43, 45, 68, 70, 105, 206, 211
  families of offenders, 49, 127–8, 139, 140, 141, 162, 162–3, 182, 184, 202, 205, 206–7
  heroin, 110, 115, 139
  methadone, 139–40, 153, 157
  in prison, 73, 74, 108, 112, 139–40
  and psychosis, 129, 178
  Suboxone, 153–4, 156–7
  trade, 106–7, 108
  use of, 49, 51, 65, 69, 80–1, 84, 87, 88–9, 118, 123
dysfunctional families, 49, 52, 166–8, 182, 206
  intergenerational dysfunction, 167–8, 182

education
  investment in areas of need, 212
  significance for desistance, 219–22, 222–3

employment, 150
  construction industry, 56
  'dream' job, 152
  of ex-offenders, 212
  indigenous prisoners, 222, 223
  job training, 212
  loss of, 132
  significance in desistance, 43, 56, 60, 62, 70–1, 79, 84, 85, 88, 94, 95, 98, 131–2, 152, 210
  youth unemployment, 4–5
environmental traps, 179, 180
Erikson, E. H. (1982), 6, 7
'ethical' offender *see* personal morality of offender
ex-offenders as mentors, 230–1

Fader, J. J. (2013), 210
family/intimate relationships, 63, 80–1, 111, 121, 146, 159, 165–6
  negative relationships, 63, 75–6, 77, 78, 79, 84, 91–2, 99, 102, 113, 165–6
  rejection of offender, 163, 167, 206–7
family support for offenders, 82–3, 119–20, 138–9, 176, 184–5, 210
  families' own problems, 129, 133–4, 166–8, 176, 179, 192–3, 202, 203
  influence rejected, 106–7
  support for families, 65–6, 212
  see also dysfunctional families; NSOs
Farrall, S. (2004), 210
Farrington, D. (2007), 20
father/father figure
  help from, 38–9
  lack of, 71, 74–5, 79, 87–8, 90, 115, 118–19, 184–5
  relationship with, 118–20, 123–4, 125, 206–7
fatherhood, 38, 42–3, 44, 57, 60, 71, 72, 78, 110–11, 151, 158, 174
  access to children, 79, 80–1, 99, 100, 101–2, 113, 153, 160
fear of incarceration, 39–40, 46–7, 60
Flinders Foundation Studies Program, 222

foster care, 141, 163, 183, 207, 213
  respite care, 213–16
foster carers, 82–3, 92, 206
'fuck it' mentality, 50–1, 112, 123, 132, 162, 201, 219
injustice, 134

Gadd, D. and Farrall, S. (2004), 207
gang membership, 107, 113, 115, 142
generativity, 6–8, 213
  see also care
generativity and desistance, research project, 6–8, 26–34
  ethical aspects, 33
  relationship with participants, 31–3
  see also care
Guardianship of the Minister for Communities and Social Inclusion (GOM), 184

Halsey, M. and Groves, A. (unpublished), 5
Healy, Deirdre (2010), 230
Holland, S. et al (2007), 13
Home Detention Parole, 105, 144
  managing terms of, 153–4, 156–8
  negative effects of, 72–3, 77–8, 103, 121–2, 133, 194–5, 198
home environment *see* disadvantaged background
homelessness, 183
'hooks for change', 22, 62, 178, 212, 226, 230
hope, importance of, 112–13, 123, 126, 193, 221
housing, 55–6, 57, 62, 79, 80, 100, 150, 196, 212
humiliation/disempowerment, 204–5, 208–9, 219–20

identity change perspective, 22–3
identity and sense of self, 26, 57–9, 136, 151–2, 155–6
  criminal, 109–10

incarceration
  as chosen option, 77, 81
  costs, 16–18, 215–16
  experience of, 24, 118, 132–3, 135, 208–9
  fear of, 39–40, 46–7, 60
  and generativity, 23
  negative effects, 79, 97–8
  official objectives, 31
  personal costs, 38, 55, 84, 101, 110–11, 123, 135
  post-release support, 55, 103
  as refuge from chaos, 135–6
incentive *see* affirmation/encouragement
indigenous populations, 4, 14, 183
indigenous prisoners, employment, 222, 223
individual
  approach to desistance, 18–19, 126, 171–2, 203, 207
  responsibility, 2
institutionalization, 23, 101, 169–70, 176
intermittent desisters, 62, 103
  case histories, 63–74, 74–81, 81–9

juvenile detention facilities, 67, 69, 70, 92–3, 96, 108, 117, 164, 185–7
juvenile offending, case histories, 64–8, 82–4, 105–9, 129–30

Katz, J. (1988), 205, 209
Kenner, Max, 220
Koestler, Arthur, 224

Laub, J. H. and Sampson, R. J.
  (2001), 229
  (2006), 11, 181
law enforcement
  heavy handed, 156–8
  sensitive non-enforcement, 50–1
learning difficulties, 63, 205, 206
Liebling, A. (2004), 23
life-course persistent offending, 8, 9–10, 177–81
literacy and numeracy, 182
loss, crime as response to, 203

McDonald, Kevin, *Struggles for Subjectivity*, 26
McNeill, F. (2006), 229
McNeill, F. and Maruna, S. (2008), 6
Mailer, Norman, *Executioner's Song* (1979), 26
managing the scorned self, 10, 204–9
Margalit, A. (1998), 208
Maruna, Shad, desistance as process, 20
  Making Good (2001), 22, 26, 231
Maruna, Shad et al.
  (2004), 57, 138
  (2004a), 23
maturational reform, 21
Matza, D. (1964/1990) 201
Meek, R. (2012), 216
mental health issues, 63, 76, 77, 102, 117, 206, 212
  lack of support for, 77, 81, 191
mentoring, value of, 174, 187, 217–19
  use of ex-offenders, 230–1
Moffitt, T. (1993), 9, 177, 178

'normal'/conventional life, desire for, 22–3, 210
'NSOs' (Nominated Significant Others), 6, 9, 30–1, 75, 76–7, 129, 167–8, 170–1, 179, 192–3, 202, 203, 227, 228
  blame and female NSOs, 65, 168
  withdrawal of support, 129
  youth workers, 168–9
  see also family/intimate relationships; stable relationships

OARS (Offender Aid and Rehabilitation Service), 55–6, 170
offending
  adolescent or life course, 8, 9–10, 108
  costs of, 16–18
  notorious, case histories, 127–41, 141–62, 162–76
  organized crime, 114–15
  persistent, 125–6
  serious, case histories, 104–15, 115–26

ontogenic theories of reform, 21
oral language competence, 171

parentification, 10, 166–7
parent incarceration, 178, 183
parenting offenders, 65, 75–6, 105, 106–7, 123, 124, 129, 130, 133, 134–5, 135–6, 168
  lack official of support, 65–6, 129
  problems of, 129, 133–4
Parker, A. and Meek, R. (2013), 216–17
Parker, Tony *Life After Life: Interviews with Twelve Murderers* (1990), 26
parole, 89, 95, 141, 150, 209
  concept of, 193–4, 195
  managing terms of, 113–14, 152, 153–4, 156–8
  obstacles to desistance, 121–2, 123, 125, 188–9, 198
  over-zealous enforcement, 192
  political aspects, 193
  see also Home Detention Parole
parole board, 72, 113–14, 123, 193–4
parole officers, 114, 174, 194
partners of offenders, problems for, 85, 110, 113, 147–8, 156, 174–5
Paternoster, R. and Bushway, S. (2009), 40
Pearson, G. and Hobbs, D. (2003), 107
peers *see* criminal peers/associates
personal morality of offender, 45–6, 145–6, 151–2, 153
personal needs versus systemic offerings, 10, 126, 171–2, 187–99, 203
post-release
  assistance needed, 170–1, 176, 187
  prior expectations/hopes, 29, 94, 138, 140, 141, 217–18
  the reality, 29, 123, 124, 127, 155, 188–91, 195–6
  see also parole
prison, purpose and use of, 196–8
Prisoner Reintegration Employment Opportunity Program (PREOP), 222–3
prison officers/correctional staff, 228, 232
  frustrated by system, 208
  negative impact of, 72, 97
  views of, 31, 139–40, 185, 188, 191, 207–8
  see also youth workers
Prison University Project (PUP), 220–2
public transport, and offenders, 86, 155

rehabilitation programs, 201
rehabilitation/reintegration, 31, 194, 198–9, 217
  circuits of exclusion, 199
  lack of priority or resources, 191, 230
  life skills needed, 155, 171, 172–3, 176
  non-criminal identity, 3
  support not control, 231–2
  use of ex-offenders, 230–1
Reich, Adam, *Hidden Truths* (2010), 27, 207–8, 209, 210, 221
reincarceration, 13–15, 124
  for minor infraction, 197–8
relationships, difficulties in forming, 156
residivism rates, 27–9
respite care, 213–16
retroflexive reformation, 231
Rose, N. (2000), 199
Ross, S. and Guarnieri, T. (1996), 19

Sampson, R. J. and Laub, J. H. (1997), 179
2nd Chance Project, 216
sexual abuse, 163, 168, 205
sexual infidelity, 175
Shapland, J. and Bottoms, A. E. (2011), 210
social affirmation, 231
social bonding, 21–2
social context of crime, 11, 24
  see also disadvantaged background
social obligation, 2
societal and systemic failure, 2, 83–4, 86–7, 127, 206, 207–9
  adequate funding, 203–4
  community based interventions, 108–9
  flawed rehabilitation strategies, 113

insensitive law enforcement, 133, 197–8
obstacles to desistance, 73, 83–4, 86–7, 88, 96, 98, 103, 109, 121–3
system incompetence/inflexibility, 146–7, 152, 232
see also Home Detention Parole; parole
sociogenic theories of reform, 21–2
sport and desistance from crime, 216–17
stable relationships, significance of, 40–3, 44, 48, 54, 56–7, 60, 70, 71, 72, 78, 93–4, 97–8, 152–3, 154, 155, 156, 158, 159, 160, 174
Step out: Youth At Risk of Re-offending Mentoring Initiative (SOMI), 217–19
Stevens, A. (2012), 213
stigma of criminality, 21, 62, 103, 176, 210, 212, 213, 219

Time for Kids, 213–16
trauma, experience of offenders, 203–4

unemployment, 4–5
intergenerational, 182

victim awareness, 137–8, 144–5
Violence Prevention Program ('VPP'), 112–13

Wacquant, L. (2010), 198–9
Ward, T. and Maruna, S. (2007), 126
Whitaker and Garbarino (1983), 138
white-collar offending, 24–5
Whyte, W. F. *Street Corner Society* (1943), 106

Yatala, G Division, 190–1
youth workers, 183
loss of, 202, 208–9
potential value of, 168–9, 173–4